DOCUMENTS AND NARRATIVES

Concerning the

DISCOVERY & CONQUEST OF LATIN AMERICA

NEW SERIES
NUMBER FOUR

Published by

THE CORTÉS SOCIETY

BANCROFT LIBRARY, BERKELEY, CALIFORNIA

MOTOLINÍA'S HISTORY

OF THE

INDIANS OF NEW SPAIN

TRANSLATED AND EDITED BY

ELIZABETH ANDROS FOSTER, PH.D.

GREENWOOD PRESS, PUBLISHERS
WESTPORT, CONNECTICUT

Library of Congress Cataloging in Publication Data

Motolinía, Toribio, d. 1568.
History of the Indians of New Spain.

Translation of Historia de los indios de la Nueva Espanã.
Reprint of the ed. published by the Cortés Society, Berkeley, Calif., which was issued as no. 4 of Documents and narratives concerning the discovery and conquest of Latin America, new series.
Bibliography: p.
1. Indians of Mexico. 2. Franciscans in Mexico. I. Title. II. Series: Documents and narratives concerning the discovery and conquest of Latin America,

new series, no. 4.
F1219.M922 1973 970.4'2 73-8449
ISBN 0-8371-6977-1

Originally published in 1950 by The Cortés Society, Berkeley, California

Reprinted with the permission of The Cortés Society, University of California, Berkeley, California

Reprinted by Greenwood Press, Inc.

First Greenwood reprinting 1973
Second Greenwood reprinting 1977

Library of Congress catalog card number 73-8449

ISBN 0-8371-6977-1

Printed in the United States of America

Preface

In making this translation I have tried, so far as possible, to keep something of the flavor of the original and yet make it easy to read. That means that I have sometimes had to break up or rearrange sentences that were too long and rambling to be clear. In places where I felt that there was some doubt about the meaning, or some obscurity in the construction, I have given the original Spanish in the notes.

It has been a pleasure to become as well acquainted with Fray Toribio as one necessarily does with an author in the course of translating his work, and I wish to thank Dr. George P. Hammond, Director of the Bancroft Library of the University of California, for having, as it were, introduced me to that very interesting and lovable person by suggesting the need of such a translation, as well as for his help in preparing the manuscript for the press.

My thanks are also offered to Dr. Frederick W. Hodge, Director of the Southwest Museum, Los Angeles, for his very great kindness and interest; to the staff of the Museum of the American Indian in New York, for their friendly assistance; to Mr. Henry R. Wagner, of San Marino, for helpful criticism and advice; to Monsignor Cummings, of St. Mary's Church, Northampton, to Mr. Miguel Zapata y Torres, Mr. Alfred Fisher, and others of my colleagues at Smith College who have most kindly answered questions, read the manuscript, and offered helpful suggestions.

Elizabeth Andros Foster

Smith College, Northampton, Massachusetts
June, 1949

Contents

BOOK TWO

BOOK THREE

Life and Works of Fray Toribio Motolinía

ELIZABETH ANDROS FOSTER

OF Fray Toribio's life before he came to New Spain we know practically nothing except that he was a Spanish Franciscan friar, first in the Franciscan Province of Santiago and later transferred to the Province of San Gabriel, and that he had probably been at some period an associate of Father Martín de Valencia, since he was chosen by the latter as one of the group of twelve friars to accompany him to New Spain. In the letter from the General of the Franciscans to Father Martín de Valencia, dated October 30, 1523,[1] Fray Toribio's name is sixth on the list, and he is included in the group described as "learned preachers and confessors."

His name as given in the above-mentioned list is Fray Toribio de Benavente, but he himself signed it to the Introductory Letter to the Count of Benavente as "Motolinía, Fray Toribio de Paredes," which would imply that he was born or lived in Paredes, a small town on the river Carrión some fifteen leagues east by north of Benavente. That he was more gen-

1. Mendieta, pp. 203 and 619.

erally referred to as Fray Toribio de Benavente is probably because he was also associated with the larger and better known "Villa de Benavente."

The story of his adoption of the name Motolinía, which has become an indissoluble part of his personality, is as follows: When the twelve friars first reached Mexico, Fray Toribio noticed that the Indians kept staring at them and saying "Motolinía, motolinía," and as he was of an inquiring turn of mind he asked the meaning of the word. Upon being told that it meant *poor,* and that the Indians were commenting on the Franciscans' bare feet and patched and threadbare habits, he at once declared that because it was the first Nahuatl word that he had learned (and undoubtedly also because of its meaning) it should thereafter be his name. From then on he always called himself Toribio Motolinía[2] and signed himself "Motolinía, Fray Toribio," giving the place of honor to the word that stood for poverty.

When, at the first chapter meeting held on July 2, 1524, within two weeks of their arrival in Mexico,[3] the twelve newly arrived friars and the five of their Order who were already there were assigned in groups of four to the towns of Texcoco, Tlaxcala, Huejotzingo, and Mexico, Fray Toribio apparently remained in Mexico with Father Martín de Valencia and three others. The first explicit mention of his presence in Mexico occurs in the *Acta* of the cabildo of Mexico dated July 28, 1525, in which he is referred to as guardian of the Franciscan monastery in that city, but he himself tells us[4] that he was present at the meeting called by Cortés to consider the use of the royal "hierro de rescate"—the branding-iron for slaves—which reached New Spain in mid-May and Mexico City some time later, and also that he was present "at everything that happened" during the troubles in Mexico[5] while Cortés was absent on his trip to Honduras, from October, 1524, to June, 1526. The fact that Cortés, before setting out for Honduras, gave special instructions to the officials left in charge in Mexico, "as well as to a certain Fray Toribio Motolinía, Franciscan, and to other good friars that they should pay great attention to the conversion of the natives and

2. *Idem,* p. 211. Bernal Díaz del Castillo, chap. clxxi (Madrid, 1928), II, p. 302, gives a different explanation of the name. According to him the name Motolinía, meaning "the poor friar," was given to Fray Toribio by "the Caciques and Señores of Mexico because everything that was given to him in charity he gave to the Indians, and sometimes went hungry himself, and wore very ragged habits and went barefoot."

3. Motolinía, *infra.* p. 170.

4. Motolinía a Carlos V, *Col. Doc. Inéd.,* VII, p. 285.

5. *Idem., infra,* p. 171.

guard against any uprising in Mexico or the other provinces,"[6] may indicate that Fray Toribio was already, in October, 1524, guardian of the monastery in Mexico.

Being an active and outspoken man and deeply interested in the welfare (both spiritual and material) of his Indian charges, he threw himself with all his energy into the struggle between the religious and civil authorities, because he felt that the latter were jeopardizing not only the salvation of the Indians, but also the whole Spanish colonial enterprise. His attitude toward the majority of the Spanish laity in Mexico, whom he habitually refers to as "the Spaniards," is made very clear throughout his *History of the Indians of New Spain.*[7]

The civil authorities, almost from the beginning, accused the friars of interfering in civil and criminal affairs and using episcopal powers which could be conferred upon them only by the king. In the case of the action taken in the above-mentioned session of the cabildo on July 28, 1525, when the accusation was made and Fray Toribio, as guardian, was required to present evidence of his authority, the civil officials were clearly in the wrong, as Fray Toribio pointed out to them, for the credentials had already been presented by Father Martín de Valencia, as custodian, and acknowledged in the session of March 9, 1525. The cabildo again acknowledged the credentials, but registered a protest against them in so far as they granted the friars authority to intervene in civil and criminal cases, this being, as they claimed, prejudicial to the royal power and to the pacification of Mexico. The papers referred to were two royal cedulas issued at Pamplona in November and December of 1523 and two Latin *bulas* from the general of the Franciscans incorporating the papal bull which gave episcopal powers to the friars until such time as bishops should be appointed for New Spain. These documents specifically gave Father Martín de Valencia full authority *in utroque foro.*[8] In this connection it is interesting to note that the above-mentioned *Acta* of July, 1525, refers to Fray Toribio as guardian of the monastery of San Francisco "calling himself vice-bishop of New Spain."

In the long struggle between the civil government and the friars it is evident that both sides were at fault and both sides had some legitimate grievances. Feelings ran high and many unfortunate things were done and

6. Bernal Díaz del Castillo, chap. clxxiv, vol. II, p. 319.
7. Motolinía, *infra,* pp. 42-43, 95, 101, 159, 164, 171-172, 188, 195, 196, 202.
8. Mendieta, *op. cit.,* p. 200 ff.

said, some of them by Fray Toribio. On several occasions he preached violent sermons against the civil authorities.

In 1524, according to Torquemada,[9] Father Martín de Valencia felt it necessary to place an ecclesiastical interdict upon the city of Mexico and remove the Franciscan group for a time to Tlaxcala because the government, as represented by Gonzalo de Salazar, had violated the sanctuary of the monastery of San Francisco by arresting some of Cortés' followers who had taken refuge there.

In 1526, at the end of January, Cortés' servant Martín Dorantes arrived in Mexico with dispatches announcing that Cortés was on the way back from Honduras and that Estrada and Albornoz were to exercise the powers of government temporarily. Dorantes went directly to the Franciscan monastery, where he was enthusiastically received by the friars and by some partisans of Cortés.[10] Fray Toribio assisted that night in collecting arms and alerting other followers of Cortés in the city.[11]

The situation in Mexico was in no way improved by the appointment, in 1527, of the first royal audiencia under the presidency of the rapacious Nuño de Guzmán, who continued the struggle against the intervention of the friars in public affairs.

In April of 1529 the audiencia ordered the arrest of some Indians of Huejotzingo, but, warned by Bishop Zumárraga, they took refuge in the monastery of which Fray Toribio was then guardian.[12] The latter was accused by the audiencia of preaching against that body and of ordering their officer to leave Huejotzingo within nine hours, under penalty of excommunication. In this order Fray Toribio described himself as follows: "I, Fray Toribio Motolinía, guardian of this monastery of San Miguel de Huexotzinco, visitor, defender, protector and judge commissary, by appointment of the bishop elect of the city of Mexico."[13] This episode with its sequelae figures largely in the long list of accusations against Bishop Zumárraga and the Franciscans sent by Nuño de Guzmán later in the

9. Torquemada, vol. I, p. 593 and vol. III, p. 57.

10. Bernal Díaz del Castillo, chap. clxxxviii, vol. II, pp. 395-396.

11. *Col. Doc. Inéd.*, vol. XL, pp. 478, 529, 545.

12. A similar case is referred to by the Dominican Fray Vicente de Santa María in a letter of 1528 to the Bishop of Osma, president of the Council of the Indies. (See Ternaux Compans, vol. XVI, p. 92.) One wonders whether the date as given is correct. Were there really two such cases in consecutive years, or should the date of Fray Vicente's letter be 1529?

13. García Icazbalceta, *Zumárraga* (Mexico, 1881), Appendix 51, p. 242, and Ternaux Compans, vol. XVI, p. 104 ff.

same month to the Council of the Indies.[14] The depositions of some of the witnesses given in this document contain odd bits of information (or misinformation) about Motolinía, for instance that he "sent six or seven hundred *castellanos* of gold from the mines to a sister of his who is married to a rascally servant of Cortés and of Benavente."

In August of the same year, 1529, a sworn statement was made by a certain Fray Juan de Paredes in which he claimed that during the government of Estrada (while Cortés was absent from Mexico) the Franciscans had plotted to seize the power and drive out all the Spanish laity because they interfered with the conversion of the Indians, and hold the land themselves, subject only and directly to the Emperor. The ringleaders of the plot were said to be the custodian, Fray Luis de Fuensalida, Fray Francisco Jiménez, Fray Pedro, and Fray Toribio Motolinía "who was coming from Texcoco with other guests."[15]

The struggle thus begun in the very year of the arrival of the friars continued with increasing bitterness during the term of the first audiencia and reached its climax in the spring of 1530 when, on March 4, the *oidores* entered the monastery of San Francisco and forcibly removed two accused men, Cristóbal de Angulo and García de Llerena, who were being held there in custody by the bishop-elect since, as ecclesiastics, they were subject to his jurisdiction and not to that of the civil authorities. After fruitless negotiations with the said authorities, on March 6th Bishop Zumárraga issued a ban of excommunication against the city. Because of the disrespect shown to the monastery, the custodian, Fray Luis de Fuensalida, removed the friars from San Francisco to Texcoco.[16]

When the second audiencia assumed control in 1530 conditions were very much improved, and the friction between civil and religious authorities was reduced to the minimum.[17] In 1531 we find them coöperating in the foundation of the town of Puebla de los Angeles, in the hope that the

14. *Col. Doc. Inéd.*, vol. XL, pp. 468 ff. See also vol. XIII, pp. 161-165, for Zumárraga's letter of Aug. 27, 1529, to the Emperor.

15. Ternaux Compans, vol. XVI, p. 109, gives the date as April 23, but *cf.* García Icazbalceta, *Zumárraga*, App. 53, p. 244, where it is given as August 23.

16. The documents in this case are to be found in *Col. Doc. Inéd.*, vol. XLI, pp. 3, 8, 12, 23, 31, and in García Icazbalceta, *Zumárraga*, App. 2, p. 43 f. Motolinía, *infra*, p. 160, refers to a case of violation of sanctuary in the monastery of San Francisco in Mexico in 1528, and to another earlier one, and says that "because of this the friars left the monastery, which remained for more than three months without friars and without sacrament." It is not clear to which case this statement applies. That there were several cases of such violation of sanctuary is evident from the testimony given in the *Sumario de la residencia tomada a don Fernando Cortés.*

17. See Motolinía's tribute to the second audiencia in his History, *infra*, pp. 192-193.

unoccupied and discontented Spaniards, of whom there were many roaming about New Spain seeking their fortunes, might be induced to acquire property and settle down to agriculture or stock raising. The first idea of the audiencia was, apparently, to settle Spaniards in the city of Tlaxcala.[18] At the beginning of 1531 they had abandoned that plan and were looking for an appropriate site "near the Province of Tlaxcala," and found a suitable one between Tlaxcala and Cholula.[19]

There has been a question as to whether this project originated with the friars or with the audiencia, and as to the part played in it by Fray Toribio. Motolinía himself does not claim any credit, nor does he even allude to having said the first Mass there.[20] He merely states that he was present at the founding.[21] According to him, the new town was built by command of the audiencia "at the instance of the Franciscan friars." Bishop Zumárraga, writing to the Council of the Indies,[22] says that it was the idea of the audiencia, submitted to the friars and approved by them. The Oidor Salmerón seems to have been the prime mover in the matter: "Some," he says, "have been timid and doubtful about doing this, but I have insisted because in my opinion the advantages are obvious."[23] He also speaks of the plan as needing further consideration and expert criticism, since it is "only the product of my own poor judgment," and says that it has been submitted to the prelates and friars and to experienced persons, who are all heartily in favor of it.[24] Certainly there is complete agreement between his ideas and those of Fray Toribio as to the desirability of establishing such a town.[25]

The evidence of the documents cited above leaves no doubt whatever that the actual date of the founding of Puebla was 1531, and not 1530, as Motolinía gives it.[26] It agrees also with the fact noted by Veytia[27] that in 1531 the Octave of Easter (the day of the founding) did fall on the 16th of April, whereas in 1530 it did not.

Motolinía's life in Mexico and its neighborhood would seem to have

18. *Col. Doc. Inéd.*, vol. XLI, p. 39, Letter of the audiencia to the Emperor, 30 May, 1530.
19. *Ibid.*, pp. 79-83, Letter of the audiencia to the Emperor, 14 August, 1531.
20. Torquemada, vol. I, p. 313; Vetancourt, vol. III, p. 148, and vol. IV, p. 271.
21. Motolinía, *infra*, p. 262; and also *Memoriales*, p. 199.
22. García Icazbalceta, *Zumárraga*, App. 6, pp. 52-53.
23. *Col. Doc. Inéd.*, vol. XIII, p. 195 ff, letter of Salmerón to the Council of the Indies, 30 March, 1531.
24. *Ibid.*
25. Compare Salmerón's letter, just cited, with Motolinía, *infra*, p. 261.
26. Motolinía, *infra*, p. 261.
27. Echeverría y Veytia, *Historia de la Fundación . . . de Puebla*, vol. I, p. 85 f.

been a busy one during the years between his arrival and 1531. We know definitely that he was guardian of the monastery of San Francisco in Mexico in 1525, that he was still there in 1526 at the time of the arrival of Martín Dorantes, and that in April of 1529 he was guardian of the monastery in Huejotzingo. Mendieta states,[28] but without mentioning the date, that he was guardian in Texcoco during a very dry year and that he organized a religious procession and prayers for rain, which were so effective that a second procession had to be arranged to obtain relief from the excessive rainfall induced by the first. Motolinía refers[29] to the same episode as having occurred in the fourth year from the arrival of the friars, *i. e.,* 1528.

In spite of these facts, there is a tradition of his having been in Guatemala during the same period. Mendieta[30] says that he became guardian of Texcoco "on his return from Guatemala," and the statement is repeated by Vetancurt.[31] The chief exponent of the tradition is Fray Francisco Vásquez. He states categorically that Motolinía travelled, preached, and baptized in Guatemala and Nicaragua during the years 1528 and 1529 and that he preached in Santiago de Guatemala on the occasion of the feast of the patron saint of the city (July 25) in 1530.[32] The statement is based on two very vague indications: one, the claim of a Guatemalan Indian to have been baptized by Fray Toribio "shortly after" the capture of the king Ahpozozli, which occurred in 1526; the other, an undated certificate signed by Fray Toribio of the reception into "our brotherhood" of one Gaspar Arias, "first alcalde of this very noble city." Arias was alcalde in 1528 and 1529, but obviously might still be referred to at any later date as "the first alcalde."[33] There are also statements to the effect that Motolinía was sent to Guatemala in 1533 by Fray Jacobo de Testera, who had been elected custodian in that year,[34] but there seems to be no very good reason for accepting them, and considerable difficulty in reconciling a trip to Guatemala at that date with the other events of Fray Toribio's life whose dates we know.

On the whole, however, the most conclusive evidence against his hav-

28. Mendieta, p. 625.
29. Motolinía, *infra,* p. 129.
30. Mendieta, p. 625.
31. Vetancurt, vol. IV, p. 271.
32. Vásquez, vol. I, p. 30-35.
33. Vásquez' statements were accepted by Sánchez García in his biography of Motolinía. Ramírez, *Noticias,* pp. li-liii, rejected the possibility of Motolinía's presence in Guatemala in 1528 and 1529.
34. Mendieta, p. 665, and Torquemada, vol. III, p. 489.

ing been in Guatemala either in 1528-30 or in 1533 is furnished by Motolinía himself, when he says in book II, chapter 8: "In many parts of this country earthquakes are frequent, as in Tehuantepec, for instance, where there were many during the half year that I spent there. *They tell me* that there are many more in Guatemala." Had he already been in Guatemala at the time of writing this, he would certainly not have said "they tell me." One can be sure that he would have said something like "and there were many more in Guatemala when I was there." This statement was obviously made after his stay in Tehuantepec with Fray Martín de Valencia.[35] Four paragraphs later in the same chapter he speaks of the year 1537 as past, so that it seems safe to conclude that as late as 1538 he had not yet been in Guatemala.[36]

After the first five or six years our knowledge of Fray Toribio's movements has mostly to be gathered from scattered statements in the *History* and the *Memoriales*. We learn from these sources that in 1531, being then over forty, he planted some date seeds in Cuernavaca, and that in 1541, while in Texcoco, he was presented with flowers produced by the trees which had grown from those seeds.[37] We have already seen that at the end of 1532 he accompanied Fray Martín de Valencia to Tehuantepec and spent six or seven months in that country, where he evidently visited the ruins of Mitla, described in the *History*, book III, chapter 5. In 1535 he was in Cholula when the third attempt was made by the friars to place a large cross on the site of an old Indian temple where two previously erected crosses had been destroyed by lightning.[38] From 1536-39, he was, by his own account, in Tlaxcala, and he tells us that he lived there for six years.[39] During at least part of this time he was guardian of the monastery. In 1540 he was living in Tehuacán,[40] so that the six years of residence in Tlaxcala presumably began in 1534. During this period he made short trips in various directions, to Cholula in 1535, as we have seen; to Quecholac in 1539;[41] in May, 1538, to Mexico to a chapter meeting;[42] in March of 1539 to Atlihuetzia, where he made investigations into the murder of the Indian

35. See letter dated Tehuantepec, 18 January, 1533, and signed by Father Martín de Valencia and other friars, among them Motolinía. *Nueva Col. Doc. Hist. Mex.*, vol. II, pp. 177-186.

36. I find that this deduction had already been made by Fray Lázaro Lamadrid in his edition of Vásquez's *Crónica*. See his note 1 on p. 31, vol. I, of that work.

37. Motolinía, *Memoriales*, p. 335.

38. *Idem, infra*, p. 89.

39. *Ibid.*, p. 72.

40. *Ibid.*, p. 141, and *Memoriales*, p. 102.

41. Motolinía, *infra*, p. 138.

42. *Ibid.*, p. 158.

boy Cristóbal and wrote his account of it.[43] In January and February of 1541 he travelled for over a month in the Mixteca country and visited Antequera, in the valley of Oajaca. By February 24th he was back in Tehuacán and had finished the "Introductory Letter" prefixed to his *History*.[44]

After February 24, 1541, we have no definite information about Motolinía until 1544. We know that he was sent by Fray Jacobo de Testera with a group of friars to Guatemala as vice commissary general with instructions to establish Franciscan monasteries there and in Yucatan; authorities differ, however, as to exactly when he went, although 1542 seems to be the most generally accepted date. It was certainly at some time between the return of Fray Jacobo de Testera, as commissary general for New Spain, from the general chapter meeting held in Mantua in 1541, and the 2nd of June, 1544, when a chapter meeting of the newly formed Franciscan custodia of the "Santísimo Nombre de Jesús de Guatemala" was called and Fray Toribio was elected its first custodian.[45]

The Franciscans were apparently well received in Guatemala, but soon came into conflict with the Dominicans, headed by Fray Bartolomé de las Casas, the recently appointed bishop of Chiapas. The situation became so bad that toward the end of September of 1545 Fray Toribio resigned his office as custodian and shortly afterwards left for Mexico with some of his companions, others of the group having gone to Yucatan. On October 21, 1545, he wrote from Xuchtepec to the officers of the city government of Santiago de Guatemala, evidently in answer to a request from them that he should come back.[46] The letter is guarded, but shows an unmistakable bitterness against the Dominicans in the reasons that he gives for withdrawing his group from Guatemala. The Guatemalan authorities were persistent, and on December 4 of the same year the officers of the city government wrote to the commissary general of the Franciscans and to the bishop of Mexico, asking to have Fray Toribio sent back to them. The request was refused by the commissary general on February 1, 1546, on the ground that Fray Toribio was indispensable in Mexico.[47]

After his return to Mexico Motolinía was appointed Vicario Provincial of his order to fill out the term of Fray Alonso Rangel, who had lost

43. *Ibid.*, p. 249.
44. *Ibid.*, Introductory Letter, p. 34.
45. Vázquez, vol. 1, p. 103.
46. Ramírez, *Noticias*, p. lxxx.
47. Vázquez, vol. 1, p. 106.

his life in a shipwreck on June 15, 1547.[48] In 1548 Fray Toribio was regularly elected to the office of provincial for the usual three-year period.[49] From then until his death we have little information about him. Mendieta mentions his being guardian of the monastery in Atrisco[50] (or Atlixco), and Cervantes de Salazar speaks of his being guardian of Tacuba,[51] but in neither case is any date given. There is also an unsupported statement to the effect that he was offered and refused the bishop's miter.[52] In 1551 he visited the monastery in Tecamachalco.[53] In August of 1554 he was in Cholula, where he and some others wrote a letter to the viceroy, Don Luís de Velasco.[54] In 1554 he was again guardian in Tlaxcala[55] and was still there on January 2, 1555, when he finished the letter to Charles V. During his guardianship there Fray Gerónimo de Mendieta, who came to Mexico as a young man in June of 1554, was a member of the community.[56] At some time before his death in August, 1569, Fray Toribio had returned to the monastery in Mexico, and his last act was to rise from his sickbed to say Mass once more in the old cloister of the church of San Francisco.[57] At the time of his death he was over seventy-eight years old[58] and was the last survivor of the original group of twelve who had come to Mexico in 1524.

The question as to when Motolinía first came into contact with Las Casas is much confused by an extremely ambiguous statement made by the former in his letter to Charles V, written probably during the last weeks of 1554 and dated January 2, 1555. The first part of this statement is clear enough. "I have known Las Casas for fifteen years" [*i. e.,* since 1539]. The rest merely obscures the matter: "before he [or it might equally well be I] came to this land [Mexico in particular, or the New World in general?] and he was going to Peru and, not being able to reach there [probably the attempt he made in 1534], stopped in Nicaragua, but was not able to stay there long and from there came to Guatemala and stayed

48. Vetancurt, vol. IV, p. 202.
49. Mendieta, p. 541.
50. *Idem,* p. 624.
51. Cervantes de Salazar, vol. II, p. 254.
52. Sánchez García, "Bio-bibliografía," p. xxv.
53. Anales de Tecamachalco, in *Nueva Col. Doc. Hist. Mex.,* vol. V, p. 272.
54. Ternaux Compans, vol. x, p. 401.
55. *Nueva Col. Doc. Hist. Mex.,* vol. I, p. 82. Mendieta used this account, but without mentioning the name of Motolinía.
56. Mendieta, p. 230.
57. *Ibid.,* p. 620.
58. Motolinía, *Memoriales,* pp. 335-336.

there even less time and then was in Guaxaca, where he was as restless as he was everywhere else and then turned up in Mexico and was at the Dominican monastery there."[59] A few lines later Fray Toribio speaks of Las Casas' turning up in Tlaxcala with a train of Indian baggage carriers at the time when the bishop and prelates of New Spain had met to consider the papal bull on baptism. This occurred at the beginning of the year 1539.[60] Las Casas himself tells us definitely that he was in Tlaxcala in 1538, on the feast of the Assumption (August 15) and not only witnessed an Indian pageant on that day, but also, at the invitation of the Franciscans, officiated at High Mass.[61] Fray Bartolomé does not mention Motolinía by name, but speaks of a manuscript lent to him by "one of the outstanding and much respected Franciscan friars, at that time guardian of the monastery of San Francisco in the city of Tlaxcala," who had compiled a detailed account of the progress made by the Indians in the Christian faith. That this friar was Motolinía becomes obvious if one compares certain chapters of the latter's *History of the Indians* and *Memoriales* with Las Casas' *Apologética Historia.*[62]

If the two men had not met before, they certainly met in the summer of 1538 or 1539. At first, relations between them were sufficiently friendly for Fray Toribio to give Las Casas free access to the material that he had collected on Indian customs, and perhaps to receive in exchange certain information from Fray Bartolomé. It is tempting to suppose that the description of the Nicaraguan volcano in *Memoriales,* chapter 68, is based on information given to Motolinía by Las Casas. Certainly the episode of the friar who had had himself let down into the crater so that he could try to get some of the molten metal appears in both accounts, and Las Casas clearly states that the report of this experiment was sent to him by the friar concerned *while he was in Mexico.*[63]

However, friendly relations between them did not last long. Both men were fighters, and, being temperamentally incompatible, they soon found themselves fighting on opposite sides, in spite of the fact that in their

59. *Col. Doc. Inéd.*, vol. VII, p. 261.

60. Motolinía, *infra,* p. 137.

61. Las Casas, p. 165. The date 1538 would appear to be incorrect. Las Casas certainly misquotes Motolinía's date in the account of the Corpus Christi celebration in chapter 63. He gives it as 1536, whereas Motolinía says 1538 (History, bk. I, chap. 15, *infra,* p. 101.)

62. *Cf.* Motolinía, *History,* bk. I, chap. 4, with Las Casas, chap. 121; Motolinía, *History,* bk. I, chap. 9, and *Memoriales,* bk. I, chap. 25, with Las Casas, chap. 138; Motolinía, *History,* bk. I, chap. 12, and *Memoriales,* bk. I, chaps. 30-31, with Las Casas, chap. 130; Motolinía, *History,* bk. I, chap. 15, with Las Casas, chap. 63.

63. Las Casas, p. 302.

championship of the Indians they were really in agreement. In many passages of the *History*,[64] Motolinía is as bitter as Las Casas himself about the exploitation of the Indians by "the Spaniards," and we have already seen that in 1529 he was actually accused of plotting to drive out of Mexico all Spaniards except the friars because they interfered with the conversion of the Indians. After the tumultuous period of the first audiencia, and as things became more settled in Mexico, Fray Toribio maintained that the attitude of the Spaniards improved greatly and that there were many of them who lived up to the obligations imposed by their privileges.[65] For Las Casas, however, all Spaniards remained cruel exploiters of the Indians.

As the New Laws (signed by Charles V on November 28, 1542) on the holding of encomiendas and repartimientos were not promulgated until the year after the completion of the *History,* the latter naturally contains no expression of feelings or opinions about the matter. The same is true of the Confesionario, a confessor's manual circulated by Las Casas in manuscript form among the clergy and friars, and suppressed by a royal order of November 28, 1548. As Motolinía was at that time provincial of the Franciscans in New Spain, it became his duty—a duty which was probably also a pleasure—to collect all copies that might still be in the hands of the friars of his order.[66] The copies thus collected were turned over to the viceroy, Don Antonio de Mendoza, and burned. When the same Confesionario reappeared, this time in printed form (Seville, 1552), Motolinía reacted violently to what he considered the injustice of Las Casas both toward the Spanish laity and toward the friars who gave them absolution and admitted them to the sacraments. In his letter to Charles V, he freely and forcibly expressed his bitter resentment of Las Casas' attitude, and flew to the defense of the Spanish laity, whom he himself had once attacked in much the same way.

That the two friars also disagreed fundamentally on the subject of administering the sacrament of baptism to adult Indians became painfully evident even during Las Casas' stay in Tlaxcala, when he refused to baptize an Indian whom the Franciscans considered well prepared.[67] The whole question of baptism, especially adult baptism, had become a matter of serious controversy between the friars who were first in the field and the later arrivals of the same or other orders, who criticized their predeces-

64. See above, note 7.
65. Motolinía a Carlos V, *Col. Doc. Inéd.*, vol. VII, p. 265.
66. *Ibid.*, pp. 259, 260.
67. *Ibid.*, pp. 262-263.

sors for simplifying the ritual and for not requiring sufficient preparation and probation in the case of adults. The former had based their practice on the instructions given them in Spain by the Franciscan minister general, Cardinal Santa Cruz, together with the interpretations and opinions of one of their number, Fray Juan de Tecto, former professor of theology at the University of Paris.[68] Finally the situation became so serious that the bishops and prelates of New Spain met with the audiencia to discuss the subject, and the problem was referred to the Council of the Indies and the archbishop of Seville, who, in turn, referred it to the Pope and ordered the friars in Mexico to carry on as they were doing until such time as a papal decision should be rendered. On June 1, 1537, Pope Paul III issued a bull[69] justifying the procedure followed by the first friars, on the ground that "they had good reason for believing that it was the right thing to do," but insisting upon certain things as essential for all future baptisms.

This bull reached Mexico during the following year and was discussed at another meeting of the audiencia with the ecclesiastical authorities on April 27, 1539.[70] It was decided to limit the baptism of adults, except in cases of urgent necessity, to the appointed periods of Easter and Pentecost, and, in order to ensure uniformity of practice, a manual was ordered drawn up for the guidance of those administering the sacrament. This action was unsatisfactory to the friars who had to deal with the great numbers of Indians that continued to present themselves for baptism. For three or four months no adults were baptized, but then the friars of the monastery of Quecholac, which Motolinía was then visiting, decided to defy orders and baptize all the Indians whom they considered worthy.[71] In 1541 a further statement was issued by the theologians of the University of Salamanca, who insisted firmly upon an adequate period of probation and instruction in Christian morality as well as in religious doctrine.[72]

To Fray Toribio and his colleagues it was of enormous importance that as many Indians as possible should be baptized and so started on the road to salvation. They undoubtedly also felt that they would have more hold over the Indians once the latter had been baptized, and could then proceed with further instruction. To Las Casas it was of equal importance that the sacrament should not be lightly administered, and that, when

68. Motolinía, *infra,* p. 134.
69. Mendieta, bk. III, chap. 37.
70. García Icazbalceta, *Zumárraga,* App. 26.
71. Motolinía, *infra,* p. 138.
72. *Col. Doc. Inéd.,* vol. III, pp. 543-553.

administered, it should be with the full ritual. Motolinía, who had borne the burden in the matter of teaching and baptizing Indians, and knew the problems involved, very humanly and understandably resented the criticisms of a man who had had little practical experience in the field.

The constant activity and hardships of a pioneer missionary's life would seem a discouraging background for literary pursuits. The early friars in New Spain had no secluded cells, nor peaceful monastic libraries in which to work, and yet Fray Toribio, undaunted by all obstacles, very soon began to write an account of the Indians, their history, their customs, and their conversion, together with a description of the country, its flora, fauna, and interesting geographical features. The account was written in intervals of leisure over a period of years. From the text itself we gather that Motolinía was working on it in 1536, 1537, 1538, and 1540, and the "Introductory Letter" is dated in 1541. The intervals of leisure, by the author's own statement, were few and far between and always subject to interruption by calls for his services. The result is that the book lacks form and coherence, is often rambling and repetitious. Fray Toribio himself was fully aware of these deficiencies, as he tells us in the eighth chapter of his third book: "I see that for lack of time even this that I have written is a mere patchwork, and that I cannot properly carry out my intention in what I have begun. For very often I am interrupted by the necessity of succoring my neighbors and by the charity which obliges me to do so, so that I am hourly compelled to minister to them."

He writes, naturally, in the style of his period, using the long, complex sentences and the numerous synonyms that so delighted his contemporaries. The sixteenth century Spanish sentence is by nature slow-moving and involved, but Motolinía's are sometimes so involved that he loses his way and misleads the reader.

In spite of this sixteenth century verbosity Fray Toribio's style is, by comparison with contemporary writers on the same subjects, remarkably straightforward and simple. It is mercifully free from the learned comparisons and pious reflections with which Torquemada and Las Casas, for instance, interlard their narratives. There is only one classical reference (to Aristotle) and only thirteen to the Bible. Only twice does our author indulge in rhetorical moralizing—once in book III, chapter 11, on Peru and the greed for gold, and once in the same book, chapter 6, when he addresses Mexico. His chief concern is to tell the reader as simply and clearly as he can about things in which he himself is tremendously interested, and about which he has taken pains to inform himself.

Motolinía's first interest, naturally enough, was in the people whose souls he had come to save, but he was interested in them also as human beings here on earth, not merely as immortal souls to be prepared for Paradise. It is obvious from what he says and from the way he says it that he really liked them and admired their good qualities, their intelligence, gentleness, and indifference to wealth. Again and again he speaks of these things. Furthermore Fray Toribio lived quite simply and humbly in the bare little Franciscan monasteries in the Indian towns, travelled barefoot, with Indian guides, over leagues and leagues of mountain trails and native roads from province to province, and met the natives with sympathetic understanding and the respect due to one's fellow men, with the result that he knew his Indians intimately and was loved and respected by them. It must have been bitterly hard work and at times discouraging, but Motolinía's patience was great—unlike that of some priests of whom he says:[73] "They would like, after working with the Indians for two days, to see them as pious as if they had been teaching them for ten years, and as they do not seem so, these priests cast them aside. Such people seem to me like a certain man who bought a very thin sheep and gave it a piece of bread to eat and then felt of its tail to see if it had grown fat." Of the priests who do not really like the Indians he says: "Those friars who are indifferent to these Indians, or have a sort of dislike for them, God makes unhappy and they live here as if in torment until the country throws them off and casts them aside as dead and useless bodies." Those words could never be said of him.

This was, however, not the only thing that held Fray Toribio in New Spain. The country itself, its marvels and its possibilities, were of the greatest interest to him. Whenever he could, he went to see the new and marvelous things he heard about. He investigated lagoons, volcanoes, springs, natural bridges, and even counted the number of rivers and streams he crossed in a day's journey. He was not a scientist, but he was interested in the kinds of trees and fruits that grow in the different climates of Mexico, in the birds and beasts that inhabit her woods and waters, in the nature of the soil, the mineral resources, the native crops, and the European plants that can be advantageously grown there. One of his favor-

73. Motolinía, *infra*, p. 137.

ite ideas was that Mexico should become the great silk-producing center of the world.

Unlike the dissatisfied Spaniards of whom he speaks who were always swearing: "as I hope to return to Spain!" Motolinía thoroughly adopted New Spain as his home and interested himself in its welfare. Hence his practical sense impelled him to approve and coöperate in the founding of the Spanish town of Puebla de los Angeles. He would even have gone farther than the original plan, and in 1555 we find him urging that advantage should be taken of the new town's strategic location to make it a real stronghold and a center of Spanish military power.[74] Such a show of force would, he believed, go far toward keeping the country at peace and safe for the Spaniards, who after all were merely a handful in comparison with the vast Indian population.

Though he believed that a show of force would be a useful protection, he by no means advocated the use of force in dealing with the natives. In fact he vigorously deprecated any sort of harsh treatment of the Indians, not only from religious and humanitarian motives, but because it was a very short-sighted policy from the point of view of the Spaniards. He repeatedly pointed out the fatal results of exploitation of the natives, already obvious in the Islands, and urged the conquerors to cherish the Indians, not only because it was their religious duty, but because it was to their advantage to develop the resources of the country, a thing which could not be done if the Indian population was exterminated by harsh treatment and a crushing burden of taxation.

In this connection he gave the highest praise to the officers of the audiencia and to the viceroy, Don Antonio de Mendoza, for their humane and enlightened attitude, but still felt that the problem of the government of New Spain had not been finally solved, and that a correct solution was a matter of vital importance to the country. A land so large and so remote could not, he believed, be effectively governed from a center of power so far away as Spain. It needed the personal presence and interest of its ruler to maintain justice and peace and to settle promptly the difficulties that were bound to arise. Motolinía's own solution of the problem is given at the end of chapter nine of his third book: a prince of the royal blood should be made ruler of New Spain and should live in his realm to ensure its loyalty and to give it good government, prosperity, and prestige.

Fray Toribio was an eye-witness of most of the scenes that he describes

74. *Ibid.*, p. 271. Also Carta a Carlos V, *op. cit.*, p. 273.

so vividly, and when he was dealing with a subject on which he did not have first-hand information he took pains to inform himself of the facts and also of the reliability of his sources. Judged by modern standards these may not always have been of the most trustworthy, but according to his lights he did his best to ensure the accuracy of his statements. Prescott, who used Motolinía freely as a source, is rather unjust to him when he says: "The most startling occurrences are recorded with all the credulous gravity which is so likely to win credit from the vulgar; and a stock of miracles is duly attested by the historian, of more than sufficient magnitude to supply the wants of the infant religious communities of New Spain."

Some apparently miraculous happenings Fray Toribio does relate as fact; one could scarcely expect anything else, given his period and his training, but he often carefully refrains from asserting an unreserved belief in alleged miracles. For instance, after reporting some visions seen by Indians, he makes this explicit statement: "Many of these converts have seen and report different revelations and visions which, considering the sincerity and simplicity with which they tell of them, seem to be true. But because it might be false I do not write them down nor do I either affirm or deny them." Of the miracles attributed to Fray Martín de Valencia after his death Motolinía says: "which, because I have not sufficient certainty about them, I neither believe nor disbelieve." A certain critical sense and independence of judgment we must undoubtedly grant him. His contemporaries and immediate successors had no doubts whatever of his value as a first-hand source of information, and speak repeatedly of his accuracy and reliability.[75]

As we have already seen, Las Casas was given access to Motolinía's manuscript, or manuscripts, in 1538 or 1539, by Fray Toribio himself, and made use of them in his *Apologética Historia de las Indias.* Alonso de Zurita, who says that he knew Motolinía for several years while he was in Mexico (between 1554 and 1564)[76] had in his possession a manuscript of Motolinía's which he used as source material for his *Relación* and later sent to Mendieta, at the request of the latter.[77] Mendieta used Motolinía's writings freely, but in only one case does he give the title of the one to which he is referring. That is in the fourth book of the *Historia Ecle-*

75. Mendieta, p. 230, "a man who for no reason whatever would speak anything but the simple truth," and p. 573, "a careful investigator."

76. *Nueva Col. Doc. Hist. Mex.*, vol. III, pp. xii and xiv.

77. *Ibid.*, pp. xxx-xxxi.

siástica Indiana, page 451, where he quotes from a work which he calls *De Moribus Indorum.* The material quoted is to be found in the *History of the Indians,* book II, chapters six and eight, and in the *Memoriales,* page 138. He also lists *De Moribus Indorum* among Motolinía's works in the fifth book, page 260, of the *Historia Eclesiástica Indiana.*

We know that the *History of the Indians* was finished in February of 1541 and we may assume that Motolinía would take the first opportunity of sending it to the Count of Benavente. There is no way of knowing to what extent it was circulated or copied in Spain, but certainly Gómara, who must have been writing in 1550 or 1551, in the last part of his *Conquista de Mejico*[78] used material from the "Introductory Letter" and from the first book. On the authority of Cervantes de Salazar, writing in Mexico about 1558 or 1559, we know that Gómara, in the first part of the abovementioned work, which deals with the conquest of Mexico, was following very closely a work of Motolinía which we no longer have. It was, in all probability, the one listed by Rebolledo[79] as *La Guerra de los Indios.* Cervantes de Salazar himself must have had a copy of this work before him while he was writing his own *Crónica de la Nueva España,*[80] for he frequently comments on the fact that in such and such a case Gómara is following or sometimes copying Motolinía, or that in a particular case he differs from Motolinía.

The earliest published list of Motolinía's works is given by Fray Francisco Gonzaga in his *De origine Seraphicae Religionis Franciscanae,* Rome, 1589, "Quarta Pars Provincia Sancti Evangeli," p. 1235: *"Scripsit non nullos libros ut de moribus Indorum; Adventus duodecim Patrum, qui primi eas regiones devenerunt et de eorum rebus gestis; Doctrinam christianam mexicano idiomate; alios item tractatus spiritualium materiarium et devotiones plenarum."* This list is a word for word version in Latin of the list given by Mendieta,[81] in which all but the first title are in Spanish. Torquemada, at the end of his life of Motolinía, simply copied Mendieta's list.[82] Mendieta also mentions[83] an account of the martyrdom of Cristóbal written by Motolinía, and refers again[84] to a brief catechism "which is

78. See Bibliography, *infra.*
79. See below, note 86.
80. See Bibliography, *infra.*
81. Mendieta, p. 620.
82. Torquemada, vol. III, p. 441.
83. Mendieta, p. 241.
84. *Idem,* p. 550.

circulating in printed form," and also to "an account which he wrote of the conversion that he and his companions effected in the Indians of this land, with other matters related to it" which he dedicated to the Conde de Benavente and concluded with a "cántico espiritual."[85] There is nothing in the nature of a "cántico espiritual" at the end of the *History of the Indians,* but the *Memoriales* does end with a brief chapter which invites "the first conquerors, the spiritual conquerors and the angels to join in "a new song of thanksgiving to the Lord."

In 1598 Rebolledo[86] was the first to mention by name the lost work of Motolinía known as *La guerra de los Indios,* and also added to the list a "treatise in Spanish on the *'Camino del espíritu,'*" probably one of the spiritual treatises mentioned by both Gonzaga and Mendieta.

Early in 1601 Fray Juan Bautista translated into Mexican and published Motolinía's account of the martyrdom of the three Indian boys, Juan, Antonio, and Cristóbal. That this was a later version of the story than that which appears in the *History of the Indians,* book III, chapter 14, is proved by the fact that the latter ends with the bringing of Cristóbal's body to Tlaxcala by Fray Andrés de Córdoba, whereas the Mexican version ends as follows: "and I, the author of this story, Fray Toribio Motolinía, moved the bones of this blessed child to the church."[87]

In 1606 Henrico Martínez,[88] in writing about the Mexican calendar, mentioned that Motolinía had written an explanation of it. Torquemada in the *Monarchía Indiana,* book X, chapter xxxvi, p. 301, repeats this statement. The *History of the Indians*[89] contains a brief exposition of the subject, but a much fuller one is to be found in the *Memoriales.*[90]

The *Memoriales* were frequently cited by both Torquemada and Herrera.[91] The same title was given in 1629 by Antonio de León Pinelo in his *Epítome de la Biblioteca Oriental, Occidental Náutica y Geográphica.* He also listed for the first time a manuscript *Relación de las cosas, idolatrías, ritos y ceremonias de la Nueva España,* which he claimed to have

85. *Idem,* p. 556.

86. Rebolledo, *Catálogo de los sanctos y varones notables desta apostólica orden,* at the end of his *Chrónica General de Nuestro Seráfico Padre Sant Francisco y su apostólica orden,* Seville, 1598.

87. From the monastery chapel where the body was first buried.

88. Henrico Martínez, *Reportorio de los tiempos y Historia Natural desta Nueva España,* Mexico, 1606.

89. Motolinía, *infra,* bk 1, chap. 5.

90. Motolinía, *Memoriales,* pp. 36 ff and 48-57; see also a reproduction of the calendar wheel at the end of the volume.

91. See Bibliography, *infra.*

seen. The same title was given by Nicolas Antonio in 1672 in his *Bibliotheca Hispana Nova.*

Robertson in his *History of America,* London, 1777, and Clavigero in the *Storia Antica de Messico,* 1780-81, were the first to use the title *Historia de los Indios de la Nueva España.* There were, according to Clavigero, several copies of this work in Spain in his day.

In 1856 Buckingham Smith, in a letter to Ramírez, mentioned a Motolinía manuscript preserved in the library of the Academia de la Historia, entitled *De los frailes que han muerto en la conversión de los Indios,* and another in the library of the Escorial, described as follows: T.2. *Anonymi Rel.—idolatrías i ritus de los Indios de la Nueva España de la conversión i aprovechamiento de los Indios, i de los frailes que han muerto en su conversión—con la vida del P. fr. Martín de Valencia de Sn.* (sic) *Juan— M. II. 21 p. 427—1 tomo fol. letra del tiempo.*[92]

In 1848 a part of our text—from the beginning through the first half of Chapter 9—appeared in Lord Kingsborough's *Antiquities of Mexico,* vol. 9, under the title *Ritos antiguos, sacrificios e idolatrías de los Indios de la Nueva España, y de su conversión a la fe, y quienes fueron los que primero la predicaron.* Ten years later the complete text was published with the title *Historia de los Indios de la Nueva España* by Joaquín García Icazbalceta in the first volume of his *Colección de Documentos para la Historia de México.* The basis of this edition was a copy made for García Icazbalceta by Prescott from a manuscript in his possession. The text was edited by José Fernando Ramírez, who also wrote the detailed and valuable introductory study of Motolinía's life and works, the best that has been done. It is from this text that the present translation was made. In 1914 another edition was published in Barcelona by Fray Daniel Sánchez García. This same edition was reprinted in Mexico in 1941.

In 1860 or 61 there appeared for sale in Madrid a manuscript which was bought for García Icazbalceta by a friend of his. It contains, besides a copy of Zurita's *Breve Relación,* a manuscript of Motolinía, without title. García Icazbalceta took it to be "a first draft of the *History of the Indians,*" "one of the rough drafts from which the author compiled the much better arranged *History of the Indians.*" In 1903 his son, Don Luís García Pimentel, following in his father's footsteps, published this manuscript in Mexico under the title *Memoriales de Fray Toribio de Motolinía,* as the first volume of a series called *Documentos Históricos de México.* It is cer-

92. Ramírez, *Noticias,* pp. cxxiv and cxxxiv.

tain from internal evidence that parts at least of the *Memoriales* are posterior to 1541.[93] It contains much of the same material as the *History,* and frequently in the same words, but it gives much more information about Indian customs and has chapters on Nicaragua and Guatemala which do not appear in the *History.* On the other hand, it lacks the life of Father Martín de Valencia and the description of plays, pageants, and processions with which the converted Indians celebrated the Christian feasts. The style is much rougher and more careless than that of the *History* and it is noticeable that whereas the latter has very few classical and Biblical quotations and allusions, and very little in the way of moralizing digression, all of these appear frequently in the *Memoriales.* It seems probable that there were at some time other copies or versions of the *Memoriales* in existence, for Torquemada in several instances when supposedly quoting from the *Memoriales* gives more material than is to be found in the text as we know it.[94]

One other important work of Motolinía—probably not known to his contemporaries, and certainly not mentioned by any of them—was discovered only in the nineteenth century. This is the famous letter to Charles V of Spain, containing Motolinía's violent attack on Las Casas. Parts of it came to light in 1805, but it was not published in full until Buckingham Smith included it in the first volume of his *Colección de Documentos para la Historia de la Florida* in 1857. Since then it has appeared in the same volume with Ramírez's edition of the *Historia de los Indios de la Nueva España* in 1858,[95] and also in volume VII of the *Colección de Documentos Inéditos del Archivo de Indias,* 1867, and in Sánchez García's edition of the *Historia* in 1914.

93. *E. g., Memoriales,* p. 345, "más de 1542 años que hay desde su (Christ's) advenimiento hasta hoy," and, p. 53, "a 8 de octubre de este año de '49 . . . Hoy a 20 de octubre" (of the same year).

94. *E. g.,* Torquemada, vol. I, pp. 324 ff., and *Memoriales,* pp. 226 ff.

95. It is interesting to read García Icazbalceta's comment on Ramírez's treatment of the relations between Motolinía and Las Casas. "I see that you have come out in favor of the latter, showing yourself rather hard on the former." This comment is followed by an expression of García Icazbalceta's own feeling about Las Casas: "In spite of all that I have read I cannot form a judgment about Fray Bartolomé . . . I believe that though he had rare and eminent qualities, he was completely lacking in the one that governs all the others . . . that is, prudence, with which the good bishop was entirely unacquainted." From a letter to Ramírez, published in *Obras de Don Joaquín García Icazbalceta,* vol. VII, *Opúsculos Varios,* pp. 313 ff.

Introductory Letter

From a Friar Minor to the Illustrious Don Antonio Pimentel, sixth Count of Benavente, about the ancient rites, idolatries, and sacrifices of the Indians of New Spain, and about the marvelous conversion which God has effected in them. This letter tells the origin of those who settled New Spain and became its rulers.

MAY the peace of our most high Lord God be always with your soul. Amen. Our Redeemer and Master, Jesus Christ, in his sermons adapted his subjects, parables, and examples to the capacity of his hearers, and following his example I say that wise courtiers should pride themselves upon the same things as their Lord and King, for to do otherwise would be the height of folly. Hence it is that when the Emperor in his court prides himself upon his prowess in the lists, all his gentlemen are jousters; and if the King inclines to be a huntsman, all the nobles hunt; and the costume that the King likes and wears, that same is worn by the courtiers.

And hence it is that, as our true Redeemer gloried in the Cross, all those of his court gloried more in that same Cross than in any other thing, like true courtiers who understood and knew that in this lay their true salvation. And hence it is that man prides himself upon nothing so much as upon his reason, which makes him a man, capable and deserving of eternal bliss, and distinguishes and sets him apart from the brute beasts. God so gloried in the Cross that He became man and determined by the Cross to redeem the human race; and since the Lord glories in the fruit of the Cross, that is, the souls of those who are to be saved, I believe that your Lordship, as a wise and loyal servant of Jesus Christ, will rejoice to hear and know of the salvation and redemption of the converts in the New World, which is now called New Spain, where, by the grace and will of God, so many and such great and rich lands are being discovered every day, where Our Lord is newly known and his holy name and faith exalted and glorified. His is all the goodness and virtue which shines forth in your Lordship and in all the virtuous princes of the world, your Lordship being no less endowed with these qualities than were all his ancestors, especially your Lordship's renowned father, Don Alonso Pimentel, fifth Count of Benavente, of good and glorious memory, in whose footsteps your Lordship in his youth is following faithfully, showing himself to be the no less magnanimous than Catholic Lord of the very famous house and noble title of Benavente.

Because of this, all of us, your servants and chaplains should work and study to serve you and show our gratitude for mercies received. I therefore beseech your Lordship to accept this little tribute, taken from my work and occupation by stealing from my sleep some hours in which I have compiled this account; a tribute which I present to your Lordship knowing that I have fallen so far short of my intention that I might be criticized by men experienced in this land, who have seen and heard all, or most, of what shall here be told. And in order that this work may not be defective in what men naturally desire to know—and it is even true that to seek out and learn secrets is the glory of lords and princes—I shall in this letter briefly state the things that seem to me appropriate to this narrative.

This land of Anáhuac or New Spain (first so called by our lord the Emperor), according to the ancient books which these natives had, written in characters and figures, for that was their form of writing [1]—and because they had no letters but only characters, and because man's memory

1. On the pictographs of the ancient Mexicans, see T. A. Joyce, ch. 4; S. G. Morley, *Introduction to the Study of the Maya Hieroglyphs;* Eduard Seler et al, *Mexican and Central American Antiquities, Calendar Systems, and History,* various articles; Bureau of American Ethnology, Bulletin No. 28.

is weak and feeble, the elders disagree in telling of the antiquities and notable things of the land, although some things have been deduced and understood from their characters respecting the antiquity and the succession of the lords who ruled and governed this great land.[2] Of this, however, I shall not treat, for it seems unnecessary to tell of persons and names which can ill be pronounced or understood. Let it suffice to say how at the time when this land was conquered by the good knight and valiant captain, Hernando Cortés, now Marquis of the Valley, the supreme king and lord was one named Moteuczoma, and called by the Indians Moteuczomatzin, a title of greater dignity.

There were, among these natives, as I have said, five books of figures and characters. The first tells of the years and seasons; the second, of their days and feasts during the whole year; the third, of the dreams, illusions, vanities and omens in which they believed. The fourth is the book of baptism and the names they gave the children; the fifth deals with their rites, ceremonies and omens connected with marriage. Of all these, one—the first—can be believed, because it tells the truth, for although barbarous and illiterate, these Indians were punctilious in counting the seasons, days, weeks, months, years and festivals—as will appear later. Also they depicted the deeds and histories of conquests and wars, and the succession of their great lords, the storms and noteworthy signs in the skies, and general pestilences, telling in what season and under what lord they occurred; and they list all the chief lords who ruled this New Spain until the coming of the Spaniards. All this they have in characters and figures which make it known. They call this book *The Book of the Number of the Years,* and according to what has been learned from it about the people who settled this land there were three different peoples, and even today there are some of the same names.[3] One group they call Chichimecas, and they were the first lords of this land. The second group was the people of Colhua. The third group was the Mexicans.

About the Chichimecas we find nothing except that they have lived in this land for eight hundred years, although it is considered certain that they are much older, but that, being a barbarous race who lived like savages, they had no way of writing or representing things. The people of Colhua, we find, began to write and make records by means of their

2. This is one of the confused sentences referred to in the Introduction. The verb of which "Esta tierra de Anáhuac" was to be the subject never appears.

3. The early history of Mexico is very confused. See authorities in note 1; also, George C. Vaillant, *Aztecs of Mexico,* and references therein.

characters and figures. We do not find that these Chichimecas had houses or villages or clothing or corn or any other kind of grain or seeds. They dwelt in caves and in the forests, and lived on roots, venison, rabbits, hares and snakes. They ate everything raw or dried in the sun; and even today there are people who live in this way, as the bearer [4] of this letter will tell your lordship at greater length, for he, with three other companions, escaped from the expedition of Pánfilo de Narváez and was for more than seven years in captivity among the Indians as a slave. Then they escaped and other Indians guided and served them during a journey of more than seven hundred leagues and looked upon them as men come down from Heaven. And they discovered a great deal of land north of New Galicia, whither men are now going in search of the Seven Cities.[5] Messengers and letters have already come telling how they have discovered an infinite number of people. The first part of that land is called the province of Cíbola. It is believed that it will be the gateway to further explorations.

These Chichimecas recognized one man as chief and obeyed him above all others. They took only one wife and she must not be related. They had no blood sacrifices nor idols, but they worshipped the sun and considered it a god, to whom they offered birds and snakes and butterflies. This is all that people have succeeded in finding out about these Chichimecas.

The second were the people of Colhua. It is not known certainly whence they came, except that they were not natives, but came thirty years after the Chichimecas were living in the land, so that there is a record of them going back seven hundred and seventy years. It is known that they were an intelligent people, that they worked and cultivated the soil, and that they began to build and construct houses and towns, and finally began to enter into communication with the Chichimecas and to intermarry with them, although it is known that this lasted only one hundred and eighty years.

4. Either Andrés Dorantes or Alonso del Castillo Maldonado. The other two members of Pánfilo de Narváez's disastrous expedition to Florida (1528) who succeeded in reaching Mexico were Alvar Núñez Cabeza de Vaca, who returned to Spain in 1537 and stayed there till 1540, when he went on an expedition to South America, and the negro Estebanillo, who accompanied Fray Marcos de Niza as guide on the latter's expedition in search of Cíbola (March to April, 1539) and was killed by the Indians.

5. The expedition led by Francisco Vásquez de Coronado, 1540-1542, which made the first exploration of the southwestern part of the United States of today. See *Narratives of the Coronado Expedition, 1540-1542,* edited by George P. Hammond and Agapito Rey (Albuquerque, 1940); or George Parker Winship's translation printed in the 14th Annual Report of the Bureau of American Ethnology, Washington, 1896.

The third, as I mentioned, are the Mexicans, whom I will discuss later. Some think that they are the same race as the Colhuas, and the reason for this belief is that their languages are identical, although it is known that these Mexicans were the latest in time and had no ruling lords,[6] but were governed by captains. The people of Colhua seemed to be of a higher class. Both peoples came to the lake of Mexico. The Colhuas came in from the east and built a town called Tollantzinco, seventeen leagues from Mexico, and from there they went to Tollan, twelve leagues north of Mexico, and moved on, continuing to make settlements, toward Tetzcoco, which is on the shore of the lake of Mexico, five leagues across and eight leagues around. Tetzcoco is to the east and Mexico to the west, and the lake is between them. Some people claim that Tetzcoco is called Colhua, out of respect for those who settled there. Later the power of Tetzcoco was as great as that of Mexico. From Tetzcoco they came to build Coatlichan, which is a little more than one league from Tetzcoco, on the shore of the lake and between east and south. From there they went to Colhuacan, to the south. Mexico is two leagues north of it, reached by a highway. There in Colhuacan they settled down and stayed for many years. Where the city of Mexico now stands there were at that time bogs and swamps, except for a small part which was dry and formed a sort of little island. There the Colhuas began to build a few straw huts, although they kept the seat of their power in Colhuacan and their chief lived there.

In this middle period came the Mexicans, and they also came in by the pass of Tollan, which is to the north of Mexico; and they came toward the west, making settlements until they reached Azcapotzalco, slightly more than a league from Mexico. From there they went to Tlacopán and Chapultepec, where there is an excellent spring whose waters flow into Mexico, and from there they settled Mexico.

While the Mexicans were living in Mexico, the center of their power, and the Colhuas were settled in Colhuacan, one of the leading Colhuas, becoming ambitious of power, treacherously killed the lord, who was the thirteenth ruler since their settlement, and made himself master of all the land. Being a shrewd man and wishing to reign undisturbed, he tried to kill the son of the lord whom he had assassinated; but the youth, by a

6. Spanish: *señores principales.* The words 'lords' and 'principal men' have been used throughout to translate the Spanish *señores* and *principales,* which are themselves attempts to render the Aztec terms *tecuhtli, tlatoani, tlatocapilli.* See Molina, *Vocabulario.*

For the social organization of the Aztecs see the articles by A. F. Bandelier and T. T. Waterman.

stratagem of his mother, was able to escape death, and went to Mexico. There he lived for many days, and grew and came to be a man, and the Mexicans, taken with his attractive personality, arranged alliances with him, so that he contracted polygamous marriages with twenty women, all daughters and relatives of the leading Mexicans. By these wives he had many children from whom are descended all the chief men of the Mexican district. Fortune was as favorable to him as it had been unfavorable to his father, for he came to be the lord of Mexico and also of Colhuacan, though not of the whole of it. During his lifetime he made over the lordship of Colhuacan to one of his sons, and he himself remained to give lustre to Mexico, where he ruled and held sway for forty-six years. After the death of this lord, who was called Acamapitzli, he was succeeded by a son even more valiant than his father, for by his skill he conquered many towns. And he was succeeded by a brother whose vassals killed him treacherously, and largely through his own fault, for he lived a very irregular life.

This third lord was succeeded by another brother called Itzcoatzin who was very fortunate and won many battles and conquered many provinces and built many temples and increased the power of Mexico.

He was succeeded by another lord named Huehue Moteuczoma, which means Moteuczoma the elder, who was a grandson of the first lord. It was the custom among these people for brothers to inherit the power, if there were brothers, and after the brothers the succession passed to the son of the eldest brother.[7] In some places, however, it was customary for the son to succeed the father but the succession of the brothers was more usual and was the custom in the larger realms such as Mexico and Tetzcoco.

Moteuczoma the elder having died without male issue, he was succeeded by a legitimate daughter whose husband was a near relative. Their son and heir was Moteuczomatzin, who was reigning at the time that the Spaniards came to this land of Anáhuac. This Moteuczomatzin reigned

7. Gómara (p. 434) says: "There are many ways of inheriting among the people of New Spain, and a great difference in this respect between nobles and commoners. The general custom among kings and the great Mexican lords is that brothers inherit rather than sons; next in succession come the sons of the oldest brother, and after them the sons of the first heir. If there were no sons or grandsons the nearest relatives inherited." Torquemada (vol. II, p. 358) says: ". . . and this last (*i. e.*, the succession of brothers) was inviolable in this Mexican state, brother always succeeding brother." Also see below, p. 144.

in greater prosperity than any of his predecessors, because he was a wise man who knew how to make himself respected and feared, so that he was the most dreaded lord of all who ruled this land. This suffix-*tzin,* the final syllable of the names of the lords mentioned here, is not a part of the name, but is added out of courtesy and as a mark of dignity, as this language requires.

This Moteuczoma knew through his prophets and soothsayers that his glory, triumph and majesty were not to last many years, and that in his time strangers would come to rule this land. For this reason he lived in sadness, as befits the meaning of his name, for Moteuczoma means a melancholy man, stern, grave and modest, a man who makes himself feared and respected, and all of these qualities were indeed characteristic of him.

These Indians, besides recording in characters and figures the things I have mentioned, and especially the succession and lineage of the lords and of the leading families, and the noteworthy things that happened in their time, had also amongst them persons of excellent memory who remembered and could relate everything that they were asked. One of these men I met; a very clever man, I thought, and with an excellent memory, and he, briefly and without contradictions, told me about the beginning and origin of these natives, giving me his opinion and that of the books considered amongst them as most authentic. This man, then, says that these Indians of New Spain originated in a place called Chicomoztoc, which in our Spanish tongue means Seven Caves, and that a certain lord[8] of this town had seven[9] sons, of whom the first born and eldest settled Cuauhquechollan and many other towns, and his line went on settling the country until they reached Tehuacán, Cozcatlán, and Teutitlán.

From the second son, named Tenoch, came the Tenochas, who are the Mexicans, and so the city of Mexico is called Tenochca.

The third and fourth sons also settled many provinces and towns as far as where the city of Los Angeles now stands, where there took place great battles and encounters such as were usual at that time. From there

8. Torquemada (vol. I, p. 32) gives the name of the father as Iztac Mixcoatl and states that the six sons by his first wife were Xelhua, Tenuch, Ulmecatl, Xicalancatl, Mixtecatl, and Otomitl. By his second wife he had one son, Quetzalcoatl.

9. One would expect six, instead of seven, since he is speaking here of the sons of the first marriage. *Siete* for *seis* is a very easy error to make, particularly as *siete* has just been used with *cuevas* (the Seven Caves).

they pushed forward to the site now occupied by Xicalanco, a much frequented town, in which many merchants from different parts and distant lands used to meet to make contracts. I remember having seen another town of the same name in the province of Maxcalzinco, which is near the port of Vera Cruz and was settled by the Xicalancas. Although the two are on the same coast, there is a long distance between them.

From the fifth son, called Mixtecatl, came the Mixtecas. Their land is now called Mixtecapán, and is a great realm. From the town nearest to Mexico, called Acatlán, to the farthest one, which is Totetepec on the coast of the South Sea, the distance is nearly eighty leagues. In this land of Mixteca there are many provinces and towns, and though it is very mountainous it is all settled. It forms some valleys and plains, but there is no plain in the whole country more than one league wide. It is a thickly settled territory and rich, with mines of gold and silver, and many excellent mulberry trees. It was for this reason that they first began the culture of silk here, and, although it is only a short time since the business was started in New Spain, they say that there will be a harvest this year of more than fifteen thousand pounds of silk. It is very good silk, and the experts who handle it say that the *tonotzi* [10] is better than the *joyante*[11] of Granada, and the *joyante* of New Spain is an extremely good silk.

It is a healthy country. All the towns are high and in dry places. The climate is temperate, and it is worth noting that silk can be raised all the year round, without missing a month. Before I wrote this letter, in the present year of 1541, I spent more than thirty days in this region I speak of, and in the month of February I saw silk-seed in many places, some of it about to hatch. I also saw worms in all stages, the little black ones, white ones, worms which had moulted, some once, some twice, and some three and four times, big worms, already out of the baskets [12] and on the trays,[13] some spinning and some in the cocoon, and some moths laying eggs. Three things are to be noted in what I have said: first, that the seed can be hatched without placing it next to the body, or between coverings, as is done in Spain; second, that in no season do the worms die, either from cold or from heat, and third, that there are green leaves on the mulberries the year round because of the temperate climate of the land. All

10. The Mexican name of a kind of silk.

11. A fine, glossy silk made in Granada.

12. Spanish: *panelas.* The dictionaries give no meaning for *panela* that would fit this context. There is a word *paneles,* meaning shallow baskets.

13. Spanish: *zarzos,* wicker trays, or screens.

this I venture to affirm because I have seen it myself, and I maintain that they will be able to raise two large crops of silk a year, and a little all the time, as I have said.

At the end of this land of Mixteca is the rich and most fertile valley of Oaxyecac, from which the most worthy Marquis, Don Hernando Cortés, derives his title, and in which he has many vassals. In the middle of this valley, built on a hillside, is the city of Antequera, which is rich in all kinds of cattle and well supplied with food, especially wheat and corn. At the beginning of this year I saw wheat sold there at one real the fanega, and in this country a real is worth less than half what it is in Spain. Antequera has very fine quinces and pomegranates and a great many very good figs, which last nearly all the year. The fig trees here grow very large and handsome.

From the last [of the six sons] are descended the Otomíes, called by his name, which was Otomitl. It is one of the most numerous races of New Spain. All, or most, of the summits of the mountains around Mexico are full of them. I believe that the seat of their power is Xilotepec, which is a great province, and the provinces of Tollan and Otompa belong almost wholly to them, without counting that in the best part of New Spain there are many towns of these Otomíes, from whom the Chichimecas are descended. These two races, in truth, are the lowest and most barbarous in all New Spain, but they are of suitable disposition for receiving the Faith, and they have come and still come eagerly to receive baptism and learn the Christian doctrine.

I have not been able to ascertain which of these brothers went to settle the province of Nicaragua. I know only that at a time of great sterility many Indians were driven by necessity to leave New Spain, and I suspect that it was during the four-year period when there was no rain in all the land, for it is known that at that very time a great number of canoes or boats went by way of the South Sea and landed in Nicaragua, which is more than three hundred and fifty leagues from Mexico. They made war upon the natives who were settled there and defeated them and overthrew their power. The invading Nahuas remained and settled there, and although that was only a hundred years ago, more or less, when the Spaniards discovered that land of Nicaragua—discovered in the year 1523 by Gil González de Avila—they estimated that the province had at that time a population of five hundred thousand souls. Later there was built there the city of León, which is the capital of the province. Because many people are surprised to see that Nicaragua is populated by Nahuas, who speak the same language as the Mexicans, and do not know when or by whom it was settled, I state here the manner of that settlement, for there is scarcely anyone in New Spain who knows it.

The same old man, father of those [*i. e.,* the six sons] mentioned above, married a second time, and this race believed that it had sprung from and been engendered by the rain and the dust of the earth;[14] and they also believed that the same old man and his first wife had sprung from that place called the Seven Caves and had no other father or mother. By that second wife they say that he had a son called Quetzalcoatl, who turned out to be an honest and temperate man. He began to do penance, by fasting and scourging himself, and to preach the natural law, as they say, and to teach the practice of fasting, both by precept and by example, and from that time many people in this land began to fast. Quetzalcoatl was not married and was not known to associate with any women, but lived virtuously and chastely. They say that he began the practice of sacrifice and of drawing blood from the tongue and ears, not as an offering to the devil, but as a penance for the vices of the tongue and ears. Later the devil adopted this practice for his worship and service.

An Indian named Chichimecatl tied a band or strap of leather around Quetzalcoatl's arm, up near the shoulder, and at that time and because of that tying of the god's arm they acclaimed him Acolhuatl,[15] and from him they say that the Colhuas are descended, the ancestors of Moteuczoma, lords of Mexico and Colhuacan. This Quetzalcoatl was considered by the Indians as one of their principal gods, and they called him the god of the air, and everywhere they built him an infinite number of temples and set up statues of him and painted his picture. About the origin of these natives there are different opinions, and especially about those of Colhua, or Acolhua, who were the chief lords of this New Spain; so I will set forth the different opinions for the benefit of your most excellent lordship.

The people of Tetzcoco, who in antiquity and power are not inferior to the Mexicans, are called today Acolhuas and their whole province to-

14. This sentence is confused. The text reads: El mismo viejo, padre de los arriba dichos, casó segunda vez; la cual gente creyó que había salido y sido engendrada de la lluvia y del polvo de la tierra. . .

15. From *acoli,* which means shoulder, or the bone of the upper arm. See the following paragraph. Motolinía does not make it very clear, but apparently these two paragraphs represent the rival myths of the Mexicans and the Texcocans, both explaining the name Acolhua, or Colhua, and establishing a claim to it.

gether Acolhuacán. This name they derive from a valiant captain of theirs, a native of that same province, called Acoli. *Acoli* is the name of the bone which reaches from the elbow to the shoulder, and from that bone they call the shoulder *acoli*. This captain was another Saul, valiant and great of stature, so much so that he stood head and shoulders above all the people and there was no other like him. This Acoli was so courageous, mighty, and renowned in battle that for him the province of Tetzcoco was called Acolhuacán.

The Tlaxcaltecas, who received the Spaniards and helped them to conquer New Spain, are of the Nahua people, that is, of the same tongue as the Mexicans. They say that their ancestors came from the northwest, and that to reach this land they sailed for eight or ten days. From the oldest men who came from there they had two arrows which they cherished as precious relics and considered as a very important sign to tell them whether they would win the battle, or whether they should retire while there was still time. These Tlaxcaltecas were a warlike people, as will be shown later in the third part. When they went out to battle, those arrows were carried by two captains, the most renowned in valor. In the first encounter they attacked the enemy with these arrows, shooting them from a distance, and then strove until death to recover them. If the arrows struck and drew blood, they were certain of victory and all were greatly encouraged, and with that hope made great efforts to attack and conquer the enemy. If the arrows did not strike anyone or draw blood, they retreated as best they could, because they considered it a certain omen that the battle would go badly for them.

To return to the point: the oldest of these Tlaxcaltecas hold that they come from the northwest, and from there they say came the Nahuas, the principal race and language of New Spain. Many others believe and say the same thing. Toward that part of the northwest, five hundred leagues have now been discovered and conquered, as far as the province of Cíbola, and I have a letter, written this very year,[16] telling how in the country about Cíbola they have discovered an infinite number of people amongst whom they have not found the Nahua language, whence it would appear that it is a foreign and hitherto unheard of race.

16. Probably this is the original of the *Relación postrera de Cíbola,* published by G. P. Winship (Bureau of American Ethnology 14th Annual Report, p. 566.) from a copy made by García Icazbalceta from papers in his possession, said to have belonged to Motolinía.

Aristotle in his book *De Admirandis in Natura*[17] says that in ancient times the Carthaginians sailed through the straits of Hercules, which are our straits of Gibraltar, toward the west, a journey of sixty days, and that they found pleasant, delightful, and very fertile lands. As that voyage was frequently made, and many remained and dwelt in that land, the Carthaginian senate decreed that no one, under pain of death, should make that voyage, for fear that their city might be depopulated. These lands or islands may have been those which come before San Juan, or Española, or Cuba, or perhaps some part of this New Spain. However, a land so great as this, and so thickly populated in all sections would seem rather to trace its origin from other foreign parts; and there are some indications that it comes from the division and dispersal of the sons of Noah. Some Spaniards, in view of some of the rites, customs, and ceremonies of these natives, judge them to be of the race of Moors. Others, because of some causes and conditions which they see in them, say that they are of the Jewish race; but the commonest opinion is that they are all gentiles, since we see that they practice it and consider it good.[18]

If this account should leave the hands of your most illustrious lordship, two things I beg of you in charity, for love of our Lord: one, that the name of the author be given as a Friar Minor and nothing else; the other, that your lordship have it examined in the first chapter meeting in the town of Benavente, since many most learned men meet there; for there are many things which I did not have time to reread after I had written them, and for that reason I know that the account is somewhat defective and badly written.

I pray to God that His holy grace may dwell continually in the soul of your most illustrious lordship.

Written at the monastery of Santa María de la Concepción at Tehuacán, on the day of the glorious apostle Saint Matthias, in the year of the redemption of humanity 1541.

Your most illustrious lordship's poor
and humblest servant and chaplain,

Motolinía. Fray Toribio de Paredes

17. The passage referred to is chapter 84 of the *De Mirabilibus Auscultationibus,* an opusculum *not* written by Aristotle, but included in standard editions of his works.

18. I can suggest no satisfactory translation for this clause, which reads in the original: *mas la común opinión es que todos ellos son gentiles, pues vemos que lo usan y tienen por bueno.* It is not clear to what the *lo* refers, nor what is the subject of *usan* and *tienen.*

BOOK ONE

Here begins the account of the things, idolatries, rites and ceremonies which the Spaniards found in New Spain when they conquered it, together with many other notable things which they found in the land.

CHAPTER I

Of how and when the first friars who made that journey set out; and of the persecutions and plagues which occurred in New Spain.

IN the year of our Lord 1523, on the day of the conversion of Saint Paul, which is the 25th of January, Father Fray Martín de Valencia,[1] of blessed memory, with eleven friars as his companions set out from Spain to come to this land of Anáhuac, sent by the most reverend father, Fray Francisco de los Angeles, at that time General of the Order of Saint Francis. They came with great indulgences and pardons from our very Holy Father, and at the special command of His Majesty our Lord the Emperor, to convert the Indians, natives of this land of Anáhuac, now called New Spain.

1. For more detailed information about this expedition and about Fray Martín de Valencia and his companions, see below pp. 182-183 and 187, and Fray Gerónimo de Mendieta, *Historia Eclesiástica Indiana,* p. 197 ff.

God struck and chastened with ten terrible plagues this land and all who dwelt in it, both natives and foreigners.

The first was a plague of smallpox, and it began in this manner. When Hernando Cortés was captain and governor, at the time that Captain Pánfilo de Narváez landed in this country, there was in one of his ships a negro stricken with smallpox, a disease which had never been seen here. At this time New Spain was extremely full of people, and when the smallpox began to attack the Indians it became so great a pestilence among them throughout the land that in most provinces more than half the population died; in others the proportion was little less. For as the Indians did not know the remedy for the disease and were very much in the habit of bathing frequently, whether well or ill, and continued to do so even when suffering from smallpox, they died in heaps, like bedbugs. Many others died of starvation, because, as they were all taken sick at once, they could not care for each other, nor was there anyone to give them bread or anything else. In many places it happened that everyone in a house died, and, as it was impossible to bury the great number of dead, they pulled down the houses over them in order to check the stench that rose from the dead bodies so that their homes became their tombs. This disease was called by the Indians 'the great leprosy' because the victims were so covered with pustules that they looked like lepers. Even today one can see obvious evidences of it in some individuals who escaped death, for they were left covered with pockmarks.

Eleven years later there came a Spaniard who had measles, and from him the disease was communicated to the Indians; if great care had not been taken to prevent their bathing, and to use other remedies, this would have been as terrible a plague and pestilence as the former. Even with all these precautions many died. They called this the year of the 'little leprosy.'

The second plague was the great number of those who died in the conquest of New Spain, especially around Mexico. For you must know that when Hernando Cortés landed on the coast of this country, with the energy which he always showed, he scuttled his ships to rouse the courage of his men, and plunged into the interior. After marching forty leagues he entered the land of Tlaxcallan, one of the largest provinces of the country and most thickly populated. Entering the inhabited part of it, he established himself in some temples of the devil in a little town called Tecoautzinco (the Spaniards called it Torrecilla, 'the little tower,' because it is on a height) and while there he fought for two weeks with the Indians roundabout. They are called Otomíes and are people of low condition, like peasants. A great number of them came together, for the country is thickly populated. The Indians who live farther in the interior speak the language of Mexico. As the Spaniards were fighting valiantly with these Otomíes, the news reached Tlaxcallan; whereupon the lords and principal men came out, formed a great friendship with the Spaniards, took them to Tlaxcallan, gave them presents and supplies in abundance and showed them great affection. Not content to remain in Tlaxcallan, after resting for a few days they took the road to Mexico. The great lord of Mexico, whose name was Moteuczoma, received them in peace, coming out in great majesty, attended by many noble lords. He gave many jewels and gifts to Captain Hernando Cortés and a very good reception to all his companions; and so, with his safe-conduct and agreement they went about Mexico for many days. At this time Pánfilo de Narváez arrived with many more men and horses than Hernando Cortés had. Put under the banner and command of Cortés,[2] they showed themselves very haughty and presumptuous because of their arms and numbers, but were so humbled and humiliated by God that the Indians, wishing to throw them out of the city and beginning to make war upon them, drove them out with very little difficulty. More than half the Spaniards died in the retreat from the city,[3] and nearly all the others were wounded, as were also the friendly Indians; in fact the whole force came very near to destruction and had great difficulty in getting back to Tlaxcallan, because of the many warriors who followed them all the way. When they reached Tlaxcallan they cared for their wounds and got back their strength, always showing courage; and, making the best of a bad situation, they set out on a campaign of conquest, accompanied by many of the Tlaxcaltecas, and conquered the land of Mexico. In order to conquer Mexico they had built brigantines in Tlaxcallan which can be seen today in the shipyards of Mexico. These brigantines they carried in pieces from Tlaxcallan to Tetzcoco, a distance of fifteen leagues. When they had put the brigantines together and launched them, having by this time taken many towns and won others over to fight on their side, a great number of warriors went out from Tlaxcallan to fight for the Spaniards against the Mexicans, for they had always been their very deadly enemies. In Mexico

2. After Cortés had surprised and defeated Narváez, who had been sent by Governor Velázquez of Cuba to supersede him.

3. June 30, 1520. The disastrous defeat of the Spaniards known as the "noche triste."

and on the Mexican side there was much greater strength, because all the most powerful lords of the land were in Mexico and on her side. When the Spaniards arrived they laid siege to Mexico, and by seizing all the highways and fighting on the water with their brigantines prevented assistance or supplies from reaching Mexico. The captains waged war savagely along the highways and tore down every bit of the city that they captured; before this practice was instituted, as soon as the Spaniards retired to their camps at night the Indians re-took all that the Spaniards had won during the day and re-opened the highways. Having made a practice of tearing down buildings and blocking up roads, they took the city after many days. In this war, because of the great numbers who died in both armies, men compare the number of the dead and say that it is greater than the number of those who died in Jerusalem when it was destroyed by Titus and Vespasian.

The third plague was a very great famine which came immediately after the taking of the city of Mexico. As they were unable to plant because of the great wars, some of them defending the land and helping the Mexicans and others fighting on the side of the Spaniards, and as what was planted by one side was cut down and laid waste by the other, they had nothing to eat. Although it sometimes happens that there are barren years in this country, years of little rainfall or of heavy frost, the Indians at such times eat a variety of different roots and herbs, for they can endure barren years better and more easily than other races. In this year of which I am speaking, however, there was such a scarcity of grain (which in this country they call *centli* when it is in the ear, and in the Islands they call it *maíz;* and the Spaniards use this latter word, and many others which they brought from the Islands to New Spain); corn, I say, was so scarce that even the Spaniards were in difficulties for lack of it.

The fourth plague was that of the *calpixques* or overseers, and the negroes. As soon as the land was divided, the conquerors put into their allotments and into the towns granted to them servants or negroes to collect the tributes and to look after their various affairs. These men lived, and still live, in the villages, and though for the most part they are peasants from Spain they have taken possession of the land and order the native lords around as if the latter were their slaves. Because I do not wish to disclose their defects, I shall keep silent about what I think and only say that they make themselves feared and insist upon service as if they were the absolute and natural masters. They never do anything but demand, and however much people give them they are never content, for wherever they are they infect and corrupt everything, as foul as putrid flesh. They make no effort to do anything except to give orders. They are the drones who eat the honey made by the poor bees who are the Indians, and they are not satisfied with what the poor things give them, but keep demanding. In the first years these overseers were so absolute in their maltreatment of the Indians, over-loading them, sending them far from their land and giving them many other tasks, that many Indians died because of them and at their hands, which is the worst feature of the situation.

The fifth plague was the great taxes and tributes that the Indians paid. As they had, in the temples of their idols and in the possession of their lords and chief men and in many tombs, a great quantity of gold, the accumulation of many years, the Spaniards began to exact heavy tributes from them, and the Indians, terrified of the Spaniards ever since the war, gave everything they had. As the tributes, however, were so continuous that they had scarcely paid one when they were obliged to pay another, they sold their children and their lands to the money lenders in order to meet their obligations; and when they were unable to do so many died because of it, some under torture and some in cruel prisons, for the Spaniards treated them brutally and considered them less than beasts.

The sixth plague was the gold mines, for in addition to the taxes and tributes paid by the towns which had been granted to the Spaniards, the latter began to seek for mines, and it would be impossible to count the number of Indians who have, up to the present day, died in these mines. The gold of this country was a second golden calf, worshipped as a god, for they come all the way from Castile through many dangers and difficulties to adore it. Now that they have it, please God it may not be to their own damnation.

The seventh plague was the building of the great city of Mexico, which, in the first years, employed more people than the building of the temple of Jerusalem. So many were the people engaged in the work that a man could scarcely make his way along some streets and highways, broad as they are. In the construction some were crushed by beams, others fell from heights, others were caught beneath buildings which were being torn down in one place to be built up again in another; especially did this happen when they tore down the principal temples of the devil. Many

Indians died there, and it was many years before they completely demolished the temples, from which they obtained an enormous amount of stone.

The custom of this country is not the best in the world, for the Indians do the work, get the materials at their own expense, pay the stonemasons and carpenters, and if they do not bring their own food, they go hungry. They carry all the material on their backs and drag the beams and big stones with ropes, and as they had no machinery and plenty of people, they used four hundred men to transport a stone that required one hundred. It is their custom to sing and shout as they work, and their songs and cries scarcely stopped day or night, so great was the zeal which, in the early days, they brought to the building of the town.

The eighth plague was the slaves whom the Spaniards made in order to put them to work in the mines.[4] So great was their haste, in some years, to make slaves that from all parts of Mexico they brought in great herds of them, like flocks of sheep, in order to brand them. They were not content with those who among the Indians are called slaves (for, although according to their cruel and barbarous law some may be slaves, in actual truth almost no one is), but hurried the Indians so to produce slaves as tribute—so many every eighty days—that, having exhausted the supply of real slaves, they brought their children and their *macehuales* (who are of a low social class, like farmer-vassals) and all whom they could get together, and brought them in, terrifying them into saying that they were slaves. The fact that no careful investigation was made and that branding was cheap produced so many marks on their faces, in addition to the royal brand, that they had their faces covered with letters, for they bore the marks of all who had bought and sold them. For this reason this eighth plague cannot be considered the least.

4. See Bernal Díaz del Castillo, vol. II, ch. CXLIII, pp. 27-28, and ch. CCXIII, pp. 594-596. At first royal permission was asked, and granted, to brand as slaves the Indians of towns which had shown themselves hostile and had actually killed Spaniards. They were to be given three chances to make peace, and if they still refused, could then be enslaved and branded on the face. Later, permission was asked, and granted, for the Spaniards to take slaves from the Indians as tribute and to buy and sell them as the Indians themselves did. Responsible persons were appointed to take charge of the branding irons. Bernal Díaz's comment is interesting: "I wish also to state here that it would have been better if . . . His Majesty had never given this permission . . . for certainly there were great frauds in this matter of branding the Indians." Things reached such a pitch that a year or more after the return of the Cortés expedition from Honduras Bernal Díaz, who was at that time one of the custodians of the branding iron in the town of Guazacualco, agreed with his colleague to destroy it, and then sent a message to the audiencia in Mexico telling what they had done and asking that no more slaves be branded in all New Spain. The audiencia so decreed.

The ninth plague was the service of the mines, to which the heavily laden Indians travelled sixty leagues or more to carry provisions; the food which they carried for themselves sometimes gave out when they reached the mines and sometimes on the way back before they reached home; sometimes they were kept by the miners for several days to help them get out the mineral or to build houses for them or to serve them, and when their food gave out they died, either at the mines or on the road, for they had no money to buy food and there was no one to give it to them. Some reached home in such a state that they died soon after. The bodies of these Indians and of the slaves who died in the mines produced such a stench that it caused a pestilence, especially at the mines of Oaxyecac. For half a league around these mines and along a great part of the road one could scarcely avoid walking over dead bodies or bones, and the flocks of birds and crows that came to feed upon the corpses were so numerous that they darkened the sun, so that many villages along the road and in the district were deserted. Other Indians fled to the woods, abandoning their houses and fields.

The tenth plague was the divisions and factions which existed among the Spaniards in Mexico;[5] this was the one that most endangered the country, had it not been that the Lord kept the Indians blinded. These dissensions were the cause of the execution of some Spaniards and the injury and exile of others. Some were wounded when they came to blows, there being no one except the friars to reconcile them nor to intervene. The few Spaniards left in Mexico were all passionate adherents of one party or the other, and the friars had to go out sometimes to prevent their fighting, and sometimes to separate them after they had started, exposing themselves to the shots and weapons of the combatants and the hoofs of the horses. They had to be kept from fighting both because it endangered the Spanish possession of the country and because it was known that the Indians were ready for war and had made provision of arms and were only awaiting the arrival of an expected piece of news. According to a conspiracy arranged by the Indians with those who escorted him, the captain and governor, Hernando Cortés, was to be killed on the road to Las Hibueras.[6] Cortés discovered the conspiracy very near to the spot where the assassination was to have taken place. He executed the chief men who were involved in the treason, thus putting an end to that danger. Here in

5. During the absence of Cortés on the expedition to Honduras, October, 1524, to June, 1526.
6. The form *Hibueras* is used here and below. Later the name is given as *Higueras*.

Mexico the Indians were waiting for one party of Spaniards to defeat the other in order to fall upon those who should be left and put them all to the sword. God, however, did not permit this, not wishing that what had with such difficulty been won to His service should be lost; and He Himself gave grace to the friars to pacify the belligerent factions and to the Spaniards to obey the friars as their true fathers, which they always did. The Spaniards themselves had begged the Friars Minor (for at that time there were no others) to use the powers granted to them by the Pope until such time as bishops should be appointed. Thus, sometimes by entreaty and sometimes by reproof, the friars remedied great evils and prevented many deaths.

Chapter II

How much the friars helped in the conversion of the Indians. The many idols that the Indians had and the cruel sacrifices they performed. Other things worthy of note.

The land was so devastated by the disturbances and plagues already mentioned that many houses were completely deserted and there was none which did not have its share of grief and sorrow, a condition which lasted for many years. To remedy these great evils the friars commended themselves to the most holy Virgin Mary, guiding star of the lost and consolation of the afflicted, and also took as their leader and captain the glorious Saint Michael, to whom, with Saint Gabriel and all the angels, they chant a Mass every Monday. It is still done today in some houses of the Order, and almost all the priests, during Mass, say a collect to the angels. The first year, as soon as they learned something about the land, it seemed to them that it would be well for some of them to go to Spain, both to win the favor of His Majesty for the natives and to bring back more friars, because the size of the country and the number of the inhabitants demanded it. Those who remained in the land took into their houses the sons of the lords and principal men, and with the consent of their parents baptized many of them. These children whom the friars brought up and educated turned out to be very nice and clever, and learned the good doctrine so well that they taught many others. Besides this they helped greatly by divulging to the friars the rites and idolatries and many secret ceremonies of their parents. This information was of great assistance to the friars in confounding and dissipating the errors and the blindness of the Indians.

The friars told the Indians who was the true and universal Lord, creator of heaven and earth and of all creatures, and how this God ruled and governed the universe with His infinite wisdom, and gave it all the life it had, and how, of His great goodness He wished all men to be saved. They opened the Indians' eyes and showed them that it was the devil whom they served and what his occupation was, namely to bear away to eternal damnation and its terrible sufferings all those who believed and trusted in him. And with this each friar told the Indians what he considered sufficient and most suitable for their salvation. It was very distasteful to them to hear the word God, and all the knowledge they wished was of how to give themselves over to vice and sin by taking part in sacrifices and festivals, eating, drinking, and becoming intoxicated at them, and offering to the idols their own blood, drawn from their ears, tongues, arms and other parts of their bodies, as I shall later tell. This land was a copy of hell, its inhabitants shouting at night, some calling upon the devil, some drunk, some singing and dancing. Especially at the festivals of their devils they used drums, horns, cornets and big shells.

In the drinking bouts that they very frequently had it is incredible the amount of wine they consumed and what each one of them poured into himself. Their wine, before they ferment it with certain roots which they add to it, is clear and sweet like honey and water. After it is fermented it becomes somewhat thick and has a bad odor, and those who get drunk on it smell even worse. They ordinarily began to drink after vespers; they drank so steadily, in groups of ten or fifteen with the pourers never ceasing to pour, and ate so little that by the end of the evening they were losing their wits, now falling, now sitting down, singing and shouting and calling upon the devil. It was pitiable to see men created in the image of God become worse than brute beasts; and worse still, they did not confine themselves to that one sin, but committed many others, striking, wounding, and even killing one another, though they might be friends and close relatives. Except when drunk they are so peaceful that even in a violent quarrel they merely push each other, and almost never shout, although the women do sometimes scream when they quarrel, as happens wherever there are women.

They had another form of intoxication which made them crueler. It was produced by a certain small fungus or mushroom, for there are mushrooms here as in Castile. But the ones that grow here are such that they eat them raw, and, because they are bitter, they eat with them, or drink after eating them, a little honey. Shortly afterward they see all sorts of visions, especially snakes, and, as they go completely out of their minds, they think that their legs and bodies are full of worms which are eating them alive, and thus, half raving, they rush out of the house wanting someone to kill them. With this beastly drunkenness and suffering it would sometimes happen that they would hang themselves, and also they would treat others with greater cruelty. These mushrooms they call in their own language *teonanacatl,* which means 'flesh of God'—or of the devil whom they worshipped. In this way, with that bitter food, their cruel god gave them communion.[1]

In many of their feasts they used to make balls of dough of various kinds, which they used almost as if it were the communion of the god whose festival they celebrated. But they had one which seemed more properly a communion feast.[2] In November, when they had harvested their corn and other grains, they would take the seed of a kind of plant which they call *cenizos,*[3] mix it with cornmeal dough and make *tamales,* which are round balls, and these they would boil in water in a pot. While they were cooking, some young boys would play upon a sort of drum made all of wood, without hide or parchment, and they also sang and said that those balls were converted into the flesh of Tezcatlipoca, the god or devil whom they considered greatest and to whom they attributed most dignity. Only the boys mentioned above partook of those balls, as a sort of communion or flesh of the devil. The other Indians tried to manage to eat human flesh, the flesh of those killed as sacrifices. This was usually eaten by the principal men, the merchants and the ministers of the temples, for the lower classes rarely got a mouthful. After the Spaniards made war

1. Sahagún (vol. III, p. 230) describes these mushrooms as follows: "There are certain little mushrooms in this country that are called *teonanácatl.* They grow under the dry grass in the fields and open spaces; they are round and have a tallish stem, delicate and rounded. If one eats them they have an unpleasant taste and are bad for the throat and intoxicating. They are good as a remedy for fever and gout; one should eat not more than two or three. Those who eat them see visions and have a feeling of nausea. If eaten in any quantity they act as an aphrodisiac." Mr. Henry R. Wagner tells me that these mushrooms are undoubtedly the ones known as "peyotes."

2. On this subject see Frazer, pt. V, vol. II, ch. X, *Eating the God.*

3. According to Ramírez (*Historia de los Indios,* I, p. 25, note 5) the manuscript here reads *gemujos.* The Kingsborough text reads *xenixos.* Gómara (p. 446) calls this plant *ajenjos* (wormwood), but says that it is different from the kind that grows in Spain.

on them, and from the time of the taking of Mexico until the country was pacified, even the Indians who were friendly to the Spaniards often ate the flesh of those whom they killed, for the Spaniards could not always forbid it, but, sometimes, because they needed the support of the Indians, tolerated the practice, although they abhorred it.

CHAPTER III

Continues the subject of the preceding chapter and tells of the devotion which the Indians began to show for the sign of the cross, and how it began to be used.

In all this time the friars were not slothful in assisting, by prayers and supplications, the Faith and those who were fighting for it, and especially zealous were Father Fray Martín de Valencia and his companions, until there came another father, Fray Juan de Zumárraga, who was the first bishop of Mexico.[1] He expended much care and diligence in the decoration and adornment of his cathedral church, upon which he spent for four years the whole income of the bishopric. At that time no prebends were provided in the church but all the money was spent in building and ornaments, for which reason it is as richly decorated and adorned as one of the good churches of Spain; Fray Juan de Zumárraga, however, had plenty of difficulties which at last made him return to Spain. But before he left he had aroused in the people a great reverence for the symbol of the cross, of which they began to paint a great many; and as this land has very lofty mountains, they also made very great and lofty crosses which they worshipped, and as they gazed upon them some were cured of the idolatry from which they still suffered. Many others were by this holy symbol delivered from temptations and evil visions which appeared to them, as shall be told in its proper place.

The principal ministers who served and offered sacrifice in the temples of the idols and the old lords, as they were accustomed to being served and to enjoying all the land—for they were not merely masters of their wives and children and estates, but of all they wished and thought, every-

1. The first bishops in New Spain were appointed in 1528, Fray Juan de Zumárraga as bishop of Mexico and Fray Julián Garcés as bishop of Tlaxcala.

thing being subjected to their will and wish and the vassals having no other will but that of the lord, and if anything, however grave, was commanded them, having no other answer than *mayuh,* which means 'so be it' —these lords and principal ministers, then, would have none of the law which opposes the desires of the flesh. God, however, remedied this by killing many of them with the plagues and diseases already mentioned; others became converted. The estates of those who died passed to their sons, who, as children, had been baptized and brought up in the house of God; so God himself put the lands into the power of those who believed in Him. He has done the same against those who oppose in many ways the conversion of these Indians.

The friars also endeavored to have churches built everywhere, and now in almost every province which has a monastery there are churches dedicated to the twelve apostles, especially to Saint Peter and Saint Paul, who, besides the churches named for them, have their images painted on every altarpiece everywhere.

In all the temples of their idols, the Indians served and honored devils, both in those of the outlying districts and in those of the city of Mexico itself—except that some of the city temples had been torn down and burned by the Spaniards. While the latter were busy building Mexico City and making homes and dwellings for themselves, they were content to prohibit public human sacrifices in their presence; but in secret and round about Mexico there were plenty of them performed. Thus idolatry was left in peace and the houses of the devils and their ceremonies were preserved and their service continued. At this time the governor, Don Hernando Cortés, had gone to Las Hibueras, and there were those who, seeing the offense that was being committed against God, wrote to him and asked him to order the sacrifices to the devil to cease, because as long as they were not suppressed preaching would be of little avail and the work of the friars would be in vain. In this matter the governor at once took adequate action. But since each man had his own affairs to consider (as has already been said), idolatry went on in spite of Cortés' orders until the first day of the year 1525, which that year fell on a Sunday. On that night in Tetzcoco, where the teocallis or temples of the devil are most numerous and largest, fullest of idols, and best served by chief priests and ministers, three friars, from ten o'clock at night until dawn, frightened and put to flight all those who were in the abodes and halls of the devils. That day, after Mass, they preached to the Indians, strongly condemning their homicides and ordering them, in God's name and the King's, not to indulge in these practices, and telling them that unless they obeyed they should be punished as God commanded that such transgressors should be.

This was the first battle against the devil; later he was attacked in Mexico and its villages and surroundings and in Cuautitlan. Also, when in Tlaxcallan they began to tear down and destroy idols and set up the crucifix, they found amongst the idols the image of the crucified Christ and of His blessed Mother, the very images that the Christians had given them, thinking that they would worship them alone. It may have been that, having a hundred gods, they wanted to have a hundred and one;[2] but the friars knew very well that the Indians continued to worship what they were in the habit of worshipping. Then they saw that the Indians had some Christian images on their altars along with their devils and idols; and in other places they had the Christian image displayed and the idols hidden behind a partition or a wall or inside the altar; for this reason the friars took the images away from them, as many of them as they could find, and told them that if they wished to have images of God or of Saint Mary, they should build a church to house them. At first, out of deference to the friars, they began to ask for images and to make hermitages and shrines, and later churches, and place the images in them; but with all this they always tried to keep their temples whole and sound, although later, as things progressed, they began to lay hands on them and take stone and wood from them to build churches, and so the temples were left desolate and destroyed, and the idols of stone, of which there were infinite numbers, not only were broken and knocked to pieces, but came to serve as foundations for churches, and as some of them were very large they were the best thing in the world for the foundation of so great and holy a work.[3]

Only He who counts the drops of the rain and the sands of the sea can number the dead and the depopulated lands of Haiti (now called the

2. There is obviously a lacuna in the text at this point. Torquemada (vol. III, p. 61), who is following Motolinía pretty closely, has this: ". . . images which the Spaniards had given them, thinking that they would be content with them; but, being accustomed to the worship of many gods, they put these images with the figures of the devil and worshipped them together; and being accustomed to have many gods, if they had a hundred, they wanted a hundred and one . . ."

3. It is interesting to note that Cortés regretted the wholesale destruction of Indian temples and idols. In the summary of the evidence taken during the trial of Cortés in 1529 we find at least two witnesses who testified that he "showed great annoyance, because he wanted those temples of the idols to remain as a memorial," and that "he regretted that they had destroyed the Indian idols." *Sumario de la Residencia,* (vol. I, p. 232, and vol. II, p. 156).

Island of Española), of Cuba, San Juan,[4] Jamaica, and the other islands. And, the thirst of their greed unslaked, the Spaniards went on to discover the innumerable islands of the Lucayas [5] and of Mayaguana [6]—which they said were mines of gold,[7] with very fine looking and intelligent inhabitants and friendly Indians[8]—and all the coast of the mainland, killing so very many souls and sending them almost all to hell, treating men worse than beasts, and esteeming them less, as if they really were not created in the image of God. I have seen and known plenty of natives of this land, and have been confessor to some of them, and they are men of good sense and good consciences; why then should not the others have been so too, if the Spaniards had not been in such a hurry to kill and exterminate them? Oh, how wise it would be in New Spain to open one's eyes and take warning from those who have perished in these islands! I use the name New Spain of the country from Mexico to Peru, and all that has been discovered from New Galicia to the north. All of this land, as much of it as has not already been destroyed, should take warning and fear the judgment which God will execute for the destruction of the Islands. Let it suffice that there are already in this New Spain many towns laid waste, at least along the coast of the North Sea and also on that of the South Sea, and wherever there were mines when the land was first allotted; and many other towns far from Mexico are only half alive.

If anyone should ask what has been the cause of so many evils, I would answer: covetousness, the desire to store in one's chest a few bars of gold for the benefit of I know not whom. For such possessions, I say, will not reach the third heir, since every day we see that they disappear out of one's grasp and vanish like smoke or like fairy treasure; and at the most they last only until death, and then, because the wretched body must be covered with vain and ill-judged pomp and foolish clothes, the wretched soul is left poverty-stricken, bare, and ugly. How many, many souls, because of this wretched and disordered greed for the gold of this land are burning up in hell! Please God that it may grow no worse! And yet, bad

4. Puerto Rico.

5. The Bahamas.

6. Also spelled Mariguana. One of the large islands of the Bahamas.

7. Spanish: herrerías, literally 'iron foundries.' Used here figuratively, I think, to mean an inexhaustible source of supply.

8. The text appears to be corrupt at this point. According to Ramírez, *Historia de los Indios* (vol. I, p. 27, note 4) the manuscript reads: *y hermanos domésticos guaridos,* which makes no sense. He has used instead the reading of the Kingsborough edition: *sus domésticos guatiaos,* and explains *guatiaos* as the word used in the Islands for friendly Indians.

as conditions are, I know and in fact see every day that there are some Spaniards who would rather be poor in this land than have much gold from mines and the sweat of the Indians, and for this reason there are many who have given up the mines. I know some others who, not satisfied with the way in which men are enslaved here, have freed their slaves. Others are modifying and diminishing the tributes and treating the Indians well. Others do without them because the practice goes against their consciences. Others, not wishing to be accountable for the sweat of the poor, demand nothing but the modified tribute, and pay for all other services, such as meals, messengers and burden-carrying. And these I would consider true neighbors; and so I say that he who would consider himself really a neighbor and would behave accordingly should do as these Spaniards are doing.

Chapter IV

Of how some of the Indians began to come to be baptized, and of how they came to learn the Christian doctrine, and about the idols that they had.

Now that the preachers were beginning to have some facility in the language, and preached without books, and as the Indians no longer called upon or served their idols except in distant and secret places, many of them came on Sundays and feast days to hear the Word of God. It was necessary to begin by explaining to them who is the living God, the All Powerful, Who knows neither beginning nor end, Creator of all things, Whose wisdom has no bounds, the highest Goodness, Who created all things visible and invisible, and preserves them and gives them being. After this, they were told whatever else seemed most suitable at the time. With this it was necessary to explain to them who Saint Mary was, because up to that time they had named only Mary or Saint Mary and thought that when they spoke this name they were naming God. They also used the name Saint Mary for all the Christian images they saw. When this had been explained, and also the immortality of the soul, they were told who the devil is in whom they believed, how he kept them deceived, what evil qualities he has, and the care that he takes to prevent any soul from being saved. When they heard this there were many who became so alarmed and terrified that they trembled to hear what the friars were saying, and some poor wretches, of whom there are an abundance in this land, began to come to baptism and to seek the kingdom of God, seeking it with tears and sighs of great importunity.

These Indians were always very scrupulous about supplying wood to the temples of the devil, for they always had, in the courts and halls of the temples, many braziers of different kinds, and some very large. Most of them stood before the altars of the idols and burned every night. They also had certain round houses or temples of the devil, some large and some smaller, according to the size of the town. The entrances were made like the mouth of hell, and painted with the mouth of a fearful serpent with terrible teeth and fangs. In some cases the fangs were represented in relief, so that to see this sight and then go in filled one with fear and horror, especially in the 'hell' that stood in Mexico, which seemed to be a copy of hell itself. In these places perpetual fire burned night and day. The houses or 'hells' that I am talking about were round and low and had their floors on a level with the ground so that one did not go up steps to them as one did to the other temples, of which there were also many round ones. The temples, however, were high and had altars, and one went up to them by long flights of steps. These round temples were dedicated to the god of the wind, who was called Quetzalcoatl. Some Indians were deputed to bring wood, and others to watch and keep the fires burning. They did almost the same thing in the houses of the lords, where, in many parts of the country, they built fires. Even today they do it to some extent, and watch over the houses of the lords, but not as they did in the old days, for they no longer do a tenth part of what they used to do.

At this time a different fire, the fire of devotion, began to kindle in the hearts of the Indians when they learned the Ave María, the Pater Noster, and the catechism. To make them accept the teaching more readily, and find some pleasures in it, the friars gave them the Per signum Crucis, the Pater Noster, the Ave Maria, the Credo and the Salve, with the Commandments, in their own tongue and set to music in a simple and pleasing tune. They were so eager to learn, and there were so many of them, that they were fairly piled up in the courtyards of the churches and shrines and in their own sections of the town, singing and learning prayers for three or four hours on end; and their haste was so great that wherever they went, by day or by night, one could hear them on all sides singing and reciting the whole catechism. The Spaniards were amazed to see the fervor with which they recited it and the eagerness and haste with which they learned it. They learned not only these prayers but many more which they now know and teach to others along with the catechism. In this and in other things the children were a great help.

Now that the friars were thinking that everything was done because idolatry had been abolished in the temples of the devil and the people were coming to learn the Christian doctrine and be baptized, they discovered the most difficult thing of all, and the one that took the longest to destroy. This was that at night the Indians continued to meet and call upon the devil and celebrate his feasts with many and diverse ancient rites, especially when they sowed the corn and when they harvested it,[1] and every twenty days, which was their month.[2] The last day of each twenty was a general festival throughout all the land. Each one of these days was dedicated to one of their chief devils, whom they honored with various human sacrifices and many other ceremonies. They had eighteen months, as will be explained later, and each month was of twenty days, and when these eighteen months were over there were left five more days, which they said were useless,[3] and belonged to no year. These five days were also days of great ceremonies and feasts, until the beginning of the year.[4]

Besides these they had other days in memory of their dead, when they mourned for them, and after eating and getting drunk they called upon the devil. And this was the manner of these days: they buried and mourned the dead man, and then twenty days later they mourned him again and offered food and roses[5] on his tomb, and after eighty days they did the same thing again, and repeated it every eighty days. After a year they

1. For description of various corn ceremonies, see below, bk. I, ch. VII. For a discussion of the whole subject, see Frazer, Pt. V, "Spirits of the Corn and of the Wild"; also S. G. Morley, *The Ancient Maya.*

2. See below, bk. I, ch. V, for Motolinía's account of the Aztec calendar. Sahagún (vol. I, pp. 363-373) discusses the subject in much greater detail.

3. Spanish: *andaban en vano,* a translation of the Aztec term *nemontemi.*

4. Gómara (pp. 429 and 446), probably following Motolinía, also speaks of the festivals celebrated on these five days. Sahagún (vol. I, p. 111), however, says that these days were considered unfortunate and nothing was done on them. He mentions no festivals, nor do any of the other authorities that I have been able to consult.

5. Throughout his book Motolinía uses the word *rosas* to mean simply 'flowers.' Sometimes it stands alone as here and on pp. 54 and 55. At other times it forms part of the phrase *rosas y flores,* in which the two words seem to be synonyms. The Spaniard, even today, does not, as a rule, know the names of flowers or trouble to distinguish one from another; in the sixteenth century and earlier, *rosas y flores* seems to have been a set phrase meaning nothing but 'flowers.' One finds it in the charming *serranilla* of the Marqués de Santillana, whose beautiful herd girl of La Finojosa is to be found in a 'green meadow full of roses and flowers.'

mourned the dead and made offerings every year on the anniversary of his death. This they did for four years, and then they stopped entirely and never thought of the dead man again to pray for his soul. All their dead they called *teotl fulano,* which means 'God so-and-so,' or 'Saint so-and-so.'

When merchants or other persons came from a distance their friends and relatives made a feast for them and got drunk with them. They thought it a great thing to go far away from their lands and there exercise their skill and ingenuity and come back having proved themselves men, even though they brought back nothing more valuable than their persons. Also when someone finished building a house they gave him a feast. Others worked for two or three years and acquired as much as they could in order to give a feast to the devil, in which they would not only spend everything they had but even borrow, so that they had to go into service and work another year or two to pay off their obligations. Others who had no money to give such a feast would sell themselves and become slaves so as to be able to give a feast some day to the devil.

At these feasts they provided hens, dogs, and quail for the ministers of the temples, and bread and wine, and plenty of it, for they all left the feast drunk. They would buy quantities of roses and tubes of perfume, cocoa (which is another good beverage), and fruit. In many of these feasts they would give the guests blankets, and in the majority of them they would dance night and day until they were either drunk or exhausted. Besides this they had many other feasts with different ceremonies, and on the nights of these feasts all was shouting and calling upon the devil. No human power or wisdom was sufficient to abolish these feasts, for it was very hard for the Indians to relinquish the customs in which they had grown up. These customs and idolatries, at least the majority of them, it took the friars two years and more to overcome and uproot, with the favor and aid of God and by the means of the sermons and admonitions which they constantly addressed to the Indians.

Not long ago they came to tell the friars how the Indians concealed their idols and put them in the pedestals of the crosses, or under the stones in the steps, so that they might pretend to be adoring the Cross and in reality adore the devil. They tried to shelter there the life of their idolatry. The idols that the Indians had were very many, and to be found in many places, especially in the temples of their devils and in the courtyards and in lofty places such as groves and high ridges, and in the high passes and on steep hills, wherever there was a spot high or pleasing or suitable for a resting place. Those who passed by would offer blood from the tongue or ears, or a little incense of the kind they have in that land, which is called copal. Others would offer roses that they gathered along the road; and when they had nothing else they would scatter some blades of grass or a few straws. In those places they stopped to rest, especially the burden-carriers, for they carry very large and heavy loads.

They also had idols near the waters, mostly near springs, where they built their altars with a portico covering the steps; and at many important and copious springs they would have four of these altars arranged in the form of a cross, facing each other with the spring in the middle, and into the water they would throw much copal and paper and many roses, and some water worshippers made offerings there of their own blood. Near great trees, such as big cypresses or cedars, they made the same altars and sacrifices. In the courtyards of their devils, before the temples, they took pains to plant and grow cypresses, plane trees or cedars. They also built those altars, small but with steps and roof, at many cross roads and in the different quarters of their towns and on the hillsides. In many other places they had buildings like oratories, in which they had a quantity of idols of different forms and figures. All these were public, and even in many days they could not all be completely destroyed, both because they were so numerous and in so many different places, and because the people made new ones every day. In one place the Spaniards broke a great many idols, and when they went back they found that new ones had been made and put up; for, as the Indians do not have to seek stone cutters to make the idols for them, nor picks to work the stone, nor anyone to mould them—since many Indians are skilled workmen and carve one stone with another—the Christians could not exhaust the supply of idols nor destroy them entirely.

They had idols of stone, of wood, and of baked clay. They also made them of dough and of seeds wrapped in dough, and they had some big, some bigger, and medium-sized ones, and small and tiny ones. Some were like bishops with their miters and staffs, some of which were gilded and some set with turquoise in various ways. Others were figures of men, and these, in place of the miters, had on their heads mortars into which wine was poured, because these figures represented the god of wine.[6] Others had different distinguishing symbols by which one recognized the particular devil represented. Others were figures of women, also of many

6. The name of this god was *Ometochtli.*

sorts; and others were in the shape of wild beasts: lions, tigers, dogs, stags, and all the beasts that live in the forests and in the fields.

They also had idols in the form of snakes, and these of many different forms, long and coiled and others with a woman's face. Before many idols they offered vipers and serpents, and before others, strings of vipers' tails, for there are certain very large vipers which have on their tails rings with which they make a noise, for which reason the Spaniards call them 'bell snakes.' Some of them are very savage. They have ten or eleven of these knobs or rings and their bite is fatal, the victim living scarcely twenty-four hours. There are other very large snakes, as thick as a man's arm. These are reddish and are not poisonous; on the contrary they are highly esteemed by the great lords as food. These are called 'stag snakes,' either because they resemble the stag in color, or because they station themselves in a path and lie in wait for the stag. Seizing hold of a branch the snake winds its tail around the stag and holds it, and though it has no teeth or fangs it sucks its victim's blood from the eyes and nose. No one man ventures to catch these snakes, because the snake would squeeze him to death, but if there are two or three men, they pursue the snake and tie it to a big stick. It is much esteemed as a present for the lords. There are idols also of these snakes.

They also have bird idols, eagles, for instance, and very commonly one sees idols of an eagle and a tiger. There are idols of owls and night birds, of others such as the hawk, and of all birds that are large or beautiful or savage or of especially precious plumage. The principal idol was that of the sun, and they had them also of the moon and stars, of the big fish and alligators, even of toads and frogs, and of other big fish, and these, they said, were the fish gods. From one town on the lake of Mexico the Spaniards took some idols of these fish, which were big ones made of stone, and later, when they returned there, they asked for some fish to eat, and the people answered that they had taken away the fish god and so the inhabitants could catch no fish.

Fire, air, water, and earth were worshipped as gods, and of these they had painted images, and for many of their devils they had shields and bucklers, and painted on them the figures and arms of their devils with their emblems. Of many others they had figures and idols, some carved and some painted, even of butterflies and fleas and grasshoppers, and the images were big and well executed.

After destroying these public idols, the friars went after the ones that were enclosed, as if imprisoned, in the pedestals of the crosses, for the devil could not remain near the Cross without suffering great anguish. All these idols they destroyed, for although there were some bad Indians who hid the idols, there were other good ones who had been converted, and as this practice of concealing the idols seemed to them evil, and an offense against God, they reported it to the friars; but even among the converted Indians there were some who tried to argue that it was not right to report this. This task of destroying the idols was very necessary, to prevent offenses against God, and keep the glory that is due to Him from being given to the idols, as well as to protect many from the cruel sacrifices whose numerous victims died in the forests, or at night, or in secret places; for the Indians were very tenacious of this custom, and even though they no longer sacrificed as much as they used to, they still, at the instigation of the devil, sought opportunities to do so. As will soon be told,[7] the sacrifices and cruelties of this land and people surpassed and exceeded all others in the world, as one reads and as shall here be told. But before I begin to tell the cruelties of their sacrifices, I shall tell the method they have of dividing the time into years and months, weeks and days.

CHAPTER V

Of the variable elements in the year, and how in some nations the year begins differently; of the name that the Indians gave to the child when it was born; and of their method of counting the years, and the ceremonies that they performed.

DIFFERENT nations used different methods in the calculation of the year, and so it was in this land of Anáhuac; and, although there are in this country, because of its great size, different peoples and tongues, in the parts that I have seen they all calculate the year in the same way. The better to understand what time is, you should know that time is a quantity of the year, which means the rate of movement of the variable elements; and these variables are ten, namely: year, month, week, day, quadrant, hour, point, moment, ounce, and atom.[1] The year has twelve

7. See below, bk. I, chs. VI-XI, inclusive.

1. This account of the variable elements is apparently taken from the *De proprietatibus rerum* of the Franciscan Bartholomaeus Anglicus, a popular encyclopedia written about 1230-1240, of

months, or fifty-two weeks and one day, or three hundred and sixty-five days and six hours. The month has four weeks, and some months have two days more, others, one, except February. The week has seven days, and the day has four quadrants. Each quadrant consists of six hours, and the hour, of four points. The point has ten moments; the moment, twelve ounces; the ounce has forty-seven atoms, and the atom is indivisible. The Egyptians and Arabs began the year in September, because in that month the trees have ripe fruit, and they believe that at the beginning of the world the trees were created in fruit, and that September was the first month of the year. The Romans began the year in January, because it is then, or shortly before, that the sun begins to approach us. The Jews began the year in March, because they believed that the world was created at that season, with flowers in bloom and the grass green. Modern Christians, out of reverence for our Lord Jesus Christ, begin the year at his holy Nativity, and others at the time of the blessed circumcision.

The Indians of New Spain, at the time that this land was conquered and entered by the Spaniards, began their year at the beginning of March,[2] but as they do not know about leap year, they vary their year through all the months. They had a year of three hundred and sixty-five days. Their month was of twenty days, and they had eighteen months and five days in a year, and the last day of the month was amongst them a day of great solemnity. The names of the months[3] and the days are not given here because they are very complicated, and can scarcely be written; perhaps I will give the figures by which they were known and by which the Indians reckoned them. These Indians of New Spain had a week of thirteen days which they indicated by the following signs or figures: the first, besides the name which it had like all the others, was designated by a swordfish, which is a fish or marine creature; the second, by two winds; the third, by three houses; the fourth, by four water-lizards, which are also marine creatures; the fifth, by five snakes; the sixth, by six figures of death; the

---

which Book IX treats of the divisions of Time. For three centuries this work enjoyed a great popularity and was translated into various languages. A Spanish translation by Vicente de Burgos was published at Toulouse in 1494 and later at Toledo in 1529. See G. Sarton, *Introduction to the History of Science,* Carnegie Institution of Washington, Publ. no. 376, vol. II, under Bartholomaeus Anglicus. The *De proprietatibus rerum* would undoubtedly be known to Motolinía. (For assistance in tracking down this information I am indebted to Mrs. Margaret Grierson of the Smith College Library.)

2. According to Sahagún (vol. I, p. 84) the first day of the first month corresponded to February second.

3. For the names of the eighteen months, see Sahagún, vol. I, pp. 84-109.

seventh, by seven stags; the eighth, by eight rabbits; the ninth, by eagles;[4] the tenth, by ten dogs; the eleventh, by eleven monkeys; twelfth, by twelve brooms;[5] the thirteenth, by thirteen reeds. Their weeks were counted by thirteen days, but the names of the days were twenty,[6] all named with their names and indicated by their figures or characters. And by this same count they counted their market days, for they held some every twenty days, some every thirteen days, and some every five days. The last mentioned practice was and is the most usual, except in the big towns, for these had their market every day, and the market-place full from mid-day on. They are as exact in the calculation of these market or fair days as the merchants of Spain are in knowing the fairs of Villalón or Medina. They had, as we do, experts in this calculation of the months, years and principal festivals, who were well versed in the computations. This calendar of the Indians had for each day its idol or devil, with the names of male or female deities, and all the days of the year were full, like the calendars of Roman breviaries, which have a saint for every day.

All children, when they were born, took the name of the day on which they were born, such as 'one flower,' 'two rabbits.' This name was given to them on the seventh day after birth, and then if it was a male child, they put an arrow[7] into his hand, and, if it was a female child, a spindle and weaving stick (shuttle), as a sign that she should be diligent and housewifely, a good spinner and a better weaver. The arrow signified

4. Motolinía either confused the ninth sign, which all the other authorities give as *atl* (water), with the fifteenth, *quauhtli* (eagle), or carelessly wrote *águilas* (eagles) for *aguas* (waters).

5. Spanish: *escobas* (brooms). The twelfth sign (Aztec *malinalli*) is rendered by Sahagún (vol. I, p. 305) as *heno* (hay). Torquemada, volume II, p. 304, translated it as "a certain medicinal herb." Joyce (p. 61) gives it as grass. Seler (*Chronology*, B. Am. Eth., Bulletin 28, p. 4) says that *malinalli* means *escobilla* (a little brush or broom). Both *escoba* and *escobilla* have botanical meanings. They are the names of certain of the Artemisias, which would explain Torquemada's translation.

6. The seven day signs not given by Motolinía are: 14, ocelot; 15, eagle; 16, vulture; 17, motion; 18, flint knife; 19, rain; 20, flower.

As the week had only thirteen days, but all twenty signs were used, it follows that for twenty weeks each succeeding week began with a different day sign (but always with the numeral 1). The twenty-first week began again with the first day sign, *e.g.*

Week I	1 swordfish	to	13 reeds
Week II	1 ocelot	to	13 deaths
Week III	1 stag	to	13 rains
Week IV	1 flower	to	13 brooms, etc.

This gave a cycle of 260 days divided into twenty groups of thirteen, each group "ruled" by one of the twenty day signs. The 260 day cycle (known as *tonalamatl*) was not a calendar. It was quite independent of the 365 day year and was used by the experts for divination and the determination of lucky and unlucky days.

7. See below, bk. II, ch. III. In some parts of the country the boy was given a shield and an arrow, and the girl a broom.

that the boy should be valiant to defend himself and his country, for wars were very common every year. On that day the relatives and neighbors rejoiced with the father of the child. In other parts of the country, as soon as the child was born the relatives came to greet it and spoke the following words to it: "You have come (into the world) to suffer; endure, then, and suffer." Having done this, each one of those who had greeted the child put a little lime on its knee. And on the seventh day after birth they gave it the name of the day on which it was born. Then three months later they presented the child in the temple of the devil, and gave him his name, retaining the one he already had. On this occasion also there was a banquet. Then the calendar expert told them the name of the devil which belonged to the day of the child's birth. On the names of these devils they based a multitude of omens and divinations, prophesying the fates that were to befall the individual in his lifetime, both in the matter of marriages and of wars. The sons of the principal lords were given a third name, designating their rank or office. These names were given to some when they were boys, to some when they had reached young manhood; or sometimes at the death of the father the son inherited the estate and the name of the rank which his father had held.

It is not to be wondered at that the Indians gave their days the names of beasts and birds, since the days of our months and weeks come from the gods and the planets, a thing for which the Romans were responsible.

In this land of Anáhuac they counted the years in groups of four, in the following manner:[8] They made four 'houses' with four signs; the first sign, which was *a rabbit,* was placed in the south; the second, which was *two reeds,* was placed to the east; the third, which was *three flints,* or sacrificial knives, to the north; and the fourth, which was *four houses,* to the west.[9] Then, beginning the count with the first year, and in the first 'house,' they counted the years by their names and signs up to thirteen years, which ended in the same 'house' in which they began, the 'house' of the *rabbit.* Going three times around the circle of 'houses,' that is, three 'olympiads,'[10] the last time around has five years and the first two, four

8. Torquemada (vol. II, p. 300 ff.) discusses in some detail the Aztec chronology, and in speaking of what he calls "the wheel of 52 years" which served also as a pictographic chronicle says: "I have in my possession . . . one of these wheels, with complete explanation, made by Father Toribio Motolinía." See also Sahagún, vol. II, p. 226, and Joyce, Plate VIII (photograph and diagram of the great Mexican Calendar stone).

9. The points of the compass or 'world-directions' were of great importance in the Mexican calendar. See Joyce, pp. 78-79.

10. The four-year period of Greek reckoning.

years each, which makes thirteen all together, and this period of thirteen years we might call an 'indiction.'[11] In the same way they made three more of these 'indictions,' going through the four 'houses' so that they made in all four 'indictions,' each one of thirteen years, which all together made up an 'hebdomad'[12] of fifty-two years, the beginning of the first 'hebdomad' falling always in the first 'house.'[13]

Very noteworthy ceremonies and festivals were held on the last day of those fifty-two years and on the first day which began the new year and new 'olympiad.' On the last day of the last year at the hour of vespers, in Mexico and all its territory, and in Tetzcoco and its provinces, at the order of the temple ministers, all fires were extinguished with water in the temples of the devils as well as in private houses. Even in certain places (the 'hells' that I have mentioned above)[14] where fire was kept perpetually burning, it was extinguished on that day. Then certain ministers of the temples of Mexico went out two leagues to a place that is called Ixtlapalapa and ascended a hill upon which stood a temple of the devil held in great reverence and devotion by Moteuczoma, the great lord of Mexico. In that place, then, at midnight, which was the beginning of the year of the following 'hebdomad,'[15] these ministers kindled new fire with a stick which was known as the fire stick.[16] Then they lighted a torch, and before anyone kindled a fire for private use, they bore it with great zeal and haste to the principal temple in Mexico. There they placed the fire before the idols, and then brought a captive taken in war and, sacrificing him before the new fire, they cut out his heart, and the chief minister sprinkled the fire with blood as a sort of benediction. When this ceremony was finished

11. The indiction of Christian reckoning was really a period of fifteen years.

12. The reason for the use of the term hebdomad for the 52 year cycle seems rather obscure, since groups of seven do not occur at all in the Mexican calendar. The only possible connection seems to be that the 52 years suggest the 52 weeks which, in our reckoning, make up a year. Torquemada (vol. II, p. 303) also uses hebdomad, and so does Sahagún (vol. I, p. 365).

13. Spanish: *comenzando siempre el principio de la primera hebdómada en la primera casa.* This must be a careless blunder, for the sense demands either "the beginning of the hebdomad" or "the beginning of the first year of the hebdomad."

14. See above, bk. I, ch. IV.

15. Spanish: *principio del año de la siguiente hebdómada.* One would expect . . . *del primer año.*

16. According to Sahagún (vol. II, p. 269) the new fire was kindled on the breast of a captive who had been taken in war. As soon as the fire was kindled the captive was sacrificed. Torquemada (vol. II, p. 294) says that the fire was kindled on the breast of *a freshly sacrificed captive,* "en la misma herida." Motolinía does not mention the captive, and Gómara explicitly states that the sticks used for kindling the fire are placed on the ground. Gómara's information is mostly second-hand and much less to be relied upon than Sahagún's.

and the fire was, as it were, blessed, there were people from many places waiting there to carry new fire to the temples of their towns. This they did, first asking permission of the great Mexican prince or pontiff, who was a sort of pope; and they bore it with great zeal and speed. Although the town might be many leagues away, they went so fast that they very shortly brought the fire there. They performed the same ceremony in the provinces far distant from Mexico, and it was performed everywhere with great joy and rejoicing. As soon as the day dawned a great festival was held in all the land, but principally in Mexico, and in Mexico alone they sacrificed four hundred men.

CHAPTER VI

Of the festival called Panquetzaliztli, and the offerings and human sacrifices that were made then. How they cut out the hearts and offered them to the idols and then ate the flesh of the victims.

IN those days of the months that I have mentioned above, and on one of them which was called Panquetzaliztli[1] and was the fourteenth, dedicated to the gods of Mexico (especially to two of them who were said to be brothers and gods of war, strong to kill and destroy, subject and conquer);[2] on this day, then, as on a very great festival, they made many sacrifices of blood drawn from their ears or tongues, which was a very common practice. Others sacrificed blood drawn from their arms or breasts or other parts of the body. Drawing a little blood to sprinkle before the idols, as one sprinkles holy water with one's fingers, or, letting blood from the ears or tongue fall on pieces of paper and then offering them as sacrifices was a general custom everywhere, but each province had its own custom about letting blood from other parts of the body. Some drew blood from the arms and some from the breast, so that by the scars one could tell from which province a man came.

1. Panquetzaliztli is the name of a month, not a day, as Motolinía's sentence might lead one to believe. According to him and Gómara it was the 14th month. Sahagún, vol. I, p. 105, however, gives it as the 15th, its first day corresponding to November 9.

2. According to Gómara, these were Huizilopuchtli and Tezcatlipoca, but Sahagún (*loc. cit.*), who is much more reliable on the subject, calls it the festival of Huizilopuchtli, with whom was associated the god Painal.

Besides these and other sacrifices and ceremonies, they sacrificed and killed many victims in the manner which I shall now describe. They had a stone about one and a half meters long, almost a span and a half wide and a good span thick. Half of this stone was sunk in the ground at the top of the steps before the altar of the idols. On this stone they laid the unhappy wretches on their backs to sacrifice them. The chest was arched up and very tense, because their hands and feet were tied. The principal priest of the idols, or his lieutenant, who were the ones who usually performed the sacrifice (if there were sometimes so many to be sacrificed that these two got tired, their places would be taken by others already skilled in the method of sacrifice), rapidly and with great force cut open the tense chest with a cruel flint knife, and quickly cut out the heart.

This knife is made of flint which they use to strike sparks for fire. It is shaped like the tip of a lance and is not very sharp, for as it is a very hard stone that splits, it cannot be made very sharp. I mention this because many people think that the sacrificial knives were the black stone knives,[3] of which there are many here that are made with an edge as sharp as a razor and cut as smoothly as a razor, but very quickly get nicked.

The priest who performed this evil deed then struck the heart against the outer part of the threshold[4] of the altar, leaving a bloodstain there. The heart fell to the ground and lay there a while throbbing. Later they placed it in a bowl before the altar. At other times they took the heart and raised it toward the sun, and sometimes annointed the lips of the idols with the blood. Sometimes the hearts were eaten by the old priests; sometimes they buried them. Then they took the body and rolled it down the steps. When it reached the bottom, if it was the body of a prisoner taken in war, the one who made the capture and his friends and relatives carried it off and prepared the human flesh with other food and the next day had a feast and ate it. The man who took the prisoner, if he had the means, that day gave blankets to his guests. If the victim was a slave, they did not roll the body down the steps, but carried it, and had the same kind of feast and banquet as with the prisoner of war, although not so great a one. There were other festivals and days of greater ceremonies that solemnized them, as will appear in accounts of those other festivals.

As to the hearts of the sacrificial victims: as soon as the heart was

3. Obsidian.

4. The Spanish word is *umbral,* which means both 'threshold' and also the beam that is put across the top of an opening for a door or window, *i. e.,* 'lintel.'

cut out the priest of the devil took it in his hands and held it up as if he were showing it to the sun. Then he held it up to the idol and placed it in a painted wooden vessel bigger than a porringer. The blood he caught in another vessel and gave it to the principal idol as if to drink, smearing it upon the lips, and afterwards he offered it similarly to the other idols and images of the devil.

In this festival they sacrificed either slaves or prisoners taken in war, usually the former; and the number varied according to the town, in some twenty, in some thirty, and in others forty or up to fifty or sixty. In Mexico they sacrificed one hundred and upward.

On another one of the days that I spoke of they sacrificed a great many, though not so many as in the festival just mentioned. Let no one think that any of those whom they sacrificed by killing them and cutting out their hearts, or by any other form of death, were voluntary victims. On the contrary, they were sacrificed by force, bitterly mourning their death and frightful suffering. The other sacrifices, the drawing of blood from the ears, tongue, or other parts of the body, were almost always voluntary. Some of those whom they sacrificed, they flayed;[5] in some places two or three, in some four or five, in others ten, and in Mexico as many as twelve or fifteen. Then they put on the skins, which were left open in the back and across the shoulders, and having put them on as well as they could, like a man putting on a doublet and hose, they danced in that cruel and frightful dress. As all sacrificial victims were either slaves or prisoners taken in war, it was the custom in Mexico to keep for that day some one of the prisoners who was a lord or some important personage. This victim was flayed so that his skin might be worn by Moteuczoma, the great lord of Mexico. Wearing that skin, Moteuczoma danced with great gravity, thinking that he was doing a great service to the devil whom they were honoring that day. And many people went to see this as a most marvellous thing, because in other towns it was not the lords, but other leading men who put on the skins of the flayed victims.

On another day, during another festival, in each part of the country they sacrificed a woman and flayed her, and one man put on her skin

5. Motolinía is apparently referring to the festival of the god Xipe celebrated at the end of the second month, Tlacaxipeualiztli. Gómara (p. 444) speaks of Montezuma's taking part in the festival, clad in the skin of one of the sacrificial victims. Sahagún does not mention it. The flaying sacrifice seems to have been performed exclusively in honor of agricultural deities and especially of Xipe, the god of sowing. The symbolism seems to be that of vegetation in the early spring, apparently dead, but containing the germ of life within. See Joyce, pp. 37-38.

and danced with all the other men of the town, he in the woman's skin and the others in their feathers.[6]

There was another day on which they held the festival of the water god. Twenty or thirty days before the time of the festival they bought two slaves, a man and a woman, and made them live together as husband and wife. On the day of the festival they dressed the man with the robes and insignia of the god, and the woman with those of the goddess, wife of that god. Thus dressed they danced all that day until midnight, when they were sacrificed. These victims they did not eat, but threw them into a pit like a grain cellar which they had for this purpose.[7]

CHAPTER VII

Of the very great cruelties that were committed on the day of the god of fire and of the god of water. Of a drought in which it did not rain for four years.

IN another festival,[1] in some places—Tlacopán, Coyoacán, and Azcapotzalco, for instance—they erected a great round pole ten fathoms long, made an idol out of seeds, wrapped it and tied it with strips of paper and put it on top of the pole. This pole and idol they erected on the day before the festival and danced around it all day. On the morning of the festival they took some slaves and some prisoners of war, and brought them tied hand and foot and threw them into a big fire prepared for this cruelty. They did not allow the victims to burn to death, not out of any sense of pity, but to make their torture greater,[2] for after taking them out of the fire they sacrificed them and cut out their hearts. In the afternoon

6. Apparently the festival celebrated in the eleventh month, Ochpaniztli, in honor of the goddess Toci, mother of the gods and goddess of the ripe corn, healing herbs, doctors, and midwives.

7. Gómara (p. 445), whose description of this festival corresponds with Motolinía's, says that this was the festival celebrated at the end of the sixth month, Etzalqualiztli. The account of the Etzalqualiztli festival given by Sahagún (vol. I, pp. 92 and 143-154) is, however, entirely different.

1. The festival of the tenth month, Xócotl Huetzi, described in much greater detail by Sahagún, vol. I, pp. 97 and 169-174.

2. The intention was not merely to increase the torture of the victims, as Motolinía supposes, but to maintain the fire god in full vigor by feeding the fire with living victims who must be taken out before they died. In many of the ceremonies described by Motolinía and others, the victims evidently impersonated the god, and being killed in their youthful vigor were supposed to keep the god always young and strong.

they pulled down the pole and all struggled to get some part of the idol to eat, for they believed that it would make them valiant in battle.

Another day was celebrated everywhere,[3] a day dedicated to the god of fire,[4] or to fire itself, which they regarded and worshipped as a god, and not one of the least important. On that day they took one of the prisoners of war and dressed him in the robes and garments of the fire god; he danced in reverence to the god, and then was sacrificed with the other prisoners of war.

But much more frightful than the general practice is what they did here in Cuautitlán, where I am writing this, where it seems that the devil showed himself more cruel than in other places. On the day before one festival in Cuautitlán they set up six great trees, like the masts of ships, with steps leading up to them, and on that cruel night—followed by a yet more cruel day—, they beheaded two female slaves at the top of the steps before the altar of the idols. Up there they flayed their bodies and faces and cut out their thigh bones. In the morning two of the leading Indians put on the skins, even the skin of the face, like a mask, and took the thigh bones, one in each hand, and slowly came down the steps, roaring like savage beasts. Down below in the courtyards a great crowd of people, all apparently terrified, cried: "Our gods are coming, our gods are coming!" When the two men reached the foot of the steps the people began to beat their drums, and to the backs of the men dressed in the skins they attached a quantity of paper, not folded, but sewed in the form of wings, a matter of some four hundred sheets. To each of them they gave a quail, already sacrificed and beheaded, and tied it to his lip,[5] which was pierced. And thus the two danced, and many people sacrificed before them and offered them great numbers of quail, for it was also for the latter a day of death. And as the quail were sacrificed they were thrown before the two dancers, and there were so many that they covered the ground where they trod, for more than eight thousand quail were sacrificed that day. Everyone made great efforts to get them for

3. Gómara, who follows Motolinía very closely in many of his descriptions of Indian customs, identifies this festival (p. 445) as the one celebrated in the eighteenth month, Izcalli. The account of the Izcalli festival given by Sahagún (pp. 109 and 206-212) is, however, quite different.

4. Xiuhtecuhtli.

5. The Spanish text has *bezo,* which means 'lip,' especially a thick lip. Torquemada, who at this point is following Motolinía very closely, also says that the quail was hung from the lip. Gómara either did not understand, or did not like, this detail, for he changes it and says (p. 446): "They tied a sacrificed quail to each of the masked men through holes made in *the skin of the arms (brazos)* of the dead women."

this festival, to which people came from Mexico and from many other towns. At noon they took all the quail and divided them among the ministers of the temples and the principal lords. The two men dressed in the women's skins did nothing but dance all day.

On this day there was committed another greater and unheard of cruelty, which was that at the top of the six poles which they had erected on the day before the festival they bound and fastened to crosses six men, prisoners of war, and down below there stood around them over two thousand men and boys with their bows and arrows. As soon as those who had bound the captives to the poles came down, a shower of arrows was fired at the victims, and then, shot full of arrows and half dead, they were quickly untied and allowed to fall from that height. The violence with which they struck the ground broke and shattered all the bones in their bodies, and then they were made to suffer a third death, being sacrificed by having their hearts cut out. After that they were dragged away and their heads were cut off and given to the ministers of the idols. The bodies were carried off like sheep, to be eaten by the lords and principal men. On the following day they feasted on that unutterable food, and all danced with great rejoicing.

Once during the year, when the corn was about one span high,[6] in the towns which had lords of high rank whose houses were called palaces, they sacrificed a boy and a girl of three or four years. These were not slaves, but the children of leading men, and the sacrifice was made on a mountain,[7] in honor of an idol which they said was the god of water and gave them rain.[8] When there was a scarcity of water they prayed for it to this idol. In the case of these innocent children they did not cut out their hearts, but cut their throats, wrapped them in blankets, and put them into a stone chest like an ancient sarcophagus and left them thus in honor of that idol, whom they consider a very important god. His principal temple or house was in Tetzcoco, together with the gods

6. Motolinía mentions three special corn festivals, this one and two more on the following page. The first two evidently were intended to propitiate the rain gods. There were others which he does not describe. The great importance to the Mexicans of the agricultural and rain deities is at once obvious when one reads Sahagún's accounts of the month festivals (vol. I, pp. 84-212).

7. Spanish: *monte*. It is very difficult to tell whether Motolinía distinguishes between *monte* (a wood, or wooded hill) and *montaña* (mountain), or between *montaña* (mountain) and *sierra* (mountain range). He seems to use them rather indiscriminately.

8. Tlaloc. One of the most important of the Mexican deities. No less than five of the twenty month festivals were dedicated to him and to his associates, the Tlaloque and the goddess of running water, Chalchiuhtlicue or Matlalcue, who was supposed to be the wife of Tlaloc and sister of the Tlaloque.

of Mexico. He stood at the right and the gods of Mexico at the left. Both altars were raised upon a foundation, and each had three stories. I went to see them several times. These temples were the highest and largest in all the land, and larger than those of Mexico.

On the day of Atemoztli[9] they took many painted papers and carried them to the temples of the devils, and also *óllin,*[10] which is the gum of a tree that grows in the hot country. When the tree is punctured it exudes white drops which are collected and make a substance that thickens and turns black, like soft pitch. Of this substance they make the balls that the Indians use, which bounce more than the inflated balls of Castile, and are of the same size and a little firmer. Although they are much heavier they go so fast and bounce so high that they seem to have quicksilver in them. The Indians frequently offered this *óllin* to the devils, both on pieces of paper, upon which they let black drops of *óllin* fall as they burned it (pieces of paper with those black drops and others with drops of blood were given as offerings to the devil), and by smearing the *óllin* on the cheeks of the idols so that some had a crust two or three fingers thick upon their faces, and being ugly to start with, they certainly looked like figures of the devil, dirty, hideous, and foul. On that day relatives and friends joined in groups to take their food and to eat in the houses and courtyards of the devil. In Mexico, on this same day, they took a little boy and a little girl out in a very small boat, and in the center of the great lake offered them to the devil and sank them with the *acalli* or boat, and those who took them out returned in other bigger boats.

When the corn was knee high they levied an assessment for a certain day. With this they bought four slave children, five or six years old, and sacrificed them to Tlaloc, the god of water. They put them into a cave and shut it up until the next year, when they did the same thing again.[11] This cruel sacrifice began at a time when there was a four-year period with no rain, and scarcely anything green was left in the fields. To placate Tlaloc, the water god, and in order to make it rain they sacrificed these four children. The ministers who performed these sacrifices were the priests of most dignity and importance among the Indians. They wore their hair long, like Nazarenes, and as they never cut it or combed it,

9. The sixteenth month festival, in honor of Tlaloc.

10. Both Sahagún and Torquemada spell this *ulli,* and both of them speak highly of the medicinal qualities of the gum, which Motolinía does not mention.

11. The festival of the third month, Tozoztontli.

and went about much of the time black, and with long dirty hair, they resembled the devil. This long hair they called *nopapa,* and this was why the Spaniards called these ministers *papas,* or 'popes,' when they might more truly have called them the devil's cruel executioners.

Hueytozoztli.[12] This day was when the corn was waist high. Then each one took some stalks from his own fields and wrapped them in blankets, and before those stalks offered food and *atole,* which is a drink that they make out of the corn meal dough.

They also make offerings of copal, a kind of incense which is the sap of a tree. At a certain season of the year they puncture the tree so that the liquid will flow, and underneath, or tied to the tree itself, they place some leaves of the maguey. (I shall tell later[13] what the maguey is, and there is a great deal to say about it.) The sap falls on the maguey leaves and solidifies in cakes like the cuttlefish bone of the silversmiths. This copal mixed with oil makes a very good turpentine. The trees from which they get it are pleasing and beautiful to look at and have a pleasant perfume. Their leaves are very small. The tree grows in the hot country, in high places where it can get plenty of air. Some say that this copal is genuine myrrh. To return to the offering: in the afternoon they take it all to the temples of the devils and dance all night before the devil, praying him to preserve their cornfields.

Tititl.[14] On this and the following day, and their respective nights, they all danced before the devil and sacrificed to him many captives taken in wars with distant tribes. As the Mexicans said, they had some nearby provinces that were hostile and at war with them, like Tlaxcallan and Huexotzinco, which they had more for the sake of keeping in training for war and having a convenient supply of captives for sacrifices, than with any idea of making war on them and exterminating them. To be sure, the others said the same things about the Mexicans, and captured and sacrificed as many of the latter as the latter did of them. There were other distant provinces where they made war occasionally, or once a year, and on these occasions they sent out regularly organized companies. One of these provinces was the province and realm of

12. The fourth month.
13. See below, bk. III, ch. XIX.
14. The seventeenth month.

Michuachapanco, which the Spaniards now call Pánuco.[15] On this particular day they sacrificed these captives and not the ones from nearby provinces nor slaves.

CHAPTER VIII

Of the festival and sacrifice held by the merchants in honor of the salt goddess. How they represented the coming of their god, and how, once a year, the lords went to the mountains to hunt game to offer to their idols.

THE merchants held a festival, not all together, but those of each province separately. For this they obtained slaves to sacrifice, and they got them very cheap because the country was densely populated. On that day many died in the temples which belonged particularly to the merchants, and in which they held great sacrifices on many other occasions.[1]

They had other feast days on which all the lords and principal men of each province assembled in the provincial capital to dance. They dressed a woman in the robes of the salt goddess,[2] and thus dressed she danced all night, and at nine o'clock in the morning they sacrificed her to that goddess. On that day they burned in the braziers a great quantity of the incense that I have mentioned.[3]

On another festival they prepared several days beforehand great supplies of food, as each one's slender resources allowed him to do, for they are very generous, even though they pay for it by fasting, so as not to appear empty handed before their god. When the food was ready they had a sort of Advent day, and when the day arrived they carried the

15. Motolinía either confuses Michoacán with Pánuco, or Michuachapanco was some long-forgotten town in the Pánuco district.

1. In the city of Mexico the merchants had their special temple to their god Yacatecutli in the great temple enclosure. According to Sahagún (vol. I, p. 226) their annual festival was celebrated there in the seventeenth month, Tititl.

2. The festival of the salt goddess Vixtocioatl occurred in the seventh month, Tecuilhuitontli. Motolinía does not make it clear whether the whole of this paragraph refers to one and the same occasion, or whether the dancing mentioned in the first sentence is part of some other festival. Gómara's account (p. 445) definitely connects the two, but Sahagún (vol. I, pp. 93 and 154-157), though he describes in detail the ceremonies in honor of Vixtocioatl, makes no mention of the dancing by "the lords and principal men of each province."

3. *Copal.* See above, bk. I, ch. VII.

food to the temple of the devil, saying: "Our god comes; behold, he comes. Our god comes; behold, he comes."[4]

One day in the year the lords and principal men went out to make sacrifices in the temples in the mountains.[5] Men went all over the country hunting, to get beasts and birds to sacrifice to the devil—lions, tigers, and coyotes. The latter are small animals half-way between the wolf and the fox, neither quite wolves nor quite foxes. There are a great many of them and they bite so savagely that it is only a very special dog that will kill one fighting tooth to tooth. They hunted deer, hares, rabbits, quail, and even snakes and butterflies, and brought all the game to the lord, who paid each man according to what he brought, giving first the garment that he had on, then another which he had there ready to give. This payment was made not as a price, nor because of conscientious scruples—for never a scruple did they have about it—nor in return for services rendered, but solely out of a liberality by which they thought that they would greatly please the devil. Then they sacrificed everything that they had been able to catch.

Besides the festivals already mentioned there were many others, and each province had its own customs and each devil was served in his own way with sacrifices and fasts and other diabolical offerings, especially in Tlaxcallan, Huexotzinco, and Cholollan, which were independent principalities. In all these provinces, which are adjacent and of one stock, they worship one god whom they regard as the greatest and whom they call by three different names.[6] The ancients who settled these provinces were all of one lineage, but after they had multiplied they broke up into separate realms and there were great factions and wars between them. In these three provinces there were always a great many sacrifices and very cruel ones, because, as they were surrounded by provinces under the dominion of Mexico which were their enemies, and as they were continually at war among themselves, they had men who were skilled in war and of great courage and strength. This was especially true of

4. The festival of the twelfth month, Teotleco, which means 'the coming of the gods.' The gods having supposedly left the country for a season were now returning. Tezcatlipoca (god of youth) was believed to arrive before the rest and Yacatecutli (the traveling merchants' god) a day after the others.

5. The festival of the fourteenth month, Quecholli.

6. Quetzalcoatl, in all probability. See below, bk. I, ch. XII. He was essentially a Toltec god, and the people of the three towns mentioned were of Toltec stock, or at least had a large admixture of Toltec blood. Also the ruins of the great pyramid of Quetzalcoatl in Cholula indicate that he was especially revered there. What the three names were to which Motolinía refers, I do not know.

Tlaxcallan, which is the largest of these provinces and has the most alert, bold, and warlike population. It is, in fact, one of the strongest and biggest and most populous provinces of New Spain, as will be shown later.[7] These natives were in the habit of taking in their wars captives to be sacrificed to their idols, and for this reason, when fighting, they rushed in and grappled with any of the enemy whom they could seize and dragged them out and bound them cruelly. In this way the valiant showed and distinguished themselves.

These people had many other festivals marked by great ceremonies and great cruelties which I do not remember well enough to write the truth about them, although I lived for six years amongst them and heard and learned many things. I did not, however, inform myself so as to be able to write about them.

In Tlaxcallan there were many lords and important personages and much military training, and they always had a sort of garrison. All the prisoners that they took, besides many slaves, were killed as sacrifices. The same was true of Huexotzinco and Chololllan. This Chololllan was considered to be a great sanctuary, like another Rome, in which there were many temples of the devil. I was told that there were more than three hundred. I saw it all filled with towers and temples of the devil, but I did not count them. Because there were so many temples they held many festivals during the year, and some people came from more than forty leagues away; and each province had its halls and lodging houses for the festivals.

CHAPTER IX

Of the tortures which the ministers called tlamacazques inflicted upon themselves, especially in Tehuacán, Cozcatlán, and Teutitlán; and of the fasts which they kept.

IN addition to the sacrifices and festivals of which I have spoken, there were many other private sacrifices which were constantly being performed, especially by those ministers whom the Spaniards call *papas*. These men inflicted tortures upon themselves, on various parts of the

7. See below, bk. III, ch. XVI.

body, and at certain festivals they pierced the upper part of their ears with a sharp little black stone knife which they made like a surgeon's lancet, as sharp and with as thin an edge. Many Spaniards use these knives to bleed themselves or others, and they cut very smoothly, except that the point sometimes breaks, if the blood-letter is not skillful. (In this country many men endeavor to have a knowledge of blood-letting and horse-shoeing and many other trades which in Spain it would not be considered honorable to learn, even if in other respects they are vain and self-conceited—although, to be sure, the Spaniards in this country are the best and most unassuming people one could find in the world.) To return to our subject; through the hole which they made in their ears or tongues they would draw a reed as thick as one's finger and as long as one's arm. A great many of the ordinary people, both men and women, would draw or pass through holes in their ears or tongue straws as big as stalks of wheat, and others used the spines of the agave or *metl* (I will explain later[1] what this is), and all that they thus covered with blood, as well as the blood which they could catch on pieces of paper, they offered to the idols.

In Tehuacán, Teutitlán, and Cozcatlán, which were frontier provinces and carried on wars in many places, they made very cruel sacrifices of captives and slaves.[2] The tlamacazques, or young priests, inflicted upon themselves one of the strangest and cruelest tortures in the world. They cut between the skin and the flesh of the *membrum virile* and made an opening so large that they could pass through it a rope as thick as one's wrist, the length of the rope depending upon the devotion of the penitent. Some were ten fathoms long, some fifteen, and some twenty. If anyone fainted under this cruel and senseless torture, they told him that his lack of courage was due to his having sinned with a woman, for the priests who performed this mad and senseless penance were unmarried youths; and it was no wonder that they fainted, for it is well known that circumcision causes the most intense pain in the world. The other people of the town made sacrificial offerings of drops of blood which they drew from their ears and arms and from the tip of the tongue. The most devout, both men and women, had their ears and tongues torn and mutilated, and one can see it in many of them even now. In the three provinces

1. See below, bk. II, ch. XIX.

2. This sentence is quite out of place in this paragraph. It would be better placed at the beginning of the paragraph on p. 76, "the heads of those whom they sacrificed." Neither of these passages really belongs in this chapter, which deals not with sacrificial ceremonies, but with forms of penance practiced by the priests and ministers.

which I mentioned, the ministers of the temples and all those of their household fasted eighty days every year. They also observed their Lenten seasons and fasts before the festivals of the devil, especially the priests of whom I spoke, eating only corn bread and salt, and drinking water. Some of their periods of fasting were of ten days, some of twenty, and others of forty, and occasionally one, like the fast of Panquetzaliztli in Mexico,[3] was of eighty days, in which some fell ill and died, since their cruel god did not allow them to show themselves any mercy.

These *papas* were also called 'firegivers,' since three times a day and three times during the night they would go with their censers to throw incense on fire or on coals. When they swept the temples of the devil they did it with feathers instead of brooms, walking backwards so as not to turn their backs upon the idols. They ordered the whole town, even the boys, to fast, and they fasted two, four, five, and even ten days. These fasts were not general, but each province fasted according to its customs and the intensity of its devotion.

In certain towns of the province of Tehuacán the devil had perpetual chaplains who always watched and spent their time in prayers, fasting, and sacrifice. This perpetual service was divided into four-year periods, and the chaplains were also four youths who were expected to live for four years a life of privation and penance. They entered the house of the devil as the priest enters the church for a *treintanario cerrado*.[4] Each one was given one thin cotton blanket and a *maxtlatl*,[5] a sort of scarf which they gird about their loins and use as a breech clout, and they had no other clothing either day or night, even though it is fairly cold at night in the winter. Their bed was the hard earth and their pillow a stone. They fasted for all those four years, abstaining from meat, fish, salt, and chili; they ate only once a day at noon. Their meal consisted of a tortilla, which, to judge from their description, must have been of about two ounces, and they drank a bowl of a beverage called atole. They ate nothing else, neither fruit nor honey nor anything sweet, except every twentieth day, these being their feast days, like our Sunday. On these days they might eat anything they had. Each year they were given new clothing. Their occu-

3. See above, bk. I, ch. VI. The penitential period preceding the festival began one day after the end of the eleventh month, Ochpanztli. See Sahagún, vol. I, p. 105, where he says that the penitential period was forty days, and p. 192, where he says eighty days.

4. A series of thirty Masses said on thirty consecutive days, the celebrant passing the whole thirty day period shut up in the church.

5. Spanish: *un maxtlatl, que es como toca de camino con que se ciñen y tapan sus verguenzas.*

pation was to be continually in the dwelling and presence of the devil. For the night watch they were divided into groups of two; one night two watched without sleeping and the other two slept, and the next night they changed. They spent their time singing many hymns to the devil, and at times they drew blood from various parts of their bodies and offered it as a sacrifice; and four times during the night they offered incense. Every twenty days they performed the following sacrifice: they cut a hole in the upper part of the ear and drew through it sixty reeds, some thick and some as thin as a finger, some as long as one's arm, others measuring a fathom, and others the length of a javelin.[6] All these rods, when stained with blood, they placed in a heap before the idols, and at the end of the four years they burned them. They counted, if I am not mistaken, eighteen times eighty (to calculate the four year period), for there were five days in the year which they did not count;[7] but they counted eighteen months of twenty days each.

If any of these penitents, or chaplains of the devil, died, they immediately put another in his place; and it was considered an omen that there would be a great mortality and that many lords would die, so that that year they all lived in terror, for they are people who put great faith in omens. The devil often appeared to these chaplains—or they pretended that he did—and then they told the people what the devil had said to them —or whatever they pleased—and what the wishes and commands of the gods were. What they usually said that they saw was a head with long hair. The great lord Moteuczoma took great pleasure in hearing of the exercises and visions of these penitents, for it seemed to him a very special service and acceptable to the gods.

If it was found that any of those penitents had, in those four years, had carnal relations with a woman, a great meeting was held of priests and populace and the youth was sentenced to death. The execution took place not by day, but during the night. In the presence of all they beat him over the head with cudgels until the skull was crushed; then they burned his body and threw the ashes to the winds so that they should be scattered and no memory be left of that man,[8] for that act at such a time was considered an enormity which no one should mention.

6. Spanish: *como varas de tirar.*

7. See above, bk. I, chs. IV-V.

8. Gómara (p. 449) definitely associates the penitential practices of these 'perpetual chaplains' with Quetzalcoatl: "that no memory might remain of that man, since he could not spend four years without commerce with women, *when Quetzalcoatl, in memory of whom he undertook the penance,* spent his whole life without it."

The heads of those whom they sacrificed, especially prisoners of war, were skinned, and if the captives were lords or personages of importance, they skinned the heads, hair and all, and dried them in order to keep them.[9] There were many of these dried heads at first, and, except for the fact that they had some beard, no one would have taken them for anything but the heads of five- or six-year old children. The reason for this was that they were cured and dried. The skulls were placed on poles which were erected in the following manner at one side of the temples of the devil: They put up fifteen or twenty poles, more or less, about four or five fathoms high above the ground, and sunk more than a fathom in the earth. These were rounded beams, placed in a straight line about six feet apart, and all of them were full of holes. The skulls were pierced through the temples and strung on slender rods which were then stuck into the holes bored in the beams I have mentioned above; and so they had skulls by the five hundreds, by the six hundreds, and in some places by the thousands. If some of them fell, they put up others, for they were very cheap, and to have those racks very full of skulls showed that they were great warriors and very devout in sacrificing to their idols.

When they were to dance at solemn festivals they painted and blackened themselves in many ways.[10] For this purpose, on the morning of the day when there was to be a dance, professional painters, both men and women, came to the *tianquizco* or market with a quantity of colors and their brushes, and painted the faces, arms, and legs of those who were to dance according to the fancy of the individual or the requirements of the solemnity and ceremony of the festival.[11] Thus smeared and painted they went off to dress themselves in different costumes, and some made themselves so hideous that they looked like devils, and thus they served and celebrated the devil. In this same manner they painted themselves when they went out to fight, if they were at war or if there was a battle.

At the back of the principal temples there was a separate room for women, not closed, for they were not in the habit of using doors, but very modest and secluded. These women served in the temples because of vows that they had made. Some, out of devotion, promised to serve there a

9. See above, note 2.

10. See also below, bk. I, chs. X and XI.

11. The painting was pretty thoroughly conventional and traditional. certain colors and certain arrangements of stripes and painted areas being definitely associated with certain deities. See Sahagún, vol. I, bks. I and II, for the description of the gods and the adornment of priests and victims at the great festivals.

year, or two, or three, others made a similar vow at the time of some illness. All of them, or at least the majority, were young virgins, although there were a few old women who, out of devotion, wished to die there and spend their last days in penance. These old women were the guardians and teachers of the girls; and because they were in the service of the idols both old and young women were much respected.

As soon as they entered their hair was cut. For greater modesty and in order to be always ready for the service of the idols they slept in their clothes, all in one hall; and their occupation was to spin and weave, for the service of the temple, colored blankets and blankets with woven designs. At midnight they went with the older women to throw incense on the braziers that stood before the idols. At the principal festivals they all went in procession on one side and the priests on the other until they stood before the idols, at the foot of the steps. Both men and women marched in such silence and recollection that they neither raised their eyes from the ground nor spoke a word. Although most of these women were poor, their relatives gave them food and all that they needed to make blankets and to cook hot food, which they offered in the morning to the idols, tortillas and chickens stewed in a sort of small saucepan. They said that the idols consumed the smell and the steam of the food —the priests consumed the rest. These girls had a sort of mistress or mother superior who called them together at appropriate times and held a meeting as the abbess does with her nuns. She imposed penances upon any who had been negligent (for this reason some Spaniards called these girls nuns), and if any girl so much as smiled at a man they gave her a severe penance. If it was found that any one of them had carnal relations with a man, when the truth of the matter was established both were killed. They fasted all the time that they were in the temple, having one meal at noon and a supper at night. On feast days, when they were not fasting, they ate meat. They swept their own special part of the precinct, the lower court before the temples; the upper part was always swept by the ministers, in some places with costly feathers and without turning the back toward the idols, as I have said before.[12]

All these women were here serving the devil for their own interests: some that the devil might grant them favors, others that he might grant them long life or riches, others to learn to be good spinners and weavers

12. See above, this chapter.

of rich blankets.[13] If anyone committed a carnal sin while in the temple, however secretly, she believed that her flesh would rot, and she did penance so that the devil might conceal her sin. In some festivals they danced very modestly before the idols.[14]

CHAPTER X

Of a very great festival, with many ceremonies and sacrifices, which was held in Tlaxcallan.

AFTER I had written the preceding chapter I came to dwell in this monastery in Tlaxcallan, and when I asked questions and made inquiries about their festivals they told me of a remarkable piece of cruelty which I shall now relate.

In this city of Tlaxcallan, among many other festivals, there was one in honor of the principal devil[1] whom they worship, which was held every year at the beginning of March. The one that was held every four years was a solemn festival for the whole province, but this other that they held they called the Year of God.[2] When the year came the oldest minister or tlamacazque of these provinces of Tlaxcallan, Huexotzinco, and Chollollan arose and preached and exhorted them all[3] saying: "My sons, the year of our lord and master has come; strive to serve him and do penance, and let him who feels himself too weak for this leave within five days. If he departs at ten days and gives up the penance, he shall be considered

13. According to Sahagún (vol. I, p. 253) and Torquemada (vol. II, pp. 188-191) these girls were dedicated to the temple service by their mothers twenty to forty days after birth. When the girl reached the age of discretion she was told of the vow that had been made on her behalf, and went willingly to the temple to begin her service. She remained there until a marriage was arranged for her.

14. Sahagún mentions these temple women, *cioatlamacazque,* as dancing at the festival of the goddess Xilonen, on the tenth day of the eighth month, Veytecuilhuitl, also as taking part in the festival of the eleventh month, Ochpaniztli.

1. Camaxtli (or Camaxtle). See below, p. 82. The god of the provinces of Tlaxcallan and Huexotzinco. A war god closely related to the Mexican Huitzilopuchtli and to Mixcoatl of the Otomíes, and occasionally identified with them.

2. The meaning of this sentence is not clear. Apparently "this other" must refer to the *yearly* festival, and yet the special name *year of god* and the words of the following sentence "when the year came" would seem to refer to the festival celebrated every fourth year. Gómara (p. 447) makes it clear that his account (which corresponds exactly with this one given by Motolinía) is of the quadrennial celebration.

3. All the priests and ministers.

unworthy of the house of our god and of the company of his servants, and be degraded, and all that he has in his house shall be taken from him." On the fifth day the old priest rose again in the midst of the other ministers and said: "Are all here?" And they answered "Yes" (or that one or two were absent. There were very rarely any absences.) "Well, then, let us now with all our hearts begin the festival of our lord."

Then they all went to a great mountain which is four leagues from this city, two of them up a very laborious ascent. Near the top, but a little before reaching the summit, they all remained in prayer while the old priest went on up to where there was a temple of the goddess Matlalcueye[4] and presented an offering of some stones which were a sort of emerald,[5] and big green feathers[6] of which they make good feather ornaments. He made also offerings of much paper and native incense, beseeching the god and the goddess,[7] his wife, by this offering to give them courage to begin their fast and to finish it without breaking down, and strength to do penance. When he had made this prayer he rejoined his companions and they all returned together to the city.

Then came other lesser temple servants who were scattered about the land serving in other temples and brought many loads of rods as long as one's arm and as thick as one's wrist, and placed them in the principal temple. These men were given a good meal. Then came many carpenters who had fasted and prayed for five days, and they smoothed and prepared those rods. When they had finished their work they were given a meal outside of the temples. When they had gone, there came the experts who were to make the knives. They also had fasted and prayed. They made many knives with which the penitents would pierce their tongues, and as soon as they made them they placed them on a clean blanket, and if a knife broke as it was being made, they said that it was because the maker had not kept his fast well. No one who has not seen how they make these knives can understand how they do it. This is the way: first they cut a piece of the stone that they use for knives, which is as black as jet. They cut it about the length of a span or a little less, and shape it round and as thick as the calf of the leg. Then they hold

4. The name under which Chalchihuitlicue, goddess of running water, was worshipped in Tlaxcala.

5. Chalchihuitl. See below, bk. III, ch. VIII.

6. Feathers of the *quetzal,* or trogon.

7. Matlalcue or Chalchihuitlicue was the wife of Tlaloc, the god of rain and thunder. These deities were associated with mountain tops, since it is there that the rain clouds gather. Just why they were invoked in this 160 day fast in honor of Camaxtle I do not know.

it between their feet and tap the edges of the stone with a stick. At each blow they split off a little, thin knife with sharp edges like a real knife. They will get over two hundred knives from one stone, and some lancets for bloodletting as well.

They put the knives on a clean blanket and perfumed them with their incense, and when the sun had set all the priests assembled and four of them sang devil's hymns to the knives, playing upon their drums. When they had sung for a while, both voices and drums were silent, and then the same four priests sang again without the drums, this time a very sad song, and tried to arouse devotion, and wept—I think because of what they would soon suffer. When this second song was over the priests were all ready, and then an expert, skillful as a surgeon, pierced the tongues of all of them in the middle, making a good hole with the knives that had been blessed. Then that old and leading priest drew through his tongue four hundred and five rods, of those which had been fashioned by the carpenters after prayer and fasting. The other priests of long standing and great courage used in the same way four hundred and five rods each, some as thick as the thumb and others somewhat thicker. Some were as thick as the space that one can encircle with the thumb and forefinger. Other, younger priests used two hundred rods—a mere nothing! This was done on the night which marked the beginning of the fast preceding the great festival, that is, one hundred and sixty days before the feast. When they had finished that slight refreshment[8] of passing the rods through the hole in the tongue the old priest sang again, although he could scarcely move his tongue; but thinking that he was rendering a great service to his god, he did the best he could.

Then they fasted eighty days at a stretch, and every twenty days each man drew through the hole in his tongue as many more rods as on the first occasion, until the eighty days were over. At the end of these eighty days they took a small branch and placed it in the courtyard where everyone could see it, as a signal that all were to begin the fast. Then they took all the rods that they had drawn through their tongues, all stained with blood, and offered them before the idols. They planted in the ground ten or twelve stakes, each one of five or six fathoms in length, so that within the enclosure they could put the rods which they were offering as a sacrifice, of which there were many, since there were many priests.

The remaining eighty days before the festival everyone fasted, the

8. Spanish: *colación*. Sarcastic.

lords as well as all the people, both men and women; and during this fast they ate no *ají* (chili), which is one of their principal articles of diet, and one which they always eat in all this land and in all the Islands. They also refrained from bathing, a practice to which they are much addicted; and from intercourse with their wives; but those who had meat might eat it, especially the men.

The fast of the entire population began eighty days before the festival, and in all that time the fire must not be extinguished and it must not go out day or night in the houses of the principal lords. If there was carelessness about this, the lord of the house in which the fire went out killed a slave and sprinkled his blood on the brazier or hearth that had gone out. During the second eighty days those devout people, to keep their tongues from murmuring, drew through them every twenty days other little rods about six and a half inches long and as thick as a duck's quill. This was done to the accompaniment of much singing by the priests. During this period the old priest went every night to the aforementioned mountain range and there offered to the devil much paper and incense and many quail. He was accompanied by only four or five, for the others, who were more than two hundred, remained in the halls of the temple occupied in the service of the devil. Those who went to the mountain neither stopped nor rested until they returned to the temple. During these days of the fast the old priest went out to the towns of the district, as if to his benefice, to collect the customary donations.[9] He carried a branch in his hand and went to the houses of the lords, where they offered him much food and many blankets; he refused the food, but took the blankets.

Four or five days before the day of the festival they adorned and prepared the temples, and cleaned and white-washed them. The third day before it, the priests all painted themselves, some black, some red, others white, green, blue or yellow, and thus painted they danced for a whole day at the back of the principal house or temple of the devil. Then they adorned the statue of that devil of theirs, which was three times the height of a man, and very hideous and fearful. They also had a small idol[10] which, they said, had come with the ancients who settled this land and province of Tlaxcallan. This idol they placed beside the big statue,

9. Spanish: *hornazo*. Gifts made on Easter day to the priest who has preached the lenten sermons.

10. Representing the god Paynal (or Painal), a sort of messenger or adjutant of Huitzilopuchtli, with whom Camaxtle is more or less identified. See above, note 1.

and held it in such reverence and fear that they dared not look at it. Even though they sacrificed quail to it, so great was their respect that they did not dare to raise their eyes to look at it.

They also put upon the big statue a mask which they said had come with the little idol from a town called Tollan, and from another called Poyauhtlán, of which they assert the same idol was a native.[11] On the eve of the festival they again made offerings to him. First they placed on the left arm of the big idol a shield beautifully adorned with gold and feather work, and in his right hand a long arrow, or dart, whose head was of flint, the size of a metal lance-head.[12] They also offered him many blankets and *xicoles,* which is a garment like a cape without a shoulder cape, and dressed him in a long open robe like the cassock of a Spanish priest. This robe had a border of cotton dyed in the thread and of rabbit's hair spun and dyed like silk. Then they brought in the offering of food, which consisted of many rabbits, quail, snakes, locusts, butterflies, and other things that fly in the fields. All this game was offered alive and then sacrificed before the idol. After this, at midnight, one of the priests who served there came dressed in the insignia of the devil, and lighted new fire. When this was done they sacrificed one of the most important captives that they had for that festival, and this victim they called the child of the sun. Afterward there began the sacrifice and slaughter of the prisoners of war in honor of the great idol. They also at the same time named other gods, by way of commemoration, and offered them some of those whom they sacrificed.

As I have already explained the method of sacrifice I shall give now merely the numbers of those sacrificed. In that temple of that great idol called Camaxtli, which is in a district named Ocotelolco, they killed four hundred and five, and in another section a half a league from there, up a great hillside, they killed fifty or sixty more. In twenty-eight other parts of this province the sacrifices were in proportion to the size of the towns, so that the number of victims sacrificed on this day reached eight hundred in the city and province of Tlaxcallan alone. Afterward each man

11. This sentence is far from clear. Does it really mean that they came both from Tollan and from Poyauhtlán? Does "the same idol" refer to the big statue of Camaxtle or to the little one of Paynal? Gómara's statement (p. 448) is of interest as helping to clear up this confusion. He says: "a mask which they say that the first settlers brought from Puyahutla . . . of which place Camaxtle himself was a native."

12. Spanish: *saeta.* From the size of the head it would seem more likely that the weapon is the javelin or dart, thrown by means of the *atlatl* (spear-thrower), especially as the *atlatl* is one of the characteristic attributes of Camaxtle, Mixcoatl, and Huitzilopuchtli.

carried away the bodies of those whom he had brought alive to the sacrifice, leaving part of that human flesh for the priests, and then they all began to eat, with that human flesh, the chili which they had not tasted for nearly half a year.

Chapter XI

Of other festivals held in the province of Tlaxcallan; of the festival celebrated by the Chololtecas in honor of their god, and why the temples were called "teocallis." [1]

On the same day many others of the provinces of Huexotzinco, Tepeyacac, and Zacatlán died as sacrificial victims, for in all those provinces they honored the great idol Camaxtli as their principal god; and they did this with almost the same ceremonies as the Tlaxcaltecas,[2] except that in no province did they sacrifice so many or such great numbers as in this one. The reason for this was that Tlaxcallan was larger and had many more warriors, who were bolder and more valiant in killing the enemy and in taking prisoners. For they tell me that there were men who had killed and captured over one hundred and others who had taken eighty or fifty. All these prisoners were taken and kept in order to sacrifice them. When that evil day was past they made further commemoration of their god on the day following, and sacrificed to him fifteen or twenty captives more. They also had many other festivals, and especially the last day of each month, that is, every twenty days. These festivals they celebrated with different ceremonies and killings similar to those of the other provinces of Mexico. In this point also did this province exceed the others, namely that more children were annually killed and sacrificed here than in any other part of the country. As far as I have been able to make out they sacrificed these innocent children to the god of water.

In another festival they tied a man to a very high cross and shot arrows at him.[3] In another they tied a man lower down and killed him by stabbing him, as one does a bull, with rods of ilex-wood as long as one's

1. This subject is not discussed, either in this chapter or elsewhere in the book.
2. See above, bk. I, ch. x.
3. See above, bk. I, ch. VII.

arm and very sharp. Almost identical ceremonies and sacrifices were practiced in the provinces of Huexotzinco, Tepeyacac, and Zacatlán at their principal festivals, for they all recognized as the greatest of their gods, Camaxtli, which was the great statue that I mentioned.

Here in Tlaxcallan on another day of a festival they sacrificed and flayed two women. The skins of these victims were then put on by two swift-footed young men chosen from among the priests or ministers, and thus dressed these two went about the temple courtyard and through the town in pursuit of the lords and principal men, who on this festival wore fine, clean blankets, and they ran after them, and if they caught them, took their blankets from them; and so, with this sport, the festival ended.

Among many other festivals which were celebrated in Chalollan in the course of the year there was one, held every four years, which they called the year of their god, or devil.[4] The fast began eighty days before the festival. The principal tlamacazque, or priest, fasted for four days, eating each day only a tortilla so small and thin that it was very little even for a snack and cannot have weighed more than an ounce, and drinking only a little water with it. During those four days this priest went alone to pray for the help and favor of the gods, so that he and his fellow priests might be enabled to fast and celebrate the festival of their god. The fast, and what they did in those eighty days, was very different from the other fasts. On the day on which the fast began all the ministers and officers of the house of the devil, who were very numerous, went into the houses and lodgings that stood in the courtyards and before the temples, and to each one was given an earthen censer with its incense, and agave thorns, which prick like big pins, and also black paint. They all sat down in order against the wall and no one got up from there except to attend to physical necessities, and thus seated they kept watch during the first sixty days, for they never slept except early in the night for the space of two hours. From then on they watched all night until sunrise, when they slept again for an hour. All the rest of the time they kept watch and made offerings of incense, all putting incense on to the braziers simultaneously. This they did many times during both day and night. At midnight they all bathed and washed themselves and then painted themselves black again with the black paint that was provided.

During those days they also offered frequent sacrifices of their own

4. According to Gómara (p. 448), whose account agrees closely with Motolinía's, this festival with its fast was in honor of Quetzalcoatl.

blood, which they drew from their ears with the above-mentioned agave thorns. They were kept supplied with these, which they used both to draw blood and to keep themselves awake. If any nodded with sleep, there were guards who went about waking them and saying: "Here is something with which to wake yourself up and bleed yourself, and then you will not go to sleep." And it was to their advantage not to do so, for if one of them went to sleep outside of the specified hours, others came and punctured his ears cruelly and smeared the blood on his head and broke his censer, as a sign that he was unworthy to offer incense to the god. They took his blankets and threw them into the privy and said to him that because he had broken the fast and gone to sleep during the fast of his god one of his sons or daughters would die that year; and if he had no children, they said to him that someone would die whose death would grieve him greatly.

During this time no one could go out, for they were shut in as if for a *treintanario cerrado;*[5] nor did they lie down to sleep, but slept seated. After sixty days of this harsh and intolerable penance, during the other twenty days they did not bleed themselves so often and they slept somewhat more. The men who have kept this fast say that they suffered tortures in resisting the desire for sleep and that they were very much distressed by not being able to lie down. On the morning of the festival all the priests went to their houses, and their families had new blankets ready for them, very brightly colored. With these they all returned to the temple and rejoiced as at a great festival. They held many other ceremonies which, not to be prolix, I shall omit. It is enough to know the cruelties which the devil practiced in this land and the suffering in which he made the poor Indians pass their lives, only to bear them off at last to everlasting torment.

5. See above, bk. I, ch. IX.

CHAPTER XII

Of the form and nature of the teocallis (temples) and their great number; and of one more important than the others.

THE nature of the temples of this land of Anáhuac or New Spain is something the like of which was never seen or heard, both as regards their size and workmanship, and all the rest.

A thing which rises to a great height must also have a great foundation, and of this nature were the temples and altars of this land, whose number was infinite. I make note of them here so that those who come to this land in the future may know this, for the memory of them is now almost dying out. These temples are called teocallis. We found that in all the land they were built in this manner. A great square courtyard was made in the best part of the town; in the big towns the courtyard was a crossbow shot from corner to corner, and in the smaller towns, smaller. This courtyard was surrounded by a wall, often battlemented, whose gates opened on to the principal streets and highways, for they made the roads so that they should lead to the courtyard; and, to give greater honor to their temples, they laid out their roads by surveyor's lines so that they ran absolutely straight for a league or two. It was a sight worth seeing to look from the top of the principal temple and see how, from all the lesser towns and districts, the roads came in very straight and ended in the courtyards of the temples.

In the highest part of this courtyard there was a great square-cornered foundation. For the purpose of this description I measured one of these foundations in a medium-sized town called Tenanyocan and found that it was 240 feet [1] from corner to corner. All of this they filled with solid masonry. On the outside it was of stone; the inside was filled with stone or clay and adobe or well-tamped earth. As the wall increased in height it sloped inward, and at a height of nine to twelve feet they began to construct set-backs, for they did not build their walls plumb. Since it gives greater strength, they always built inward; that is to say, the foundation was broad, and as the walls went up they came nearer together, so that at the top of the teocalli they had been narrowed and built in, both by the use of set-backs and by the slope of the walls, as much as forty-two to forty-eight feet on each side. The top of the foundation was from two

1. Spanish: *cuarenta brazas;* the *braza* is about six feet.

hundred four to two hundred ten feet square. The western face of the foundation had steps leading up; and above, on the top, they built two big altars, placing them so far to the east that there was only room to walk behind them. One of these altars was placed at the right and one at the left, but each had its own walls and covered house like a chapel.

In the big teocallis there were two altars, in the others only one, and each of those altars had its own super-structure. The big temples had three stories above the altars, each set back and very high; the main foundation was also very high, so that they showed from a great distance. Each of these chapels had its own walls and one could walk all around it. In front of these altars they left a great open space where the sacrifices were held; the foundation alone, without the structures which covered the altars, was as high as a great tower. The teocalli of the city of Mexico, as I have been told by people who have seen it, had over one hundred steps. I saw them myself, to be sure, and counted them more than once, but I do not remember the number. The one in Tetzcoco had five or six steps more than the one in Mexico. The chapel of Saint Francis in Mexico is a vaulted building and reasonably high, but when one went up and looked at the city from the top of the building it was obvious that the temple of the devil was much higher; and the view of Mexico and the surrounding towns from the top of it was a sight worth seeing.

In these same courtyards, in the big towns, there would be ten or fifteen other fair-sized teocallis, some bigger than others but nowhere near so big as the main temple. Some of these faced each other, some faced the east, others south, and in each of them there was only one altar with its chapel. For each of these temples there were halls and rooms occupied by the tlamacazques or ministers, who were very numerous, and by the servants who brought water and wood, for before these altars there were braziers which burned all night, and there were fires in the halls as well. They kept all these temples very white and polished and clean, and some of them had little gardens with flowers and trees.

In most of these big courtyards there was one other temple constructed in this manner: after they had built the square foundation and made the altar, they surrounded the latter with a high circular wall surmounted by a spire. This was the temple of the god of air, of whom we said that he had his principal seat in Cholollan.[2] Throughout this province

2. This has not been said explicitly anywhere. Motolinía probably had in mind what he said in bk. I, ch. VIII, forgetting that he did not mention Quetzalcoatl by name in either passage.

there were many of those temples. This god of the air they called in their language Quetzalcoatl, and said that he was the son [3] of that god of the big statue,[4] and a native of Tollan, whence he had gone out to build up certain provinces and had disappeared. They were always expecting him to come back, and when the ships of Don Hernando Cortés, Marquis of the Valley and conqueror of this New Spain, appeared and they saw them sailing in the distance, they said that their god was coming at last; and because of the high white sails they said that he was bringing his temples over the seas. Later, when the Spaniards disembarked, the Indians said that it was not their god, but many gods.

The devil was not content with the temples already mentioned, but in every town and in each of its outlying districts, a quarter of a league out, they had other small courtyards with three or four temples. In some places there were more and in some only one; on every little hill or ridge there would be one or two and along the roads and in the cornfields many other little ones. They were all whitewashed, so that they showed up clearly and looked very big, and in the well-populated parts of the country it seemed as if everything were full of houses and especially of these devil's courtyards, so that it was really a sight worth seeing; and there was a great deal to see when one went into them. Those of Tetzcoco and Mexico were superior to all the others.

The Chololtecas began an extremely large temple, so large that the foundation alone, which is all that now remains, must be a good crossbow shot from one corner to the other, and it would be a good crossbow indeed that could shoot an arrow from the foot of it to the top.[5] Even so the natives of Cholollan point out that it used to have an even broader base and was much higher than it now appears. They began this temple with the intention of making it higher than the highest mountains of the land, even though the highest ranges of all New Spain are visible from here, that is to say, the volcano [6] and the white sierra, which is always covered with snow.[7] As they persisted in carrying out their mad attempt God confounded them as he did the builders of the Tower of Babel, causing a great stone shaped like a toad to fall there during a terrible storm

3. Compare this version of Quetzalcoatl's parentage with that given in the Introductory Letter, above, p. 32.

4. Camaxtle. See above, bk. I, chs. X and XI.

5. The great pyramid of Quetzalcoatl, 177 feet high and covering an area of nearly 45 acres.

6. Popocatepetl.

7. Iztaccihuatl.

which struck the place. From that time they ceased to work upon the temple. At the present day the building is so remarkable that if it were not apparent that the structure is of stone and clay, and in parts of cut stone, mortar, and adobe, no one would believe that it was not a small mountain. Many rabbits and snakes are to be found there, and in some parts, corn is planted. On the top of it there was a small old temple. They tore it down and set up in its place a tall cross, which was shattered by a thunderbolt, and when they erected another and still another they too were shattered in the same way. I was present on the third occasion, which was during the past year, 1535. They therefore dug off and excavated a great deal of the top of the mound and found there many idols and idolatrous offerings to the devil.[8] So I confounded the Indians by saying that because of the many sins committed in that place God did not wish his cross to stand there. Later they put up a big bell which had been blessed, and no storms or thunderbolts have come since they installed it.

Although the Spaniards conquered this land by force of arms (in which conquest God showed many marvels—that so great a land should be won by so few when the natives had many weapons, both offensive and defensive); and although the Spaniards burned some temples of the devil and broke some idols, it was very little in comparison with what remained; God has therefore showed His power still more in having held this land with such small numbers as the Spaniards had. Many times when the natives had the opportunity to recover their land with great facility and ease, God blinded their understanding, and at other times when they have been bound and united for this purpose (*i.e.,* the recovery of their land), and all in agreement, God miraculously upset their plans. If God permitted them to begin this undertaking, they would easily be able to carry it out, being all united and of the same mind and having many Spanish weapons. When this country was first conquered there was great division, and some groups were hostile to others. On the one hand the Mexicans were divided against the people of Michuacán, and the Tlaxcaltecas against the Mexicans, and on the other were the Huaxtecas of

8. Gabriel de Rojas in his *Relación de la ciudad de Chohollan* (MS., 1581) gives a different version: ". . . the Friars, thinking that there was some mystery in this (*i. e.,* in the fact that the cross was destroyed by lightning) had them dig on the top of the hill, and they found a lot of big sea shells which the Indians formerly used as trumpets. And anyone who takes into consideration the nature of thunderbolts and the fact that a great many strike in this city and district will not think it a miracle (as some historians claim) that lightning should twice have destroyed that cross, since it stood, as I have said, forty *varas* higher than the highest building in the city." (Quoted by Ramírez as a note in *Historia de los Indios,* bk. 1, p. 66.) See also Las Casas, p. 347.

Pango or Pánuco. But now that God has brought them into the fold of His church and into obedience to the King of Spain, He will bring in also those who are still missing and will not permit more souls in this land to go astray and be damned, nor will He permit more idolatry.

The first three or four years after Mexico was taken the Blessed Sacrament was kept only in the monastery of St. Francis, and later the second church in which it was placed was in Tetzcoco. As they gradually built the monastery churches, they put the Blessed Sacrament in them and the apparitions and illusions of the devil ceased. Formerly the devil had often appeared and deceived and frightened many and led them into all manner of errors, asking the Indians why they did not serve and worship him as they used to do, since he was their god, and saying that the Christians would soon go back to their own land. For this reason, during the first years, they always believed that the Spaniards would go, and waited for their flight, and certainly thought, because of what the devil told them, that they were not there to stay. At other times the devil told them that that year he wanted to kill the Christians, but as he could not do it he told the Indians to rebel against the Spaniards and that he would help them. For this reason some towns and provinces did revolt, but it cost them dear, for the Spaniards, aided by the loyal Indians, at once attacked them and destroyed them and made them slaves. Sometimes the devil told them that he would give them no water or rain, because they had angered him. It was in this that his deceit and falsehood were most obvious, for it has never rained so much nor have they had such good rainstorms as since the Blessed Sacrament was brought to this land; before that they had many sterile and difficult years. This is recognized by the Indians and is the reason why this country is so serene and peaceful, as if the devil had never been worshipped in it. It is wonderful to see in what tranquillity the natives enjoy their lands and with what solemnity and joy they treat the Blessed Sacrament and what solemn festivals they hold in honor of it, getting together the greatest possible number of priests and the best possible ecclesiastical ornaments. The town where the Blessed Sacrament is newly established invites the neighboring and friendly towns to a great festival, and they encourage and stimulate each other in the service of our true God.

The Blessed Sacrament is most reverently and devoutly placed in its monstrance, well made of silver, and besides this the tabernacle is gracefully adorned inside and out with beautiful gold and feather work.[9] This land has many excellent masters of this art, so much so that in Spain and Italy people would consider them as of the very first class and would look at them in open-mouthed astonishment, as newcomers do here. If any poor or ill-designed examples of this work have reached Spain, the fault lies with the painters who first make the sample or sketch; after him comes the *amantecatl,* for this is what they call the skilled craftsman who applies the feathers. From this name *amantecatl* the Spaniards came to call all craftsmen *amantecas,* but properly it applies only to the feather workers, for the other craftsmen all have their own names. If these feather workers are given a good colored sketch, they turn out their feather work just like it; and as the painters have achieved a high degree of excellence they make very perfect and beautiful figures and designs in gold and feathers. They adorn the churches very well and are taking more and more pains about it. The churches, which at first were small and not very well built, are being improved and enlarged; the tabernacle for the Blessed Sacrament especially is made so beautiful and so rich that it surpasses those in Spain. Although the Indians are almost all poor, the lords give very liberally of what they have to adorn the place which is to hold the Body of Christ, and those who have nothing divide the cost up among them and earn it by their labor.

CHAPTER XIII

Of how they celebrate the great feast days and other festivals of the year; and the various ceremonies that they observe.

THEY celebrate with great solemnity and rejoicing the feast days of Our Lord and of Our Lady and of the principal saints of their towns. They adorn their churches very prettily with what hangings they can get, and what they lack in tapestry they make up with branches and flowers. They cover the floor with reeds, rushes, and mint, which has increased incredibly in this land, and where the procession is to pass they erect

9. In bk. III, ch. XIX, Motolinía describes the method of making feather mosaic. A more detailed description is given by Sahagún (vol. v, pp. 217-225). Las Casas (p. 160) also has a great deal to say about it. For a brief description in English, see Joyce, pp. 245-46.

triumphal arches made of roses and with ornaments and garlands of the same flowers. They make many cone-shaped bouquets of flowers which are well worth seeing, and for this purpose all the people of the land make great efforts to have rose gardens. When they do not have gardens it sometimes happens that they send for flowers some ten or twelve leagues, to the warm country, where there are almost always roses, and very sweet smelling ones. The Indian lords and principal men, adorned and dressed in their white tunics and blankets embroidered with feathers, and with bouquets of roses in their hands, dance and sing in their own tongues hymns of the feast which they are celebrating. The friars have translated these hymns for them and their song leaders have set them to their own kind of rhythm, and they are pleasing and well sung. These dances and songs begin, in many places, at midnight, and they have fires in the churchyards. In this land the churchyards are very large and handsome because the people are numerous and cannot all get into the churches; for that reason they have their chapel out in the churchyard so that all can hear Mass on Sundays and feast days, and the churches are used for weekdays. After Mass they also sing for a great part of the day without much effort or weariness.

The whole course to be traversed by the procession is lined along both sides with interwoven branches even though it be one or two cross-bow shots in length, and the ground is strewn with reeds, rushes, leaves, and roses of many kinds,[1] and at intervals there are well-adorned altars.

On Christmas night they build many fires in the churchyards and on the flat roofs of their houses, and as there are many such roofs, and as the houses stretch out for a league or two or more, the town looks, at night, like a starry sky. And they usually sing and beat drums and ring bells. For the people of this land have already made a great many bells that inspire much devotion and give great joy to the people, and especially to the Spaniards. On that night the Indians come to the divine offices and hear their three Masses, and those for whom there is no room in the church do not go away, but stay at the door or in the churchyard praying and behaving as if they were inside. In this connection I will tell a thing which, when I saw it, in one way made me laugh and in another aroused my wonder. One day, as I went into a church which is some distance

1. Spanish: *de muchas maneras*. Separated by a comma from *roses*. If one accepts that punctuation the phrase may mean 'variously:' "variously strewn with reeds, etc." The punctuation is probably that of the editor, not of the author.

from our monastery, I found that the people of the town or parish had got together and, a short time before, had rung their bell, at the same time and in the same manner as it is rung elsewhere to call people to Mass; then, having recited the Hours of Our Lady, they repeated their catechism and then chanted their Pater Noster and Ave María. Then, ringing the bell as at the Offertory[2] they prayed silently and rang the bell again as at the Sanctus and beat their breasts before the crucifix and said that they were hearing Mass in intention, because they had no one to say it for them.

The feast of Epiphany is also celebrated by them with great rejoicing, for it seems to them as if it were their own; on that day they often represent the scene of the offerings brought by the three kings to the Child Jesus. They make the star appear from very far away, for they need no one to teach them how to make cords with which to pull it along, as all of them, big and little, know how to twist cord. And in church they have Our Lady with her lovely Son in the manger before whom they offer on that day wax and incense and doves and quail and other birds which they seek especially for that occasion; up to the present their devotion to this feast is constantly increasing.

At the feast of the Purification, or Candlemas, they bring their candles to be blessed; after they have sung and walked in the procession with them they greatly prize what is left, and keep it to use in case of illness and as a protection against thunder and lightning, for they have a great devotion to Our Lady, and because the candles were blessed on her day they treasure them greatly.

On Palm Sunday they trim their churches with branches and more particularly the places where the branches are to be blessed and where Mass is to be said. So many people come that many loads of branches would hardly suffice, even if each individual were given only a small bit; and especially in the big provinces, even though the branches were distributed in many different places, the danger of suffocation from crowding as they come to receive the branches is so great that, all other means having been tried, it has seemed best to bless the branches in their hands as they bring them. It is a sight to see the different ornaments that they put on their branches. Some bring them adorned with crosses made of

2. Spanish: *ofrenda.* Covarrubias gives *oferta* as the equivalent of *ofertorio,* meaning that part of the Mass in which the priest offers the sacrifice, beginning with the words *Suscipe sancte Pater. Ofrenda* is not given, but I assume that it must be used here in that sense.

flowers of a thousand different kinds and colors; others have roses and other flowers of many kinds and colors fastened to the branches, and as the branches are green and they hold them up high it looks like a flowering grove. Along the road they set up big trees; in the places where the trees actually grow along the road the children climb up into them, and some cut branches and throw them into the road as the procession passes, and others sing from the tops of the trees. Many others throw their clothing and blankets upon the road, and there are so many of these that most of the way the priests and bearers of the crosses walk upon blankets. The Indians keep the branches very carefully after they have been blessed, and a day or two before Ash Wednesday (of the following year) they bring them to the church door, and as there are many of them, they are piled up and burned, and provide plenty of ashes to be blessed. The ashes are received very devoutly by many of the Indians on the first day of Lent (during which season many of the men abstain from intercourse with their wives), and in some places men and women dress in black on that day. On Holy Thursday and the two following days they come to the services, and at night they scourge themselves.

All of them, both men and women, belong to the brotherhood of the Cross, and not only on this night, but on all the Fridays in the year and three times a week in Lent they scourge themselves in their churches, the men on one side of the church and the women on the other. They do this before the bell rings for the Ave María, and many days in Lent they do it after nightfall. When they are troubled by drought or illness or any other adversity they go about from church to church, carrying their crosses and torches and scourging themselves. But the scourging on Holy Thursday is a notable sight here in Mexico, both that of the Spaniards and that of the Indians, who are innumerable—in some places five or six thousand and in others ten or twelve thousand. In Tetzcoco and Tlaxcallan there are apparently some fifteen or twenty thousand, although when people are in procession the numbers appear greater than they really are. The truth is that they march in seven or eight ranks and men, women, children, the lame and the halt all take part.

Amongst the cripples I saw one this year who was a remarkable spectacle, for he had both legs shriveled from the knee down, and crawling along on his knees and his right hand he scourged himself with the other, when it was hard enough for him to get about on his knees, using both hands to help himself. Some use wire scourges, and other make them of cord, which sting no less than the wire ones. They carry a great many torches of pine knots well bound together which give a great deal of light. Their procession and scourging is most edifying to the Spaniards who are present; so much so that they begin either to scourge themselves or to carry the cross or to hold the torches, and I have seen many Spaniards weeping as they followed the procession. As they go along they all sing the Pater Noster and Ave María, the Creed, and the Salve Regina, for many of them everywhere know how to sing them. After the scourging they refresh themselves by bathing with hot water and chili pepper.

The feast of the Apostles they celebrate with great joy, and on All Souls' day, in almost all the Indian towns, they give offerings for their dead. Some bring corn, others blankets, others food: bread, poultry, and in place of wine, cocoa; and each one brings what wax he has and can spare, for though they are poor they take liberally from their scanty means and get enough for at least a little candle. They are the people in the world who worry themselves least about acquiring property for their children and leaving it to them. Very few of them will go to hell for matters of inheritance or wills, for whatever land or huts they inherited, that they leave to their children, and are contented with a small dwelling and less property, for, like the snail, they can carry all their property on their backs. I do not know from whom in this land our Spaniards got the idea, but they come from Spain very poor, with only a sword in hand, and within a year have more luggage than could be carried by a whole drove of mules, for all the houses have to be gentlemen's houses.

Chapter XIV

Of the offering which the Tlaxcaltecas make on Easter day; and of the natural disposition which the Indians have for salvation.

In this monastery of Tlaxcallan, in the year 1536, I saw an offering which I have never seen in any part of New Spain, nor do I believe that it exists elsewhere. To describe it would take a greater skill than mine to enhance and give value to what I believe God values greatly. What happened was as follows: Beginning with Holy Thursday the Indians begin to bring offerings to the church of the Mother of God, placing them before the steps where the Blessed Sacrament is; that day and Good Friday they keep coming, a few at a time, with their offerings, but from Holy Saturday at Vespers, and all through the night, so many people come that it seems as if no one could be left in the whole province.

The offerings consist of blankets such as they use for clothing and covering. Some poor people bring blankets four or five spans long and a little less in width, which may be worth two or three maravedis apiece; some even poorer people offer still smaller ones. Some women offer little cloths[1] like those used with the Pax,[2] and for that purpose they are indeed used afterwards. They are all woven in patterns, of cotton or rabbit's hair, and there are many of them and of many different kinds. Most of them have a cross in the middle, and these crosses are very different one from another. Others have in the middle a shield with the five wounds, woven in colors. Others have the names of Jesus or Mary, with fringe or embroidery all around. Others are of woven designs of roses and other flowers, well arranged.

This year a woman offered on one of these cloths a crucifix woven double-faced, although when you looked closely one side seemed more like the right side than the other; and it was so well done that all who saw it, both friars and laity, thought very highly of it, saying that anyone who could do that could weave tapestry. They bring these blankets and cloths folded, and, approaching the steps, they kneel and when they have done reverence they take out and unfold their blanket, take it by the corners with their two hands outstretched and, having raised it to their foreheads, they raise their hands two or three times and then lay the blanket upon the steps and retire a short distance, bending their knees once more, like chaplains who have given the pax to some great lord, and there they pray again. Many of them bring children, for whom they also bring offerings and put the offerings into the children's hands and teach them how to make their offering and to genuflect. To see the recollection and devotion with which they do this is enough to bring the dead to life.

Others offer copal or incense, and many candles; some bring a fair-

1. These might be either the small linen cloths used to wipe the Pax, or Osculatorium, or the veil which is used to cover it.

2. A small tablet or disk bearing a sacred emblem or picture, used since the 13th century in the ceremony of the Mass to give the kiss of peace. The Pax is kissed by the celebrant, wiped by the server, and by him presented to be kissed by the person with whom the kiss of peace is to be exchanged.

sized candle, others smaller ones, others a thin candle of two or three spans, and others a little one no bigger than your finger. As one sees them make these offerings and pray, the offerings seem like the widow's mite which was so acceptable to God, for they are taken from the Indians' means of subsistence and are given with as much simplicity and humility as if the Lord of the world were there in visible form. Others bring little crosses of a span or a span and a half or longer, covered with gold or silver and feather work.

They also offer well-made candlesticks, some very brilliant with gold and feather work with dangling silver ornaments and very valuable green feathers. Others bring cooked food in plates and bowls and present it among the other offerings. This very year they brought a lamb and two big pigs alive. The two who brought the pigs carried them tied to sticks, as they do their other burdens, and thus they brought them into the Church. It was laughable to see them, when they had reached the altar steps, take the pigs in their arms and offer them! They also make offerings of hens and pigeons, all in such great quantity that the friars and the Spaniards were astonished. I, too, often went to look, and it astonished me to see a thing so new in a world so old. They came in such numbers to bring offerings that at times they could not get through the door.

There are persons appointed to collect and store these offerings, which are taken for the poor at the almshouse that has recently been built, like the good ones in Spain. It is now fairly well endowed and is equipped to care for many poor people. There is enough wax offered to last a whole year. Then on Easter day before dawn they hold their procession with great solemnity and with much rejoicing manifested in dances and pageants. This day some children appeared in a dance, and though they were so little that children even older than they have not yet been weaned, they twirled about so much and so well that the Spaniards were helpless with laughter. Then when this is over, there is a sermon and Mass is said with great solemnity.

Many Spaniards are astonished and find it very hard to believe in the progress that the Indians have made in the faith. This is especially true of those who do not go outside of the Spanish towns, or of those who have recently come from Spain. Because they have not seen these things for themselves, they believe that all that is said about the Indians and their penitential practices is a mere fiction. They are also amazed that the natives should come from such distances to be baptized or married or to make their confession or, on feast days, to hear Mass. But when one sees these things one is impressed with the faith of these new Christians. Why should God not give His grace and His glory to those whom He formed in His own image, when they are as well disposed for it as we are? These Indians never saw devils cast out nor lame men healed, nor have they seen anyone give hearing to the deaf or sight to the blind, or resurrect the dead; and what the preachers say to them is a mystery of which, as was the case with Saint Phillip's loaves, they do not get even a crumb apiece. And yet God multiplies His word and increases it in their minds and souls, and the fruit which God produces and what is multiplied and left over is much more than what is given to them.

These Indians have almost none of those obstacles to prevent their achieving salvation which we Spaniards have and by which we are kept down, for their life is content with very little, so little, in fact, that they have scarcely enough to clothe and feed themselves. Their food is extremely poor and scanty, and their clothing the same; for sleeping most of them have not even a whole piece of matting. They do not stay awake nights to acquire or preserve riches nor do they wear themselves out to achieve position or honors. They lie down wrapped in their poor blankets and as soon as they awake are all ready for the service of God. If they wish to scourge themselves they have not the bother of dressing or undressing. They are extremely patient and long-suffering, as gentle as sheep. I do not remember ever having seen one of them bear a grudge. They are humble and obedient to all, either willingly or of necessity, and they know only how to serve and work. They all know how to build a wall or a house and how to twist rope and all the crafts which do not require much art. Their patience and endurance in illness is very great. Their mattress is the hard earth without any covering. At the most they have a worn piece of matting with a stone or piece of wood for a pillow, and many of them have no pillow but the bare ground.

Their houses are very small, some covered with a very low flat roof, some thatched with straw, others like the cell of the holy abbot Hilarion, which was more like a tomb than a house. The riches that such houses as these could hold give abundant testimony of their wealth! Fathers, children, and grandchildren live together in these little houses. They eat and drink without noise or shouting. Without quarrels or enmities they pass their lives and go out to seek what is necessary to support human life, no more. In case of a headache or an illness, if there is a doctor easily accessible amongst them to whom they can go quietly and at no great cost they do so; if not, they are more patient than Job. It is not as it is in Mexico where, if a citizen gets ill and dies, if he has been twenty days in bed, it takes all his estate to pay the doctor and the apothecary, so that there is scarcely enough left for the funeral; for the charges[3] are so high for responsories, *pauses,* and vigils[4] that the wife is left burdened with debt, or if it is the wife who dies, the husband is left ruined. I once heard a married man—and a wise one—say that if one of the couple was taken ill and death was inevitable, the husband ought to kill the wife, or the wife the husband, and try themselves to bury the deceased in any cemetery, so as not to be left poor, alone, and in debt. All these things the Indians are spared.

When an Indian woman is about to give birth to a child she has the midwife conveniently near, for they are all midwives. If it is her first child, she goes to some neighbor or relative who will help her, and waiting patiently for nature to work in her own way they give birth with less difficulty and pain than our Spanish women, many of whom have had their lives endangered and have been left in such a condition that they can never bear children again, all because labor has been artificially hastened and force has been used. If a woman bears twins, after the interval of a day—or in some places two days—during which they give them no milk,[5] the mother takes them, one in one arm and one in the other, and nurses them—and they do not die, nor are they entrusted to wet nurses. Later, each of the twins, when they wake up, knows which breast belongs to it. They do not prepare for the birth French toast[6] or honey or any of the other dainties that we consider appropriate for such occasions, but the first thing that the mother does for her children is to wash them at once in cold water without fear of its doing them harm. With all this we see and know that many of the children thus brought up naked live and are sound and well, of good constitution, strong, sturdy, merry, quick, and suitable for anything that one wishes to make of them. What

3. Spanish: *le llevan tantos derechos, o tuertos* . . . An untranslatable play on words. Derecho means a charge or tax, and also a right, and, as an adjective, straight. Fray Toribio uses the word in the first sense, and then the other senses suggest the comment that these charges are not straight or right, but crooked or iniquitous (tuertos).

4. Such, for instance, as the responsory, *Libera me, Domine, de morte aeterna,* in the Office of the Dead—originally very long, but now reduced to only four or five verses. *Pauses* made during the funeral procession at shrines. *Vigils,* the Office of the Dead.

5. See below, bk. II, ch. IX.

6. Spanish: *torrijas.*

is more to the point is that now that they have come to a knowledge of God they have few things to hinder them in following the life of Jesus Christ and keeping His law.

When I consider the entanglements and embarrassments of the Spaniards, I wish for grace to have pity on them, and much more and first of all upon myself! To see how reluctantly a Spaniard rises from his soft bed—and often it is the bright sunlight that routs him out of it—and wraps himself in a robe so that the wind may not touch him, and demands his clothes, as if he had not hands to get them himself! So they dress him, as if he were a cripple, and he says his prayers while fastening his garments—and you can imagine how much attention he gives to them. Then, because he feels a bit of cold or a breath of air, he goes to the fire while they brush his cap and doublet, and because he is so exhausted by getting from the bed to the fire, he cannot comb his hair and there has to be some one to do it for him. Then, before his shoes or slippers and cape arrive, the bells are ringing for Mass, and his horse is not ready. Sometimes he has breakfasted before he goes. You can see in what an attitude of mind he goes to Mass. But if he gets there in time to see the Elevation or the priest's Communion, he is satisfied, content not to happen upon a priest who says Mass a little slowly, because he does not want to tire his knees. There are some who have no scruples, even on Sundays and feast days. Then, when he gets back from Mass, dinner has to be right on time or else he gets out of patience. Then he rests and sleeps. You can see whether he will need all the rest of the day to attend to lawsuits and accounts and look after his mines and other sources of income.[7] Before these matters are finished it is time for supper, and at times he goes to sleep immediately after eating, unless he drives sleep away by playing some game. If this were for one year or two, and he afterwards changed his way of life, it might pass, but he ends his life in this same way, his covetousness and his vices growing from year to year, so that day and night—and almost his entire life—pass without his remembering God or his own soul, except in a few good desires which he never has time to put into execution. What shall we say, then, of those who are bogged in their vices and sins, and live in mortal sin, putting off their reformation until the moment of death when pain and grief and the wiles and temptations of the devil are so great? For at the hour of death the wiles of the Enemy are so many and so great that men can only

7. Spanish: *granjerías.* Farms, but also used to mean any income-producing business.

with difficulty remember their soul. And this comes to them as a just judgment of God, for he who in life does not remember God, in death remembers not himself.

These people whom I have been describing have great confidence in wills, and though they may owe something—or even a great deal—and be able to pay it, they think that they can fulfill their obligations by their wills; and the wills will be as well carried out by their children as they themselves carried out their fathers'. Then the approaching penalty and torment will open their eyes, which in life were closed and blinded by delights and sorrows. What I have said is meant to apply to those who are careless of their own salvation, so that they may look to themselves in time and bring themselves into an assured state of grace, charity and matrimony. Many, by the grace of God, now live in this New Spain, friends of their own souls, careful of their salvation, and charitable to their neighbors; and with this it is time to go back to our history.

CHAPTER XV

Of the festivals of Corpus Christi and Saint John which were celebrated in Tlaxcallan in the year 1538.

ON the holy day of Corpus Christi in the year 1538,[1] the Tlaxcaltecas held a very solemn festival which deserves to be recorded, because I believe that if the Pope and Emperor had been there with their courts they would have been delighted with the sight; and though there were no rich jewels or brocades there were other adornments well worth seeing—especially those of flowers and roses that God produces on the trees and in the fields—and there was plenty to look at and make one wonder how a people who up to this time had been considered as little better than brutes could know how to do such things.

1. This description (pp. 102-105) of the Corpus Christi procession and of the plays performed on the day of St. John the Baptist is used by both Torquemada (vol. III, p. 220f.) and Las Casas (pp. 162-165). They both give the date as 1536, whereas our text has it as 1538. Torquemada says that he takes the account from "a manuscript record left by Fray Toribio Motolinía." Las Casas states that the description was given to him in writing by "one of the outstanding Franciscan friars, who was at that time guardian of the monastery at Tlaxcala." "I put down," he says, "word for word, without adding or omitting anything, just exactly what he had written down in a book that he had compiled about the progress of those people in our Christian religion."

In the procession were the Blessed Sacrament and many crosses and images of the saints on their platforms. The veils of the crosses and the ornaments of the platforms were all of gold and feather work, with images of the same work, the best of which would, in Spain, be more prized than brocade. There were many saints' banners and the twelve apostles dressed with their proper insignia. Many of those who accompanied the procession carried lighted candles in their hands. All the road was strewn with reeds and rushes and flowers, and there were people who kept strewing it anew with roses and pinks.[2] There were many varieties of dances which enlivened the procession. Along the road were chapels, with their altars and altarpieces well adorned, where the procession might rest, and there many additional singers appeared and sang and danced before the Blessed Sacrament. There were ten big triumphal arches very neatly made, and what was even more striking and noteworthy was that they had the whole length of the road divided into three lanes, like the naves of a church. The central lane was twenty feet wide; along it went the Blessed Sacrament and the clergy and crosses and all the pageantry of the procession, and along the two side lanes, which were each fifteen feet wide, went all the people—and in this city and province they are not few. This division was marked by medium-sized arches of about nine feet, and there were by actual count 1,068 of these arches, for three Spaniards—and many others—counted them, considering it a noteworthy and astonishing thing. They were all covered with roses and flowers of various kinds and colors. It was estimated that each arch had a load and a half of roses (by load we mean the load an Indian carries), and that, together with the flowers in the chapels and those on the triumphal arches and sixty-six small arches, and those that the people wore and carried in their hands, made an estimated two thousand loads of roses. About one-fifth appeared to be pinks, which came originally from Castile and have multiplied here incredibly. The clumps are larger than in Spain and they bloom the whole year round. Approximately one thousand round shields made of roses were divided among the arches and the arches which had no shields had big rosettes made of something like the layers of an onion, round and very well made and with a good luster.[3] Of these there were so many that one could not count them.

2. The manuscript reads *flores* (flowers). Ramírez chose to print *rosas,* which is the reading of the Kingsborough text.

3. I have no clue to what this may be. In the Las Casas text the sentence continues thus: "so that each one seemed as if cut out of pearl, and very beautiful."

They had one very striking thing. At each of four corners or turns that the road made, there was constructed a mountain and from each mountain there rose a high cliff.[4] The lower part was made like a meadow, with clumps of herbs and flowers and everything else that there is in a fresh field; the mountain and the cliff were as natural as if they had grown there. It was a marvellous thing to see, for there were many trees: wild trees, fruit trees, and flowering trees, and mushrooms and fungus and the lichen that grows on forest trees and rocks. There were even old broken trees; in one place it was like a thick wood and in another it was more open. On the trees were many birds, both big and small: falcons, crows, owls; and in the wood much game; there were stags, hares, rabbits, coyotes, and very many snakes. These last were tied and their fangs drawn, for most of them were of the genus viper, a fathom in length and as big around as a man's arm at the wrist. The Indians catch them with their hands as they do birds, for they have a kind of herb[5] that they use for the savage or poisonous ones which puts them to sleep or makes them sluggish. (This same herb, which they call *picietl,* has also many medicinal properties.) In order that nothing might be lacking to make the scene appear completely natural, there were hunters with their bows and arrows well concealed on the mountain.[6] Usually the men who follow this calling are of another tongue, and as they live near the forests they are great huntsmen. One had to look sharply to see these hunters, so hidden were they and so covered with branches and lichen from the trees, for the game would easily come right to the feet of men so concealed. Before shooting, these huntsmen made many gestures which aroused the attention of the unsuspecting public.

This was the first day that the Tlaxcaltecas used the coat of arms which the Emperor granted them when the town was made a city. This

4. Bernal Díaz del Castillo (ch. CCI, pp. 486 ff.) describes a similar scene constructed in the *plaza mayor* of Mexico City in 1538 for the festival in honor of the peace treaty made at Aigues Mortes between Charles the Fifth of Spain and Francis the First of France.

5. Tobacco. Nicotiana rústica. Gómara (p. 445) explains how the herb was used. "They catch snakes with their hands, or rather with their feet, for the hunters tie to their feet the herb *picietl,* with which they stupify the snakes."

6. Just before this sentence Torquemada, bk. XVII, ch. VII, and Las Casas p. 163, col. 2, have the following: "On the first of these mountains was the representation of Adam and Eve and the serpent who deceived them: On the second, the Temptation of our Lord. On the third, Saint Jerome; and on the fourth, our father Saint Francis." In our text Motolinía mentions no plays in the Corpus Christi celebration of 1538, but describes an Adam and Eve play at the festival given in Easter week by the Confraternity of Our Lady of the Incarnation (see below p. 107-109), and a Temptation play, a Saint Francis play, and one on the Sacrifice of Abraham (see below p. 118-120) at Corpus Christi, apparently in the year 1539.

favor has not yet been granted to any other Indian town but this one, which well deserves it, for its people greatly assisted Don Hernando Cortés, acting for His Majesty, at the time of the conquest of the whole land. They had two banners with these arms and between them one with the imperial arms, raised on a flagstaff so high that I marveled where they could have got a pole so high and so slender. These banners were placed on the roof of their municipal buildings, so that they would seem even higher. In the procession was a part-song choir[7] of many voices with its accompanying music of flutes which harmonized with the singers, and horns, drums and bells, little and big. All these instruments sounded together when they entered and when they left the church, so that it seemed as if the heavens were falling.

In Mexico, and wherever there is a monastery, the Indians make use of all the ornaments and contrivances that they know, as well as those they have adopted from the Spaniards, and each year they take great pains and make the festival more beautiful. They go about like monkeys, looking at everything, so as to imitate whatever they see people do. Even in the crafts, they become experts just by watching and without putting hand to the work, as I shall tell later on.[8] They take out the pith of a kind of thick-stemmed herb which grows in the fields here. This pith is like a string of white wax[9] and they use it to make round or cone-shaped ornaments with a thousand designs and loops which look like the beautiful *rollos*[10] that they make in Seville. They make big carved signs with letters two spans high and then they coil it and put up the sign of the festival that is being celebrated that day.[11]

To show the cleverness of these people I will tell here what they did later on the day of Saint John the Baptist, which was the following Monday. They presented four one-act plays which it took all of Friday to write out in prose (for history is no less devoutly told in prose than in verse). In the two remaining days, Saturday and Sunday, they learned them, and represented very devoutly the Annunciation of the Birth of Saint John the Baptist made to his father, Zacharias. The play took about

7. Spanish: *capilla de canto de órgano. Canto de órgano,* in English, organum, is the early form of part singing.

8. See below, bk. III, ch. XIII.

9. Spanish: *como cera blanca de hilera.*

10. I cannot find out what these *rollos* were.

11. Spanish: *y después enróscanle y ponen el letrero de la fiesta que celebran aquel día.* The sense is obscure.

an hour and ended with a very pretty motet sung in parts. Then on another stage they represented the Annunciation of Our Lady, which was very well worth seeing and took as long as the first play. Later, in the churchyard of the church of San Juan, where the procession went, they represented upon another stage the scene of the Visitation of Our Lady to Saint Elizabeth. This was performed before Mass, as soon as the procession arrived there. It was quite a sight to see how beautifully the stages were adorned and covered with roses. After Mass they represented the Nativity of Saint John, and instead of the circumcision they baptized a week-old boy named John. Before they gave the dumb Zacharias the writing materials that he asked for by signs, it was very amusing to see the things that they brought him, pretending that they did not understand him. This scene ended with the singing of the *Benedictus Dominus Deus Israel,* and the neighbors and relatives of Zacharias, who rejoiced at the birth of the son, brought presents and many kinds of food, and set the table and sat down to eat, for by then it was dinner time.

In this connection I quote a letter written by a friar in Tlaxcallan to his Provincial[12] about the penance done and the restitutions made by the Tlaxcaltecas during Lent of last year (1539), and about how they celebrated the festivals of the Annunciation and the Resurrection.

"I do not know what better Easter greetings to give Your Grace than to tell you about the good Easter which God has given to these children of His, the Tlaxcaltecas, and to us with them, although I scarcely know where to begin. One must feel very profoundly what God has done with this people, for certainly I have been much edified during this Lent not only by the Indians of the city, but also by those from the small towns, and even the Otomíes.

"The restitutions which they made during Lent must, I believe, have been over ten or twelve thousand: restitutions of things which had been on their consciences both before and after their conversion. In some cases the things restored were poor and insignificant; in others they were greater in quantity and of real value; and in many they were of very considerable amount, golden jewels and valuable stones as well as lands and estates. One man made restitution of twelve lots of land, the smallest

12. I do not know who this friar was, or whether it would be possible to identify him. It seems unlikely that Motolinía means himself, for he is usually so straightforward that, if he were quoting himself, one would expect him to say so. The Provincial is probably Fray Antonio de Ciudad Rodrigo. See below, p. 109.

of them of four hundred *brazas,* and others of seven hundred and one of twelve hundred, with many vassals and houses on the estates. Others have given up estates which their fathers and grandfathers had taken unlawfully and without valid titles. The sons, being now Christians, unburden their consciences and give up their inheritance, although these people love their lands as others do, for they have no other means of livelihood.

"They have also done much penance, by giving alms both to the poor and to their almshouse, by fasting rigorously and scourging themselves both publicly and privately. In Lent, all through the province, they scourge themselves three times a week in their churches, and on many of these days they do it again, going in procession from church to church, as they do elsewhere on Maundy Thursday. Nor did they fail to do it on this day too, rather so many of them came that the Spaniards who were here calculated that there were twenty or thirty thousand souls. All Holy Week they were present at the services. They wept with great feeling at the Passion sermon, and many of them made their communion very reverently, often with tears, all of which was very edifying to the recently arrived friars.

"By Easter the chapel in the churchyard was finished and turned out to be a very impressive structure; they call it Bethlehem. The outside they painted at once in fresco in the space of four days, for thus the rains will never wash away the painting. On one section of the wall they painted the works of the first three days of the creation of the world; on another, the works of the last three days. Another section had the tree of Jesse with the lineage of the Mother of God, who was painted in the upper part of the picture, very beautiful; and on another our father Saint Francis. On another part of the wall is the Church: His Holiness the Pope, with cardinals, bishops, and so forth; and on the other side the Emperor with kings and knights. The Spaniards who have seen the chapel say that it is worthy to figure among the lovely rooms of the kind in Spain. It has well-wrought arches, two choirs—one for the singers and one for the musicians; and all this was done in six months. The chapel, as well as the churches, was kept very neatly arranged and decorated.

"These Tlaxcaltecas have greatly enlivened the divine service with songs and music written in parts. They had two choirs, each of more than twenty voices, and two others of flutes, with which they also played the rebec and the Moorish flutes. Besides these they had skillful drummers who played drums tuned with little bells which made a most pleasant sound." And with this the friar ends his letter.

The most important part I have left for the last, that is, the festival celebrated by the confraternity of Our Lady of the Incarnation. Because they could not celebrate it in Lent they kept their celebration for the Wednesday of the Easter octave. The first thing they did was to prepare very generous alms for the Indian poor, for, not content with those whom they have in the almshouse they went to the houses within the radius of a league and distributed seventy-five men's shirts and fifty women's, and a great many blankets and breeches. They also distributed among these needy poor ten sheep, a pig, and twenty little native dogs to be eaten with chili, as is the custom; also many loads of corn and many *tamales*[13] in place of cakes. The deputies and stewards who went about making the distribution would take nothing for their work, saying that they ought rather to give to the almshouse than to take from it.

They prepared their wax, for each member of the confraternity a *rollo*,[14] and besides these, of which there were many, they had their candles and twelve torches. And they used for the first time four new candlesticks of gold and feather work, very well made and more showy than rich. Near the door of the almshouse they had a play ready to be performed. It represented the fall of our first parents, and in the opinion of all who saw it, this is one of the most notable things that have been done in this New Spain. The dwelling of Adam and Eve was so adorned that it really seemed an earthly paradise, with different kinds of trees full of fruits and flowers, some of them natural and some of them counterfeited in gold and feathers. In the trees were many different birds, from owls and other birds of prey to little ones, and especially a great many parrots; their chattering and screaming was so loud that at times it interfered with the acting. I counted in one tree fourteen parrots, big and little. There were also artificial birds of gold and feather work which were very remarkable. The rabbits and hares were so numerous that the whole place was full of them; and there were many other small animals that I had never seen till then. There were two ocelots tethered there, very savage animals which are not exactly cats nor yet ounces. Once Eve carelessly collided with one of them and the well-bred beast moved aside. This was before she had sinned, for if it had been afterward, she would

13. See above, bk. I, ch. II.
14. See above, note 10.

not have been so lucky. There were other good imitation animals with boys inside of them. These were tame and Adam and Eve played with them and teased them. There were four streams or springs which flowed out of Paradise, each with its sign saying: Pison, Gihon, Tigris, and Euphrates.[15] In the middle of Paradise stood the tree of the knowledge of good and evil, with many and very beautiful fruits made of gold and feather work.

Round about Paradise were three big cliffs and a great mountain all full of everything that one can find on great and verdant hills, and the particular things that one finds in April and May, for these Indians have a special knack of imitating things exactly. There was no lack of birds, either small or large, especially big parrots which are as big as Spanish cocks. There were many of these, and two wild cocks and a hen,[16] certainly the most beautiful birds that I have seen anywhere. One of these cocks would have as much meat as two Spanish peacocks. They have a tuft of bristles growing out of their wattles, coarser than horsehair, and, in some old cocks, more than a span in length. These bristles are made into hyssops which last a long time.

On the cliffs also there were animals, both natural and artificial. On one of the latter was a boy dressed as a lion, tearing and eating a deer which he had killed. The deer was real and was on a ledge between some big rocks. This was a thing that attracted much attention. When the procession arrived they began the performance of the play. It took a long time, because before Eve ate the fruit or Adam consented to do so, Eve went back and forth three or four times between her husband and the serpent, Adam always resisting and pushing Eve away as if he were indignant. She, beseeching him and worrying him, said that it was evident how little he loved her, and that she loved him much more than he did her and, throwing herself into his arms, importuned him so that finally he went with her to the forbidden tree and she, in his presence, ate some and gave him some also. As soon as they had eaten they realized the evil that they had done and though they hid themselves as well as they could, they could not pervent God from seeing them, and He came, accompanied by many angels. When he had called Adam, Adam excused himself by throwing the blame upon his wife, and she by blaming the

15. See Genesis 2. 10-14.

16. Turkeys. Gómara (p. 452) calls them *gallipavos,* and says: "I give them this name because they are much like the pavón (peacock) and much like *gallos* (domestic roosters)."

serpent; and God cursed them and gave to each his penance. The angels brought two garments, very clever imitations of the skins of animals, and they dressed Adam and Eve. The most striking thing was to see them go out into exile weeping, Adam escorted by three angels and Eve by another three; as they went they sang, in parts, the psalm *Circumdederunt me*. This was so well performed that no one who saw it could keep from weeping bitterly.

There was left on the stage a cherub guarding the gate of Paradise with a sword in his hand. Then there was represented the world—another land certainly very different from the one they had left, for it was full of thistles and thorns and many serpents. There were also rabbits and hares. When the new dwellers in the world reached here, the angels showed Adam how he was to work and till the soil; and to Eve they gave spindles for spinning and making clothes for her husband and children; and, consoling the disconsolate pair, they went off singing, in parts, by way of farewell, a *villancico* whose words were:

> Oh, why did she eat
> —that first married woman—
> Oh, why did she eat
> The forbidden fruit?
> That first married woman
> —she and her husband—
> Have brought Our Lord down
> To a humble abode
> Because they both ate
> The forbidden fruit.

This play was performed by the Indians in their own tongue, and many of them grieved greatly and wept, especially when Adam was exiled and sent out into the world.

I quote another letter from the same friar to his prelate, writing him about the festival that was celebrated in Tlaxcallan in honor of the treaty of peace between the Emperor and the King of France.[17] The prelate was Fray Antonio de Ciudad Rodrigo.

"As Your Grace knows, the news came to this land a few days before Lent, and the Tlaxcaltecas wanted to see first what the Spaniards and

17. The Treaty of Aigues Mortes, July 14, 1538. See above, note 4.

the Mexicans were doing. Seeing that the latter represented the conquest of Rhodes,[18] they decided to stage the conquest of Jerusalem (and may God fulfill this prophecy in our day!). In order to give it greater solemnity they decided to leave it until Corpus Christi, which occasion they enlivened with such festivities as I shall here relate.

"In Tlaxcallan, in the city which they have recently begun to build down below on the plain, they left a big and very handsome plaza in the middle, and here they constructed Jerusalem on top of a building that they were erecting for the cabildo. The first story had already been completed, so they leveled off the top and covered the space with earth and built five towers, the principal one in the middle and one at each of the four corners, all enclosed with a battlemented wall. The towers also had battlements and were very handsome, with many windows and fine arches, all covered with roses and flowers. Our Lord the Emperor was stationed opposite Jerusalem, to the east and outside of the plaza. To the right of Jerusalem was the camp to be occupied by the army of Spain. Opposite to this was a place prepared for the provinces of New Spain, and in the center of the plaza was Santa Fé, where the Emperor was to be lodged with his army. All those places were surrounded by walls and painted on the outside to look like stone-work, with their embrasures for cannon, their loopholes and battlements, all very realistic.

"When the Blessed Sacrament reached the plaza, escorted by persons representing the Pope, cardinals, and bishops, they took their places upon a platform which had been prepared for this purpose and beautifully adorned. It stood near Jerusalem so that the entire festival should take place before the Blessed Sacrament. Then the Spanish army began to come in to lay siege to Jerusalem and, passing before the Host, crossed the plaza and pitched camp at the right. It took them some time to come in, because there were a great many people, divided into three squadrons. In the vanguard, bearing the standard with the royal arms, marched the men of Castile and León and the troops of the captain general, Don Antonio Pimentel, Count of Benavente,[19] with the banner with his armorial bearings. The main body was made up of Toledo, Aragón, Galicia, Granada, Vizcaya, and Navarre. The rear was brought up by Germany, Rome, and the Italians. There was little difference of costume between them, for as

18. For an account of this pageant, see Bernal Díaz del Castillo, ch. CCI, and Las Casas, p. 165.

19. All of the personages mentioned as taking part in the pageant were, of course, represented by Indian actors.

the Indians have never seen them and do not know about the differences, they pay no attention to them; for this reason all these actors came in dressed as Spanish soldiers, with trumpets made in imitation of the Spanish ones and drums and fifes all very orderly, drawn up in columns of five and marching in time to the drums.

"When these had marched past and gone to their camp, the army of New Spain came in from the opposite side, divided into ten companies, each one dressed in the costume that they use in war. These were very striking; in Spain or Italy people would go out of their way and be delighted to see them. They wore all the best that they had in the way of beautiful feathers, devices and shields, and all the Indians who took part in this play were lords and important men whom they call *Teuhpipiltín*. In the vanguard were Tlaxcallan and Mexico. These were very brilliantly arrayed and much admired. They carried the standard with the royal arms and the standard of their captain general, Don Antonio de Mendoza, Viceroy of New Spain. In the main army were the Huaxtecas, Zempoaltecas, Mixtecas, Colhuaques, and some companies that said they represented Peru and the Islands of Santo Domingo and Cuba. The rearguard consisted of the Tarascans and Cuauhtemaltecas.

"As soon as these had reached their camp the Spanish army came out into the field to give battle. They marched in good order straight upon Jerusalem and as the Sultan (the Marquis of the Valley, Don Hernando Cortés) saw them come, he ordered his people to go out in battle array. When they came out one saw that they were very finely dressed and differently from all the others, for they wore turbans such as the Moors use. The call to arms was sounded on both sides and the two armies met and fought with much shouting and noise of trumpets, drums, and fifes. At first victory seemed to be on the side of the Spaniards, the Moors retreating, some of them being taken prisoner and others left lying on the field of battle, although no one was wounded. When this was over the Spanish army returned in good order to its camp. Then the call to arms sounded again, the armies of New Spain and Jerusalem came out, and they fought a while; again the Moors were defeated and forced back into their city and some captives were taken back to the camp and some were left lying on the field.

"Hearing of the straits in which Jerusalem now found herself, great reinforcements of the people of Galilee, Judea, Samaria, Damascus, and all the land of Syria came, with abundant supplies of provisions and munitions, by which the people of Jerusalem were very much gladdened and so encouraged that they at once came out into the field and went straight toward the Spanish camp. The Spaniards came out to meet them and after they had fought awhile the Spaniards began to retreat and the Moors charged them, taking prisoner some of those who had not obeyed orders[20] and leaving some fallen upon the field of battle. After this the captain general dispatched a messenger to his Majesty with a letter to this effect:

" 'Your Majesty is hereby informed that the army arrived here before Jerusalem and pitched camp in a strong and secure position. Then we went out to battle against the city and those from within came out into the field; and the army of the Spaniards, servants of your Majesty, and your captains and veterans so fought that they seemed like tigers and lions; they certainly showed themselves to be valiant men, especially the people of the kingdom of León. After this there came a great reinforcement of Moors and Jews, with quantities of munitions and supplies, and the men of Jerusalem, finding themselves thus supported, came out to battle and we went out to meet them. It is true that some of our men fell, the ones who were not very well trained and had never been in the field against Moors; all the rest are full of spirit and await your Majesty's orders, to obey you in everything. Your Majesty's bondsman and servant, Don Antonio Pimentel.'

"Having seen the captain general's letter, the Emperor replied as follows: 'To my dear and well-beloved cousin, Don Antonio Pimentel, Captain General of the army of Spain. I have seen your letter by which I was very glad to learn how valiantly you have acted. You will take great care that from now on no help be allowed to reach the city, and to this end you will station all the necessary guards. You are also to let me know whether your camp is well supplied. Ascertain how I have been served by your knights, who shall receive very signal favors from me in return for their services, and commend me to all your captains and veterans, and may God guard you. Don Carlos, Emperor.'

"Hereupon the army of Jerusalem, with the help of the men who had come as reinforcements, made a sally against the army of New Spain to take vengeance for the previous encounter. As they were grieved by what had happened, they wished to avenge themselves, and joining battle, they fought valiantly until at last the people from the Islands began to

20. Spanish: *se desmandaron.*

weaken and lose ground to such an extent that, between the fallen and the captives, there was not a man left. Immediately the captain general dispatched a runner to his Majesty with a letter to the following effect:

" 'Sacred, Imperial and Catholic Majesty, ever august Emperor: this is to inform your Majesty how I arrived with the army before Jerusalem and pitched camp to the left of the city. We went out against the enemy, who were in the field, and your vassals of New Spain did very well, felling many Moors and forcing them back to the gates of their city, for your men fought like elephants and giants. After this the enemy received a great reinforcement of men and artillery, food and munitions. Then they made a sally against us and we went out to meet them; after having fought for the greater part of the day, the squadron from the Islands weakened and brought great shame upon the whole army, for as they were not skilled in war and had no arms of defense and did not know how to call upon God there was not a man of them who did not fall into the hands of the enemy. All the rest of the other companies are in very good condition. Your Majesty's bondsman and humblest servant, Don Antonio de Mendoza.'

"The Emperor's reply: 'Beloved cousin and my great captain over all the army of New Spain: Take courage like the valiant warrior that you are and encourage all your knights and soldiers. If help has reached the city be assured that from Heaven above shall come our help and assistance. Fortune varies in battle and he who is victor today is vanquished tomorrow; and he who was vanquished, on another day is victor. I have determined at once, this very night, to march all night without sleeping and be at dawn before Jerusalem. You will be prepared and with all your army drawn up in order, and since I shall so soon be with you, be consoled and encouraged. And write at once to the captain general of the Spanish forces that he too may be ready with his people, so that as soon as I arrive, when the enemy think me weary from the march, we may fall upon them and lay siege to the city. I will take the center of the line and your army the left wing and the army of Spain the right wing, so that they may not be able to escape from our hands. May our Lord guard you. Don Carlos, Emperor.'

"This done, from one side of the plaza the Emperor entered and with him the king of France and the king of Hungary with their crowns on their heads. As they began to enter the plaza they were met on one side by the captain general of Spain with half his men and on the other by the captain general of New Spain, and from all sides they came with trumpets and drums, and many of them set off rockets, which served as artillery. He was received with much rejoicing and great pomp and escorted to his camp of Santa Fé. Meanwhile the Moors showed that they had conceived a great fear, and all stayed shut up in their city. When the bombardment began they defended themselves very well. Meantime the *maestre de campo,*[21] Andrés de Tapia, had gone with a squadron to reconnoiter the country behind Jerusalem, and he set fire to a village and drove into the middle of the plaza a herd of sheep that he had captured. Each army having withdrawn to its camp, the Spaniards sallied forth again alone, and as the Moors saw them coming and saw that they were few in number, they went out against them and fought for a while. As more and more men kept coming from Jerusalem they forced the Spaniards to retreat, won the battle, and took some prisoners whom they carried back into the city. When this became known to his Majesty he at once dispatched a runner to the Pope with this letter:

" 'To our most Holy Father. O well-beloved Father, who is like you that he should possess so lofty an office upon earth? I hereby inform your Holiness that I have gone to the Holy Land and that I have Jerusalem surrounded by three armies. I, in person, am with one of them; in the second are the Spaniards, and the third is made up of Mexicans. There have been many skirmishes and battles between my people and the Moors in which my people have captured and wounded many of the Moors. After this the city received a large reinforcement of Moors and Jews, with great quantities of supplies and munitions, as the messenger will tell your Holiness. At present I am very much worried about the outcome of my journey. I beseech your Holiness to assist me with your intercessions and to pray to God for me and for my armies, for I am determined to take Jerusalem and all the other holy places or to die in the attempt; wherefore, I humbly beseech you to send us all your blessing. Don Carlos, Emperor.'

"When the Pope had read the letter he called the cardinals, and having consulted with them his answer was:

" 'My well beloved son. I have seen your letter, which has greatly rejoiced my heart, and I have given thanks to God for having thus comforted you and given you courage to undertake this holy enterprise. What

21. The officer next in importance to the captain general. He was the commanding officer of a *tercio* or *regiment.*

you wish shall at once be done, and so I command my beloved brothers the cardinals, the bishops, and all other prelates, the orders of Saint Francis and Saint James[22] and all the sons of the Church to pray for you, and that this may be effective I decree and grant a great Jubilee for all Christians. The Lord be with your soul. Amen. Your beloved father, the Pope.'

"To return to our armies. When the Spaniards saw themselves twice driven back and that the Moors had surrounded their camp, they all knelt facing the place where the Blessed Sacrament was and called upon it for aid. The Pope and the cardinals did likewise, and while they were on their knees an angel appeared at the corner of their camp and consoled them: 'God has heard your prayer and is much pleased with your determination to die for His honor and service in quest of Jerusalem, for He does not wish that so holy a place should be any longer in the possession of the enemies of the Faith. He has willed that you should encounter so many difficulties in order to test your constancy and fortitude. Fear not that your enemies shall prevail against you, and for greater surety God will send you your patron, the apostle Saint James.' This consoled them all greatly and they began to shout 'Santiago, Santiago, Patron Saint of our Spain!' Whereupon Santiago rode in mounted upon a horse as white as snow and dressed as he is usually represented in paintings. As he entered the Spanish camp they all followed him and attacked the Moors before Jerusalem. The latter, pretending great terror, took to flight and shut themselves up in the city, leaving some who had fallen on the field of battle. Then the Spaniards began to attack the city, Santiago on his white horse riding here and there all over the battle-field, and the Moors, because of the great fear that they felt, dared not even appear on the battlements. Then the Spaniards with banners flying retired to their camp. Seeing this, the other army of the Nahuas, or people of New Spain, drew up their squadrons and marched quickly upon Jerusalem as the Spaniards had not been able to enter the city.

"The Moors did not wait for them to reach the city, but sallied forth to meet them. They fought for a while, the Moors gradually winning the field until they drove their opponents back into their camp, without how-

22. The Spanish text reads *San Diego,* but it should undoubtedly be *Santo Domingo.* If written in abbreviation in the manuscript, as is probable, the two would be very easy to confuse. The two Orders chiefly concerned in the conversion of the Indians at that time were the Franciscans and the Dominicans.

ever capturing any of them. Having done this, the Moors returned with much shouting to their city. The Christians, seeing themselves vanquished, had recourse to prayer, calling upon God to help them, and the Pope and the cardinals did likewise. Then another angel appeared to them over their headquarters and said to them: 'Although you are but young in the Faith, God has wished to prove you and willed that you should be vanquished so that you may realize that without His aid your efforts are of little avail. But now that you have humbled yourselves God has heard your prayer, and shortly there will come to your assistance Saint Hypolitus, the advocate and patron saint of New Spain, upon whose day the Spaniards, with you Tlaxcaltecas, took Mexico.' Then all the Nahua army began to cry 'Saint Hypolitus, Saint Hypolitus!' Immediately Saint Hypolitus rode in, mounted on a very dark horse, and aroused and encouraged the Nahuas and went with them toward Jerusalem. From the other side also Santiago and the Spaniards came forth. The Emperor and his people took the center of the line and all together they began the bombardment, so that the people of the city, even in the towers, were helpless against the cannon-balls and arrows that were shot at them.

"Behind Jerusalem, between two of the towers there was a fairly long house of straw. At the time of the attack they set fire to this, and the attack was very vigorous on all sides of the city. The Moors were apparently determined to die rather than surrender to either Spaniards or Mexicans. Both assailants and defenders fought valiantly, hurling at each other large balls made of reeds and hollow balls of sun-dried clay filled with red ocher which made anyone whom they hit look as if he were badly wounded and covered with blood. They also used red cactus fruit. The archers had little sacks full of red ocher on the points of their arrows which made it look as if they drew blood wherever they struck. They also shot thick cornstalks at each other. While they were in the greatest heat of battle, the Archangel Saint Michael appeared upon the top of the central tower. At his appearance and his voice both Moors and Christians were filled with awe, ceased to fight, and fell silent. Then the archangel said to the Moors: 'If God considered your sins and wickedness and not His great mercy, He would already have hurled you to the depths of hell, and the earth would have opened and swallowed you alive. But because you have had reverence for the Holy Places He will show you mercy and allow you time for repentance if with your whole heart you turn to Him. Know therefore the Lord of Majesty, the Creator of all things, and believe in His most precious Son, Jesus Christ, and appease Him with tears and true penitence.' Having said this he disappeared. Then the Sultan, who was in the city, spoke to all his Moors, saying: 'Great is the goodness and the mercy of God, since He has thus deigned to enlighten us when we were greatly blinded by our sins. The time has come for us to recognize our error. Up till now we have thought that we were fighting with men, and now we see that we are fighting with God and with His saints and angels; who can resist them?' Then answered his captain general, the adelantado, Don Pedro de Alvarado, and all the soldiers with him and said that they wished to put themselves into the hands of the Emperor and that the Sultan should at once make terms so that their lives might be spared, for the sovereigns of Spain were clement and merciful. They also said that they wished to be baptized. Then the Sultan made the signal of peace and sent a Moor to the Emperor with a letter to the following effect:

"'Roman Emperor, beloved of God. We have seen clearly how God has sent you help and favor from heaven. Before I saw this I thought only of guarding my city and kingdom and of defending my vassals, and I was determined to die in the attempt. But as the God of heaven has enlightened me I recognize that you alone are captain of His armies. I recognize that all the world must obey God and you who are His captain upon earth. Therefore into your hands we put our lives, and we beseech you to come near to this city to give us your royal word and grant us our lives, receiving us with your unfailing clemency, as your natural vassals. Your servant, the Great Sultan of Babylon and Tetrarch of Jerusalem.'

"As soon as he had read the letter, the Emperor went toward the gates of the city, which were now open, and the Sultan, well accompanied, came out to receive him. Kneeling before the Emperor he swore obedience to him and tried to kiss his hand. The Emperor raised him and took him by the hand and led him before the Most Blessed Sacrament, where the Pope was. There they all gave thanks to God and the Pope received him very affectionately. The Sultan brought with him many Turks (these were adult Indians whom they had planned to have baptized) and publicly they asked the Pope to let them be baptized. His Holiness at once ordered a priest to baptize them, and they actually were baptized. Then the Most Blessed Sacrament was removed and the procession went on in order.

"For the procession of this Corpus Christi festival they had the whole road and streets so much adorned that many Spaniards who were present said: 'If any one should try to tell this in Castile they will say that he is mad and is exaggerating and embellishing it.' For the Sacrament was carried along streets all made of three rows of medium-sized arches covered with roses and flowers very well arranged and fastened. There were over fourteen thousand of these arches, not to mention ten big triumphal ones under which the whole procession passed. There were six chapels with their altars and altarpieces. The whole roadway was covered with many sweet-smelling herbs and roses. There were also three mountains, very realistically constructed, with the appropriate cliffs, and on these mountains they performed three very good plays.

"On the first, which was immediately below the upper courtyard in a lower courtyard, where there is a big open square, they represented the Temptation of Our Lord. There was a great deal in it that was very noteworthy, especially to see these things acted by Indians. One striking scene was the consultation held by the devils to see how they should tempt Christ and who should be the tempter. When they decided that it should be Lucifer, he went disguised as a hermit, but there were two things that he could not conceal, that is, his horns and his claws, for from each finger and each toe there stuck out bone claws half a span long. After the first and second temptations, the third took place on a high cliff from which the devil very proudly told Christ all the special characteristics and all the wealth of New Spain. Then he shifted to Castile, where, he said, besides many ships and great fleets that brought across the sea great riches and enormous cargoes of cloths and silks and brocades, there were other special characteristics, and amongst them many and very good varieties of wine—at which every one, both Indians and Spaniards, pricked up their ears, for the Indians are crazy for our wine. After he had spoken of Jerusalem and Rome, Africa, Europe, and Asia and had said that he would give it all to him, Christ answered: 'Get thee behind me, Satan,' and the devil fled. Although he remained concealed in the cliff, which was hollow, the other devils made such a noise that it seemed as if the whole mountain was falling down, with Lucifer, into hell. Then the angels came with food for the Lord, apparently from heaven, and after doing reverence to Him they set the table and began to sing.

"When the procession went on to the other square, they represented on another mountain how Saint Francis preached to the birds, telling them all the reasons why they should praise and bless God: because He provides them with food without need of their reaping or sowing as men have to do who earn their living with great labor; also because of the garment of beautiful and varied feathers with which God adorns them without their spinning or weaving, and because of the place which He has given them, that is, the air, through which they move and fly. The birds coming up to the saint seemed to be asking for his benediction, and he, giving it to them, charged them to sing praises to God both morning and evening. They were going away and the saint was descending the mountain when there came out across his path a savage wild beast, so ugly that it rather frightened those who saw it thus suddenly. When the saint saw it he made the sign of the Cross over it and then went up to it. Realizing that it was a beast which was destroying the flocks of the land, he scolded it gently and brought it to the town, where the principal lords were sitting on their dais, and the beast made a sign that it would obey and promised never to do any more damage in that land, and then it went away to the mountain.

"The saint, remaining there, began his sermon, saying that they should observe how the wild animals obeyed the word of God, and that men were endowed with reason and were under greater obligation to keep the commandments of God . . . As he was saying this there came out an actor pretending to be drunk, singing just as the Indians do when they are intoxicated, and as he would not stop and was disturbing the sermon, Saint Francis warned him to stop or else he would go to hell. As he persisted, the saint called the devils of a very fearful and terrible hell that was near him and they came and with much din they seized the drunkard and threw him into hell. Then the saint went on again with his sermon and there came some witches, very cleverly imitated, of the kind who with their native drugs very easily produce abortions, and as they too disturbed the sermon and would not stop, the devils came and put them also into hell.

"In this way certain vices were represented and censured in this play. Hell had a secret door by which those inside went out, and when they got out the place was set on fire and burned so terribly that it seemed as if no one had escaped and that devils and damned were all burning up. The devils and the souls of the damned cried out and shrieked, which produced a feeling of horror and fear even in those who knew that no one was really being burned. The Blessed Sacrament went on its way and another play was performed which represented the sacrifice of Abraham, of which, to be brief and as it is late, I will merely say that it was well acted. And with that the procession went back to the church."[23]

23. Las Casas (p. 165) mentions another play which he saw in Tlaxcala in 1538, representing the Assumption of the Virgin, and one representing the Last Judgment, which was given in Mexico.

BOOK TWO

INTRODUCTION

Of the conversion and progress of these Indians; and how the sacraments were first administered to them in this land of Anáhuac or New Spain. Of certain occurrences and mysterious events.

WHEN I was quite unprepared and without any thought of writing anything like this, obedience bade me write some of the notable things about these natives, the things that Divine Goodness has begun to do and is always doing in this land; and also that those who come in the future may know and understand what remarkable things have happened in this New Spain, and the trials and misfortunes which Our Lord allowed her to suffer for the great sins that had been committed here, and the faith and religion which are today preserved here and in the future will increase, if it so please Our Lord.

At first when I began to write this it seemed to me that I noticed and remembered more things ten or twelve years ago than I do now. At that time one noticed them as new and saw that God was beginning to perform His miracles and show His mercies with this people; now as one who converses and associates with a Christian and converted people, one finds many noteworthy things that seem clearly to have come by the hand of God. For, if we stop to consider, in the primitive church of God much attention was paid to some persons who embraced the Faith because they were the first, as for instance the Eunuch Cornelius and his companions. The same is true of the towns which first received the word of God, Jerusalem, for instance, Samaria, Caesarea, and others. Of Barnabas it is written that he sold a field and laid the price at the feet of the Apostle. A field is not very precious compared to what the later followers of Christ gave up, but it is recorded because it occurred at the beginning and for the sake of the example that it gave. These things aroused wonder and admiration, and because they were worthy of serving as examples men wrote them down. The first marvels that God began to perform with these gentiles, although not very great, roused more wonder than the many greater ones that came later and are still being performed today, for they are now ordinary. In this connection I shall tell here, in this second part, about some of the first things that happened in this land of New Spain, and about some of the towns that first received the Faith. Their names will be unknown in many parts of the world, though here they are all well known, being big towns, and some of them the capitals of provinces. I shall also treat in this second part of the difficulty and obstacles encountered in the administration of baptism and of the good progress made by these natives.

CHAPTER I

Which tells how the Mexicans and the people of Coatlichán began to come to be baptized and to learn the catechism.

WHEN the land had been conquered and allotted by the Spaniards, the friars of Saint Francis who were there at the time began to go about among the Indians and converse with them, at first only in the places where they had a house of the Order, as was the case in Mexico, Tetzcoco, Tlaxcallan, and Huexotzinco; for the few friars who were there at first were divided among those provinces. In each of these and in those in which the Order later had houses (there are nearly forty in this year of 1540) there was so much to tell that not all the paper in New Spain would suffice. Pursuing the brevity which is pleasing to all, I shall recount what I saw and knew and what happened in the towns where I lived and visited. Although I may say or relate something about a province, it will be of the time when I lived there; others may write of the same province and tell quite truthfully of other things that happened there, and they may be more striking and better written than what is told here, and yet it may all be accepted without contradiction.

The town to which the friars first went out to teach was Cuautitlán, four leagues from Mexico. They went also to Tepotzotlán. This they did because there was much disturbance in Mexico, and because among the sons of lords who were being taught in the House of God there were the young lords of these two towns, nephews or grandsons of Moteuczuma and among the most important members of the school. Out of deference to them the friars began to teach in these two towns, and to baptize the children. The teaching of the Faith was always continued there and these young lords were always the leaders in all good Christian practices, as were also the towns subject to them, and their neighbors.

In the first year that the friars came to this land the Indians of Mexico and Tlatilolco began to assemble, those of one parish or district on one day and those of another parish on another day, and the friars went to these meetings to teach them and to baptize the children. Shortly afterward they all assembled on Sundays and feast days, the people of each section in the center where they had their old halls, for as yet there were no churches. The Spaniards also, for some three years, held their Masses and sermons in one of these halls, which served as a church; it now houses the mint. Almost no burials were made there, but the dead were buried in the old church of Saint Francis, until later they began to build churches. For five years the Mexicans were very indifferent, either because the Spaniards had their hands full and because of the building of the city of Mexico, or because the elder Mexicans had little enthusiasm. After five years many of them woke up and built churches, and now they are very frequent attendants at the daily Masses and receive the sacraments devoutly.

In the first year of the coming of the friars, Father Martín de Valencia, of blessed memory, came to Mexico and, taking a companion who knew a little of the language, went to visit the towns of the fresh water lake whose number and location were scarcely known. They began with Xochimilco and Coyoacán, and people came from the others and urgently entreated them to go to their towns, but before they reached them the people came out to meet them, for that was their custom. The friars would find the people already assembled, and then, by writing and through interpreters they would preach to the people and baptize some children, always praying God that His holy word might bear fruit in the souls of those infidels and enlighten them and convert them to His holy Faith. The Indian lords and principal men destroyed their idols in the presence of the friars and erected crosses and designated sites for the building of their churches.

Thus these two friars went through all of the above-mentioned towns, all of them important and populous. The inhabitants asked God for instruction and baptism for themselves and their children, and when the friars saw this they gave thanks to God with great joy at the sight of such a good beginning and of so many who should be saved, as indeed proved later to be true. Then Father Martín de Valencia, of blessed memory, said to his companion: "Thanks be to God that what formerly I saw in the spirit I now see accomplished in deed and truth." He said that being one day at matins in a monastery called Santa María del Hoyo, near Gata, which is in Estremadura in the province of San Gabriel, he was reading certain prophecies about the coming of the gentiles to the Faith, and God showed him, in the spirit, a great multitude of people who were coming to the Faith, and so great was the joy that his soul felt that he began to cry aloud, as will appear more at length in the third part, in the life of the said Fray Martín de Valencia.[1] Although this holy man tried many times to go among the infidels to receive martyrdom he never succeeded in obtaining the permission of his superiors; not because they did not consider him worthy, for he was as much valued and esteemed in Spain as here, but because God thus ordained it for greater good, as a very spiritual person told him, saying that "when it was time God would grant his desire as God had showed it to him." So it was, for the general of his Order[2] called him one day and told him how he had decided to go to this New Spain with very good companions and with great powers which he had obtained from the Pope, and how because he had been elected general of the Order, this prevented his making the trip. As he considered this a matter of great importance and value he wanted to send Fray Martín and have him name any twelve companions whom he pleased. The latter accepted the mission and came, wherefore it appears that what was promised to him was no illusion.

1. For the life of Fray Martín de Valencia, see below, bk. III, ch. II.
2. Fray Francisco de los Angeles.

Among these aforesaid towns of the fresh-water lake the one which did the most to bring the friars to teach them, to collect the people, and to destroy the temples of the devil was Cuitlahuac, a cool town entirely surrounded by water; it has a large population and a great many temples of the devil, all of it built over the water, for which reason the Spaniards the first time they entered it named it Venezuela. In this town there was a good Indian who was one of the three principal lords, and being old and of most wisdom he governed the whole town. He sent for the friars two or three times and when they came he never left them, but spent a great part of the night asking them things that he wished to know about our Faith. The next morning, when the people were all assembled after Mass and sermon and the baptism of many children, most of whom were sons, nephews, or relatives of this good man I speak of, he earnestly besought Fray Martín to baptize him. In view of his being a man of excellent reason he was baptized and named Don Francisco, and afterwards as long as he lived was well known by the Spaniards.

That Indian surpassed all the others of the fresh-water lake and brought many children to the monastery of St. Francis. They turned out to be so clever that they outstripped those who had entered the school many days before them. This Don Francisco, making daily progress in the knowledge of God and in keeping His commandments, while going one day very early over the lake in a boat which the Indians call *canoa,*[3] heard a very sweet song with very beautiful words, which I saw and had written down. Many of the friars saw them and judged them to have been an angel's song. From that day on Don Francisco progressed still more and at the time of his death he asked for the sacrament of confession, and when he had made his confession he died calling continually upon God.

The life and death of this good Indian was most edifying to all the other Indians, especially those of that town of Cuitlahuac, in which churches were built. The principal one is dedicated to St. Peter, and that good Indian, Don Francisco, did a great deal in the building of it. It is a big church with three aisles, built in the Spanish manner.

The first two years the friars did not go out very much from the town where they had their residence, both because they knew very little of the

3. Las Casas, p. 182. "*Canoas* are boats made of a hollowed log, the prow narrower than the stern. They hold twenty, thirty or fifty persons, or even more. The name *canoa* belongs to this island (Haiti); the name in the Mexican language was *atcale,* from *at* (water) and *cale* (house)." Cf. below, bk. III, ch. x.

country and of the language, and because they had a plenty to attend to where they lived. The third year the people in Tetzcoco began to assemble daily to learn the catechism, and a great many also came to be baptized; as the province of Tetzcoco is very populous, the friars, both inside and outside of the monastery, were unable to keep up with the work or to help others, for many people were baptized from Tetzcoco, Huexotzinco, Coatlichan, and Coatepec. Here in Coatepec they began to build a church and made great haste to finish it because it was the first church outside of the monasteries. It was called Santa María de Jesus. After having gone about for several days among the towns under the jurisdiction of Tetzcoco, which are numerous and among the most populous in New Spain, they went on to other towns. As they did not know the country very well, when they set out to visit one town people would come out from other towns to ask them to go with them to preach the word of God, and they often came across other little villages and would find the people assembled, waiting with a meal all prepared and begging the friars to eat and to teach them. At other times they went to places where they made up by fasting for the abundance they had had elsewhere. Among the places to which they went were Otompa, Tepepolco, and Tollantzinco, which had no resident friars for a good many years after that.

Among these, Tepepolco did very well and kept growing and progressing in the knowledge of the Faith. The first time that friars came to this place was one afternoon—I omit any account of the reception which the Indians gave them—and as the inhabitants were all assembled the friars began to teach them and in the space of three or four hours many of the people, before they left, knew how to cross themselves and repeat the Pater Noster. The next day in the morning a great many people came, and when the friars had taught them and preached to them as much as was suitable for a people who knew nothing and had never heard of God nor received His word, they took aside the lord and the principal men of the town and repeated to them how God in heaven was the true Lord, creator of heaven and earth, and who the devil was whom they adored and honored, and how he deceived them, and other things of the sort. They said it so effectively that the Indians at once and in the presence of the friars destroyed and broke all their idols and burned their teocallis.

This town of Tepepolco is built on a high hill where there was one of the big and splendid temples of the devil, which they then tore down.

As the town is big and has many others subject to it, it had big teocallis or temples of the devil, and this is the general rule by which you can tell whether a town is big or small—whether it has many teocallis.

Chapter II

Of when and where they began to have processions in this land of New Spain, and of the eagerness with which the Indians come to be baptized.

The fourth year after the arrival of the friars in this country was so very rainy that the cornfields were ruined and many houses fell. Up to that time there had been no processions among the Indians, and in Tetzcoco they went out in procession with just one poor cross. As it had rained now for many days without ceasing it pleased Our Lord in His mercy and by the intercession of His Most Blessed Mother and of St. Anthony, the principal patron of that town, that from that very day the rain should cease, in order to confirm the weak and tender faith of these recent converts. After that they made many crosses and banners of the saints and other ornaments for their processions, and the Indians of Mexico went to them to get designs for the same sort of ornaments. Shortly afterward they began in Huexotzinco to make very rich and beautiful veils for the crosses and platforms for the images of the saints in gold and feather work. Then they began everywhere to adorn their churches and make altarpieces and ornaments and have processions, and the children learned dances with which to enliven the latter.

At this time, in the towns where there were friars, they went out on visitations, and people came from many towns to seek them and beg them to come; in this way the faith of Jesus Christ gradually spread and extended in many directions. Especially was this true in the towns of Eecapitztlan and Huaxtepec, where its progress was favored and assisted by the governors of those towns, for these Indians had been cured of their vices and did not drink wine. It was almost a marvel, both to the Spaniards and to the natives, to see any Indian who did not drink, because among the adult Indians, both men and women, it was the general practice to get drunk, and as this vice was the source and root of many other sins he who kept away from it lived more virtuously.

The first time that a friar went out to visit the province of Coyxco and Tlachco was from Cuauhnahuac. This house was established in the second year after the arrival of the friars and was the fifth house in order of foundation. Visiting from there through those provinces, in which there are many populous towns, they were very well received and many children were baptized. As they could not go to all the towns, when there were two near each other the people from the smaller town came to the larger one to be taught and to hear the word of God and to have their children baptized. It happened that this was the rainy season, which in this land begins in April and ends about the last of September, when the people of one town were to come to another. There was a small stream between them, and that night it rained so hard that the stream became a great river and the people could not cross. They waited there until Mass was over and the friars had finished preaching and baptizing, and then some of them swam across and went and begged the friars to come to the bank of the stream and preach the word of God to them. They went, and where the river was narrowest they preached to them, the Indians standing on one bank and the friars on the other. Then the Indians would not go away without having their children baptized, and so they made a poor little raft of reeds (on the big rivers they build rafts over big gourds, and thus the Spaniards and their luggage cross wide streams) and half in their arms and half in the water they got the children to the other side where the friars baptized them—with considerable difficulty because there were so many of them.

I believe that from the time of the conquest, which was the year 1521, down to the time in which I am writing—that is, the year 1536—more than four million souls have been baptized. I shall explain later how I know this.[1]

1. See below, bk. II, ch. III.

CHAPTER III

How the Indians hastened to come to be baptized; and of two things which happened in Mexico and in Tetzcoco.

MANY come to be baptized, not only on Sundays and on the days indicated for baptism, but every day, children and adults, the sick and the well, from all districts. When the friars go about making visits the Indians come out to meet them with their children in their arms and carrying the sick on their backs; even decrepit old people they bring out to be baptized. Many, after they have been baptized, leave their many wives and marry only one. When they come to be baptized some beg for it, others insist, others ask for it kneeling, others raising and clasping their hands, moaning and crouching, others demand and receive it weeping and sighing.

In Mexico a son of Moteuczoma, who was the great lord of Mexico, asked to be baptized, and because this son was ill we went to his house, which was near where the church of St. Hypolitus now stands. Mexico was conquered on this saint's day and for that reason a great festival is celebrated on that day in all New Spain and Hypolitus is considered the special patron of this land. They brought the sick man out in a chair to be baptized, and as the priest was performing the exorcism, when he said the words "ne te lateat Satanas" not only the sick man but also the chair in which he was sitting began to tremble so violently that, in the opinion of all of those who were present, it seemed that the devil was going out of him. This scene was witnessed by Rodrigo de Paz, who was at that time alguacil mayor [1] (because he was acting as godfather the Indian was baptized with the name of Rodrigo de Paz), and other officials of his Majesty.

In Tetzcoco as a baptized woman was going along with an unbaptized child on her back (that being the way they carry children in this country) and passing at night through the courtyard of the teocallis, which are the houses of the devil, the devil came out to her and seized the child, trying to take it from the mother, who was terrified because the child was not yet baptized nor signed with the cross. She cried aloud: "Jesus! Jesus!" and the devil at once let go of the child; but as soon as she ceased to speak

1. There is no exact English equivalent for this title. Perhaps chief constable comes fairly near it.

the name of Jesus the devil tried again to take the infant. This happened three times, until she got out of that fearful place. The very next morning she brought the child to be baptized in order that no such peril might befall him again, and so it was done. It is very striking now to see the children that come every day to be baptized, especially here in Tlaxcallan. There are days when we have to perform the baptismal service four or five times. Counting those who come on Sundays, there are weeks when we baptize three hundred children, and sometimes we baptize four or five hundred, taking in the children within the radius of a league. And if ever, out of carelessness or because of some obstacle, we fail to visit the towns two or three leagues away, there are so many to be baptized later that it is a marvel.

Also many have come, and still do come, from a distance to be baptized, bringing their wives and children, the sick and the well, the lame, the blind and the deaf, dragging along and suffering great hardships and hunger, for these people are very poor.

In many parts of this country they bathed new-born children on the eighth or tenth day and then, if the child was a boy, they put a tiny shield in his left hand and an arrow in his right hand; if it was a girl, they gave her a tiny broom. This ceremony seemed to be a sort of symbol of baptism and meant that the baptized were to fight against the enemies of the soul and to sweep and clean their souls and consciences so that, by baptism, Christ might enter.

I calculate the number of the baptized in two ways: first by the towns and provinces which have been baptized, and second by the number of the priests who have administered the sacrament. There are at present in New Spain about sixty Franciscan priests, for few of the other priests have done much baptizing. Although some have, I do not know what the number may be. Besides the sixty priests I speak of, more than twenty others must have returned to Spain, some of whom baptized numerous Indians before they went away. There were more than twenty others, now dead, who also baptized many, especially our father, Fray Martín de Valencia, the first prelate in this land who represented the Pope,[2] and Fray García de Cisneros and Fray Juan Caro, an honorable old man who introduced and first taught in this land the Castilian tongue and part singing, a very difficult task. There were also Fray Juan de Perpiñan and Fray Francisco de Valencia, each of whom must have baptized over one hun-

2. Spanish: *tuvo veces del Papa.* Fray Martín died in 1534. See below, bk. III, ch. II.

dred thousand persons. From the sixty who are here in this year of 1536 I subtract twenty who have not baptized, because they are new to the country and do not know the language. For the forty who remain I would estimate one hundred thousand or more baptisms each, for there are some of them who have baptized nearly three hundred thousand, others two hundred thousand and one hundred and fifty thousand, and others much smaller numbers; so that including those baptized by the priests now dead or returned to Spain, there must have been baptized up to the present day nearly five millions.

By towns and provinces I calculate as follows: Mexico and its dependent towns, Xochimilco with the towns of the fresh-water lake, Tlalmanalco and Chalco, Cuauhnahuac with Eecapitztlan, and Cuauhquechollan and Chietla, over a million; Tetzcoco, Otompa, Tepepolco, and Tollantzinco, Cuautitlán, Tollan, Xilotepec with their provinces and towns, more than another million; Tlaxcallan, the city of Los Angeles, Chołollan, Huexotzinco, Calpa, Tepeyacac, Zacatlán, Hueytlalpán, more than another million; the towns along the South Sea more than another million. And since this report was copied, over five hundred thousand more have been baptized, for in this past Lent of 1537, in the province of Tepeyacac alone there have been baptized by actual count over sixty thousand souls. So that, in my opinion and truthfully, there must have been baptized in the time I mention—a matter of fifteen years—more than nine million Indians.

Chapter IV

Of the different opinions that were held about the administration of the sacrament of baptism, and how it was done during the first years.

Although during the first years all the priests were in agreement as to the administration of the sacrament of baptism, later on, as there came many clergy and friars of the other orders, Augustinians, Dominicans, and Franciscans, different and contradictory opinions arose. To some it seemed that baptism ought to be administered with the ceremonies in use in Spain, and they were not satisfied with the manner in which the others administered it. Each one wanted to follow his own opinion and considered it the best and most correct, perhaps out of an excellent zeal, perhaps because we sons of Adam are all fond of our own opinions. The recently arrived always wanted to correct the work of those who had come first and, if possible, cause it to cease and be forgotten and make their own ideas prevail. The greatest evil was that those who were trying to do this took no thought and made no effort to learn the Indian language or to baptize the natives.

These different opinions and ideas were the reason why the administration of the sacrament of baptism was sometimes stopped. This could only be to the detriment of those who sought it, principally of the children and the sick, who died without remedy. Certainly these victims would have a grievance against those who were the cause of this trouble by their opinions and by the obstacles that they set up, even though they might think that their opinion was very holy and that one could ask nothing better. This same grievance would, I think, be shared by those other children and sick people who came to receive this sacrament and died while the ceremonies were being performed and before the essential words were spoken. This was in truth an indiscretion, for in the case of these last, since they wished to observe all the ceremonies, they should first have baptized the sick and then, having made sure of the principal object, they could go on and perform the usual ceremonies. In addition to what I have already said, other causes and reasons given by these men will appear in the following chapters.

The others who had come first also gave their reasons for administering baptism as they did, saying that they did it in accordance with the opinions and advice of holy doctors and learned persons and especially of a great religious and theologian named Fray Juan de Tecto, a native of Ghent, professor of theology in the University of Paris. No sounder scholar, I believe, has come to these parts, and as such the Emperor took him for his confessor. This Fray Juan de Tecto with two companions came in the same year as the twelve already mentioned and died the second year after his arrival here.[1] One of his companions, also a learned man, died at the same time. These two fathers and the other twelve discussed with great agreement the question of how they should proceed with the Indians in the matter of the sacraments and doctrine, keeping closely to certain instructions which they had brought from Spain, from very learned

1. Torquemada (vol. III, p. 424) states correctly that Fray Juan de Tecto came to Mexico a year before Fray Martín de Valencia's group, that is, in 1523.

people and from their general, Cardinal Santa Cruz. Giving causes and reasons for their procedure they cited excellent ecclesiastical authorities and laws sufficient to support their practice.

Besides this they said that they were baptizing under emergency conditions and because of the scarcity of priests, and that when there were others who could baptize they would help in the preaching and hearing of confessions. They also said that they knew by experience that for the time being, until the multitude of those who came to be baptized should diminish—many more than had been baptized in the years past—and because they had so few priests, they could not perform the service with the pomp and all the ceremonies that a parish priest can use when baptizing a single child in Spain where there are so many priests. Here in this newly converted land, how can a single priest baptize two or three thousand in a day and give them all the saliva, the breath, the candle, and the white garment and perform all the ceremonies over each one individually, and lead them into the church where there are no churches? This cannot be thoroughly realized except by those who saw the lack in past years. How can they give lighted candles when they are baptizing out in the courtyard in a high wind, and how can they give the saliva to so many? It was often very difficult to find wine for Mass and it was impossible to observe the ceremonies with all in a land where there were no churches, founts, or an abundance of priests, but one priest alone had to baptize, confess, betroth, and marry and bury, preach, pray, say Mass, learn the language, teach the children their catechism, and reading and singing.

Because it was impossible to do all this with the full ceremony they did it in the following way: at the time of the baptism they put together all who were to be baptized, placing the children in front, and said the baptismal service over all of them; with a few they performed the ceremonies of the cross, the breath, the salt, the saliva, and the white garment, and then they baptized all the children individually with holy water; and so far as I know they always kept this form. I knew of only one learned priest,[2] who thought he knew what he was doing, who baptized with a hyssop; this man was later one of those who worked to hinder the baptism of others. To return to the point, I say that when they had first baptized the children they preached again to the adults, who had been examined, and told them what they must believe, what they must abhor,

2. Spanish: *un letrado*. The term was originally applied to any student of letters; later it came to be applied more exclusively to lawyers.

what they must do in marriage, and then they baptized each one individually.

There were so many objections to this that it became necessary to have a meeting of the whole Church of these parts, bishops and other prelates as well as the gentlemen of the royal audiencia. The matter was discussed at this meeting and a report sent to Spain. This report was read by the royal council for the Indies and by the lord Archbishop of Seville, and they answered that things should be carried on as they had been begun until His Holiness should have been consulted. In truth, although there was no lack of learning, and those who came first brought, as I have said, apostolic authority and had holy and excellent theologians on their side, still it is no small thing to know the language of the Indians and to know the people, and those who have not first had at least three or four years' experience ought by no means to talk on this subject. For this reason God allows those who, as soon as they come from Spain, wish to make new laws and follow their own ideas and judge and condemn others and scorn them, to fall into confusion and act blindly and their errors to be as the beam of a wine-press and the thing they criticized to be as a straw. How often in my own experience have I seen this to be true in this land! It comes of too little fear of God and too little love of one's neighbor and overmuch love of one's own interest. For such cases the Church wisely made provision that in the conversion of certain infidels and new lands "the ministers who come last shall conform to the practice of those who came first until such time as they have a complete knowledge of the land and the people to which they come."

The language is necessary for talking, preaching, conversing, teaching, and for administering all the sacraments; no less necessary is a knowledge of the people, who are by nature timid and very bashful so that it seems as if they were born to obey. If one puts them in a corner, there they stay as if they were nailed there. Often they come to be baptized and do not dare to say so or to ask for baptism. One should not, therefore, examine them very severely, for I have seen many who know the Pater Noster and the Ave Maria and the catechism, and when the priest questions them they get upset and cannot repeat them. Now people like these should not be denied what they want, for theirs is the kingdom of heaven, since in the matter of worldly goods they barely achieve a wornout bit of matting to sleep on or one good blanket to cover them, and the poor hut they live in is tumbled down and open to the dampness of the night. They themselves are simple and without guile, not covetous, and very careful to learn what they are taught, especially in matters of the Faith. Many of them know and understand how they must be saved, and make a two or three day's journey to be baptized. The trouble is that some priests who begin to teach them would like, after working with them for two days, to see them as pious as if they had been teaching them for ten years, and as they do not seem so these priests cast them aside. Such people seem to me like a certain man who bought a very thin sheep and gave it a piece of bread to eat and then felt of its tail to see if it had grown fat.

What one can say of these people is that they are temperamentally very different from us, for we Spaniards have a heart that is big and ardent as fire, and these Indians, and all the animals of this land, are by nature tame, and because of their timidity and their temperament they are slow to express gratitude, although they are very sensible of benefits. As they are temperamentally more sluggish than we are, they are annoying to some Spaniards, but they are capable of any virtue and very capable of learning any trade or craft, and they have a great memory and a good understanding.

While things were very much at odds and there were many contradictory opinions about the manner of celebrating the sacrament of baptism and the ceremonies which must accompany it, there arrived a papal bull which ordained and established the ritual that was to be observed in this matter. The better to carry out its provisions, four of the five bishops in this country met at the beginning of the year 1539 and studied this bull of Pope Paul III. Having examined it they decided that it should be observed as follows: the catechizing they left to the discretion of the priest; the exorcism, which is the baptismal office,[3] they abbreviated as much as possible, following a certain Roman missal; they also ordered that the oil and chrism should be given to all who were to be baptized, and that this ruling should be inviolably observed by all, whether there were few or many to be baptized, except only in cases of urgent necessity.

On the question of this word *urgent* there were many differences and contradictory opinions as to just what was to be understood as urgent necessity, because in such a case a woman, an Indian, or even a Moor can baptize in the name of the Church. For this reason the baptism of adults was suppressed and in many places they baptized only children and the sick. This lasted for three or four months, until, in a monastery which

3. Spanish: *que es el oficio del baptistero.*

is in a plain called Quecholac, the friars decided, in spite of the bishops' orders, to baptize all who should present themselves. When this was known throughout that province the people who came were so many that if I had not seen it with my own eyes, I should not dare to mention it. In truth it was an enormous multitude that came, for besides the sound there were many lame and crippled, women with children on their backs, and old men, white-haired and of great age, and they came from a distance of a two or three day's journey to be baptized. Amongst them were two old women, clinging to each other, for they could scarcely walk. They stationed themselves with those who wished to be baptized, and the priest who was to baptize them and was examining them tried to turn them away, saying that they were not well taught. To this one of them answered, saying: "Would you cast me, who believe in God, out of the Church? Well, if you cast me out of the house of the God of mercy, whither shall I go? Do you not see from what a distance I have come, and that if I go back without being baptized I shall die on the road? I tell you that I believe in God; do not throw me out of His Church."

These words sufficed to get the old women, along with many others, baptized and consoled; for I am telling the truth when I say that in the five days that I was at that monastery another priest and I baptized, by actual count, fourteen thousand two hundred and some odd, giving them all the oil and chrism, which was no small task. After they have been baptized it is a wonderful thing to see them go off with their babies on their backs, so gay and happy that they seem to be fairly beside themselves with joy.

At this same time many went also to the monastery at Tlaxcallan to ask for baptism, and it was denied to them. It was the saddest thing in the world to see what they did, how they wept, and how disconsolate they were. The things they said and the lamentations they uttered were so well expressed that they filled with compassion any one who heard them and brought tears to the eyes of many of the Spaniards who were present and saw that these people had come a three- or four-days' journey in the rainy season, crossing rivers and streams with great danger and difficulty. They had very poor food and barely enough of it, in fact in many cases the food would give out on the journey. They stop wherever night overtakes them, under a tree, if there is one. In fact they bring nothing with them but trials and tribulations. The priests who were there, in view of the importunity of these Indians, baptized the children and the sick and some others whom they could not get out of the church because when they were told that they could not be baptized they answered: "Well, we are absolutely not going to leave here unbaptized, even if we have to die here." I certainly believe that if those who gave these orders [4] and those who prevented the administering of baptism had seen what was going on they would not have given an order so contrary to reason, nor would they have taken so grave a burden upon their consciences. It would be right for them to believe the men who see and handle these things daily, who know what the Indians need and understand their nature.

I have, with my own ears, heard some persons say that they did not wish to waste their twenty years or more of learning on people so nearly like brute beasts; in this it seems to me that they are wrong, for in my opinion learning cannot be better employed than in showing him who does not know it the way of salvation and of the knowledge of God. How much more must they be bound by obligations to these poor Indians whom they ought to treat as tenderly as if they were silkworms, since it is their labor and sweat that clothes and enriches those who, perchance, came from Spain without a cape to their backs.

At this same time of which I speak, amongst the many who came to be baptized there were as many as fifteen mutes; not very many in proportion to the great number of people who were baptized in these two monasteries, for in Cuauhquechollan, where they continued to baptize longer, they baptized nearly eighty thousand souls and in Tlaxcallan more than twenty thousand. These mutes made many gestures, clasping their hands, shrugging their shoulders, raising their eyes to heaven, and all to express the will and desire with which they came to receive baptism. There came also many blind people, among them two who were husband and wife, both blind and holding each other by the hand, guided by three little children whom they brought to be baptized also, and they had Christian names for all of them. After being baptized they went away so happy and joyous that it seemed to them as if their souls had recovered their sight with the new light of the grace which they had received in baptism.

4. That is, the orders restricting the administration of the sacrament of baptism.

Chapter V

Of how and when the sacraments of penance and confession began to be administered in New Spain; and of the restitution that the Indians make.

Amongst those who receive the sacrament of penance, remarkable things have occurred and still occur every day, and most of them—nearly all, in fact—are well known to the confessors; and by these things they know the great mercy and goodness of God, who thus brings sinners to true repentance. In testimony of this I shall relate some things that I have seen myself and others that have been told me by people who are completely to be trusted.

This sacrament was first instituted in New Spain in the year 1526 in the province of Tetzcoco; and it was done with great difficulty, for as the Indians were new in the Faith one could scarcely make them understand what the nature of this sacrament was, until little by little they have come to make their confessions well and truly, as will appear later.

Some of them who already know how to write bring their sins written down in great detail. They do this not once a year but at Christmas and Easter and the principal feasts, and there are many who confess even more frequently if they feel that they have sinned, and for this reason there are many who come to confession. As there are few confessors, the Indians go from one monastery to another seeking some one to hear their confessions and think nothing of going fifteen or twenty leagues. If they find confessors anywhere, then, like ants, they make a path to that place. This is very usual, especially in Lent, for he who does not do so does not seem to himself to be a Christian.

One of the first towns from which they came to seek this sacrament of penance was Tehuacán, many of whose inhabitants went to Huexotzinco—a journey of twenty-five leagues—to confession. They worked hard until they finally got friars to come to their town, and a very good monastery has been built there which has been of great benefit to all the towns of the district; this town of Tehuacán is forty leagues from Mexico, situated at the foot of a mountain range, and touches the frontiers of many towns and provinces which are visited from there. These people are docile, very sincere and of a good disposition, more so than the Mexicans. Just as in Spain the people in Old Castile and especially in the neighborhood of Burgos are more affable and of better disposition and seem to be of a different texture from those of Andalucia and of the country between Ciudad Rodrigo and Estremadura who are more astute and crafty, so one can say that the people of Mexico and its surrounding districts are like Estremadurans and Andalusians, while the Mixtecas, Zapotecas, Pinomes, Mazatecas, Cuitlatecas, and Mixes are more obedient, gentle, and temperamentally disposed to virtuous acts. For this reason the monastery at Tehuacán has done a great deal of good.

There would be a great deal to say about the towns and provinces that have come to this monastery laden with great quantities of idols, so many that it has been a thing to wonder at. Among the many who came was a lady from a town called Tetzitepec with many loads of idols which she brought to be burned. She also wished the friars to teach her and tell her what she must do to serve God. After being instructed she received the sacrament of baptism and said that she did not wish to return to her home until she had given thanks to God for the benefit He had conferred upon her and the mercy He had shown her in enlightening her and allowing her to know Him. She decided to remain there several days in order to learn and go back to her home better instructed in the Faith. This lady had brought along her two sons, for the same purpose for which she had come herself, and she gave orders that the heir should be given instruction not only so that he might fulfill his own obligations, but also so that he might teach his vassals and set them an example. Well, while this lady, newly a Christian, was occupied in this good work and filled with the desire to serve God, she fell ill and in a short time died, calling upon God and Saint Mary and asking forgiveness for her sins.

Later, in the year 1540, on Easter day I saw a very remarkable thing in this same town of Tehuacán, namely that the Indians and principal lords of forty towns and provinces had come there to attend the services of Holy Week and celebrate the feast of Easter. Some of them had come a distance of fifty or sixty leagues, though they were neither summoned nor compelled, and amongst them were people of twelve different nations and twelve different tongues. All of them, after attending the services, made special prayers to Our Lady of the Conception, for that monastery bears her name. Those who come thus for the church feasts always bring many others with them to be baptized or married or to make their confessions, and for this reason there is always a great number of people at this monastery.

Many of the Indians make restitution before they come to the confessor, considering it better to pay here, even though it leave them poor, than to pay after death. There are notable examples of this every Lent, of which I shall relate one that occurred in the first years of the conquest of this land.

An Indian went to confession owing a certain sum, and as the confessor told him that he could not receive complete absolution if he did not first make restitution, as is ordained by the law of God and required by consideration for one's neighbor, he finally brought, that same day, ten little plates of gold, each one weighing about five or six pesos,[1] which was the amount that he owed. He preferred being impoverished to being denied absolution. Although his remaining property was not, I think, worth a fifth part of what he had repaid he would rather struggle along with what he had left than go away unabsolved and have to wait in purgatory for his sons or executors to make for him the restitution that he could have made in life.

There was an important man named Juan, native of a town called Cuauhquechollan. During a period of three years he used to come with his wife and children to the monastery at Huexotzinco—a distance of eight leagues—for the principal feasts of the church year. At each feast he stayed eight or ten days during which he and his wife went to confession and received the Blessed Sacrament, and some of those who came with him did likewise. Being next in rank and importance to the lord and married to a lady of the family of Moteuczoma, the lord of Mexico, he was followed by many people, both of his own house and others who joined him because of his good example, which was so great that sometimes the principal lord, with another large retinue, accompanied him. Many of these followers were baptized, others went to confession or were married, for there was no monastery in their town until four years later. As at that time few had awakened from the sleep of their error, both natives and Spaniards were greatly edified and marvelled so much at Juan that they said he set them a great example both in the church and in his lodging.

This Juan came one Christmas and brought a shirt—shirts, at that time, being worn only by those Indians who served in the house of God—

1. The peso was both a coin and a unit of weight. It has varied in value in different periods and now varies greatly in different countries. At this time it was worth about one dollar of our money.

and said to his confessor: "I have brought this shirt so that you may bless it and put it on me; and since I have made my confession so often, as you know, I should like, if you think I am fit for it, to receive the Body of my Lord Jesus Christ, for certainly my soul greatly desires it." The confessor, as he had many times heard Juan's confession and knew how well disposed he was, gave him the Blessed Sacrament so much desired by the Indian. At the time that Juan made his confession and received communion he was well, but three days later he fell ill and shortly died, calling upon God and giving thanks for the mercies that He had shown him. Among the Spaniards this Indian's death was considered a very remarkable thing, brought about by God's secret judgment for the salvation of his soul, for he was in truth held to be a very good Christian, as he had showed by the many good works that he did during his life.

The lord of this town of Cuauhquechollan, who is called Don Martín, made great efforts to bring friars to his town, and there was established there a small but very devout monastery which has accomplished a great deal, for the people are well inclined and of a good disposition. People come there from many places to receive the sacraments.

Everywhere, but particularly in Tlaxcallan, it is remarkable to see the penance performed by the old and weary, and how eager they are to make up for the time lost while they were in the service of the devil.[2] Many old people fast in Lent, get up when they hear the bell ring for matins, and pray and scourge themselves, without anyone's making them do it. Those who have the means seek out poor people to whom to give alms, especially on feast days. This was not the custom in the old days, nor were there any beggars, for the poor and the sick used to attach themselves to some relative or to the household of the principal lord and there they stayed, enduring great hardships, and some of them died without finding anyone to console them.

In this province of Cuauhnahuac there was an old man, one of the principal men of the village, who was named Pablo, and in the time that I lived in that monastery all considered him as a model. In truth he was a person who used the curb on vice and the spurs on virtue. He spent much time in the church; one always saw him kneeling with his bare knees on the ground, and although he was old and his hair was completely white he held himself as straight and erect, apparently, as a youth. This

2. Spanish: *cuán bien se quieren entregar en el tiempo que perdieron; entregar* in the sense of *integrar,* to reimburse.

Pablo, persevering in his good intentions, came to make a general confession, though at that time few Indians were coming to confession, and immediately after confessing he was seized with his last illness. Before his death he confessed again twice and made a will in which he ordered some things to be distributed to the poor.

This making of a will was not usual in this land.[3] They left their houses and fields to their children, and the eldest, if an adult son,[4] became the owner of the estate, took care of his brothers and sisters, and as they grew up and married shared with them what he had. If the deceased's children were not yet of marriageable age, his brothers themselves came into the property, I mean the fields, and with these and the other property supported their nieces and nephews. In the case of the principal lords all their robes and blankets—which being white and thin very quickly get soiled and look old—were put away after a few days' wear and when the owner died they were buried with him. Some were buried with many blankets, some with few, depending on who they were. They also buried with the lords the jewels and stones and gold that they owned. In other parts of the country they left them to their children, and if the deceased were a lord, they knew by their custom which son would inherit.[5] Occasionally on his deathbed the father would designate one son, whichever he pleased, as his heir, and his wishes were obeyed. This was their way of making wills.

As to the restitution which these Indians make, it is very remarkable, for they give up the slaves that they held before they became Christians, arrange marriages for them, and assist them and give them a livelihood. But also they do not keep their slaves in such a state of servitude, nor work them so hard as the Spaniards do; for they keep them almost free on their lands and estates, where they work partly for their masters and

3. See above, Introductory Letter, p. 28. Also Gómara, p. 434, "It is the custom amongst the common people for the eldest son to inherit everything and to support all the brothers and sisters and nephews and nieces, provided they obey his orders. . . In other places all the children inherit and divide the inheritance amongst them."

4. The text is not very clear. It reads as follows: *el mayor, si era hombre* (if a male? or if an adult?) *lo poseía y tenía cuidado de sus hermanos y hermanas . . . si los hijos* (the deceased's) *eran por casar* (below marriageable age, minors?), *entrábanse en la hacienda los mismos hermanos* (the deceased's ? or his sons ?) . . . *y mantenían a sus sobrinos . . .*

5. See above, Introductory Letter, p. 28, and note 7. Also Gómara, p. 434: "In the case of some nobles' estates, although the oldest son inherits, he cannot enter into possession without the approval of the people or the permission of the king . . . for which reason the other sons often came into the property; and hence it must be that in the case of such estates the fathers select the son who is to inherit."

partly for themselves and have their houses and wives and children, so that they do not suffer such servitude as would make them run away from their masters.[6] These slaves were bought and sold among them, and it was a very common custom. Now that they are all Christians scarcely an Indian is sold; on the contrary many of the converts seek out the slaves that they sold and buy them back in order to free them, when they can get them; when they cannot get them many make restitution of the sum for which they sold them.

While I was writing this a poor Indian came to me and said: "I have certain debts upon my conscience. Here is a plate of gold which must be worth the amount of my indebtedness; tell me to whom I should return it. Also I sold a slave days ago and I have sought for him and cannot find him. Here is the price I received for him. Will it be sufficient to give it to the poor, or what do you bid me do?" They also give up the lands they possessed before they were converted, knowing that they cannot keep them with a clear conscience even though they inherited or acquired them according to their ancient customs. In the case of lands which are their own and to which they hold a clear title they relieve the macehuales or vassals of many taxes and tributes that they used to demand from them. And the lords and principal men try very hard to have their vassals be good Christians and live under the law of Christ.

They perform very well whatever penance is imposed upon them, however heavy it may be; many of them, when coming to confession, if not told to scourge themselves, are sorry and say voluntarily to the confessor: "Why do you not bid me scourge myself?" For they consider it a great merit, and therefore many of them scourge themselves every Friday in Lent, going from church to church. They do the same thing in times of drought or illness; I think that the place where they do it most is in the province of Tlaxcallan.

6. Slaves could even hold slaves of their own. See Motolinía (*Memoriales,* p. 325) where he quotes a letter supposedly written by a negro slave in New Spain to a slave friend of his in Santo Domingo: "Dear Friend, This is good land for slaves. Here negro have good food; here negro have slave to serve negro, and negro's slave have *navorio,* which means boy or servant. So try to make master sell you, so you come to this land; best in world for negroes."

CHAPTER VI

How the Indians wrote out their confessions in pictures and characters; and what happened to two Indian youths at the moment of death.

ONE Lent when I was in ChololIan, a big town near the city of Los Angeles, those who came to confession were so many that I could not attend to them as I wished, and I said to them: "I shall confess only those who bring their sins written down in pictures." This is a thing that they know and understand, for that was their way of writing, and I did not speak to deaf ears, for at once so many of them began to bring me their sins written down that I could not cope with them either, even though this manner of confessing was very expeditious. They pointed out the symbols with a straw, and I, with another, assisted them. In this way there was time to hear many confessions, for they expressed themselves so well in symbols and characters that I had to ask them only very little more than what they had written or depicted. Many Indian women married to Spaniards used this method of confession, especially in the city of Los Angeles, which, next to Mexico, is the best city in all New Spain, as I shall tell later, in the third part.[1]

The very day that I am writing this, which is the Friday before Palm Sunday of the present year of 1537, a youth named Benito, a native of Cholollan, died here in Tlaxcallan. He came to confession in sound and excellent health and two days later fell ill in a house far away from the monastery. Two days before he died, being very ill, he came to the monastery and when I saw him I was astounded to see how he had reached it, being so very weak. He told me that he had come to make his peace with God because he was about to die. After he had confessed he rested a little and told me that his spirit had been taken to hell, where he had suffered great torture just from terror, and while he was telling me he trembled with the fear that he still felt. He said that when he found himself in that fearful place he called upon God and begged for mercy, and then he was taken to a very happy place where an angel said to him: "Benito, God is willing to show you mercy. Go and confess and prepare yourself well, for God orders that you come to this place to rest."

A similar thing happened to another youth, a native of Chiautempan.

1. See below, bk. III, chs. XVII and XVIII.

a league distant from Tlaxcallan. This youth was named Juan de la Cruz; his duty was to know the children that were born in that town and on Sundays to collect them and take them to be baptized. When he was taken with the illness of which he died his spirit was seized and borne away by some black men, who took him along a very gloomy and toilsome road to a place of many torments. As those who were bearing him tried to throw him into these torments he began to cry aloud: "Saint Mary! Saint Mary!"—which is their way of calling upon Our Lady—"My lady, why do they throw me here? Did I not take the children to be made Christians, and carry them to the house of God? Did I not, in doing this, serve God and you, My Lady? Then, My Lady, help me and take me out of here, for I will cure myself of my sins." Saying this he was taken out of that fearful place and his spirit was returned to his body. This is corroborated by his mother who thought him dead during that period when his spirit was absent. All these and other very wonderful things were told by this youth named Juan, who died of that same illness, though he lingered for several days, very ill. Many of these converts have seen and report different revelations and visions which, considering the sincerity and simplicity with which they tell of them, seem to be true. But because it might be false I do not write them down nor do I either affirm or deny them—also because there would be many who would not believe me.

The Blessed Sacrament was given in this land to very few of the natives; scholars held different opinions and ideas on this subject until there came a bull of Pope Paul III by which, in view of the report presented to him, he ordered that the sacrament should not be denied them but should be administered to them as to other Christians.

In Huexotzinco, in the year 1528, a youth named Diego who had been brought up in the house of God and was the son of Miguel, brother of the lord of the town, was ill. During his illness, after having confessed, he begged repeatedly and with great importunity that he might receive the Blessed Sacrament. As they evaded the issue, not wishing to give it to him, there came to him two friars in the habit of St. Francis and gave him communion and then disappeared; and the sick boy Diego was greatly comforted. Then when his father came in to give him something to eat the son replied and said that he had already eaten what he desired and did not wish anything more, for he was satisfied. The father, very much astonished, asked him who had given him food. The son answered:

"Did you not see those two friars who just went out of here? Well, they gave me what I desired and had so often asked for;" and shortly afterward he died.

Many of our Spaniards are so full of scruples that they think they do right in not coming to communion, saying that they are not worthy, in which they err gravely and deceive themselves; for if it were to be by merit, not even the angels or the saints would be worthy. But it is God's will that it should suffice if you consider yourself unworthy and confess and do what you are able to. The priest who denies this to him who asks for it would commit a mortal sin.

CHAPTER VII

Of where the sacrament of marriage was first performed in New Spain; and of the great difficulty in getting the Indians to give up their many wives.

THE sacrament of marriage in this land of Añáhuac, or New Spain, was first performed in Tetzcoco. In the year 1526, on Sunday, October 14, there took place the public and solemn ceremony of the betrothal and marriage of Don Hernando, brother of the lord of Tetzcoco, and of seven of his companions, all of whom had been brought up in the house of God. For this festival many honorable persons from Mexico, five leagues away, were invited to honor and celebrate the weddings. Amongst them came Alonso de Avila[1] and Pedro Sánchez Farfán[2] with their wives, and they brought with them other honorable persons who offered gifts to the brides and grooms as is done in Spain. They brought them good jewels and also much wine—the jewel which gave most joy to all of them. Because this wedding was to be an example for the whole of New Spain, the full and solemn nuptial Mass was used, with benediction and pledges and ring, as Holy Mother Church commands. When the Mass was over the sponsors, with all the lords and principal men of the town—for Tetzcoco was very prominent in New Spain—took the newly

1. Alonso de Avila, one of Cortés' captains. Sent back to Spain with the treasure taken from Montezuma, he later returned to New Spain and died there.

2. Pedro Sánchez Farfán, one of Cortés' captains. We hear of him as a prominent citizen of Mexico in 1524-25.

married couples to the house of the principal lord. They were preceded by many people singing and dancing, and after eating they held a great *netotiliztli* or dance.[3] At that time a thousand or two of the Indians would assemble for one of these dances. After vespers had been said, when they came out into the courtyard where they danced, there was the marriage bed, beautifully decked, and there, before the bride and groom, the lords and principal men and relatives of the groom offered, as is done in Castile, household furnishings and personal adornments. The Marquis of the Valley sent one of his servants to offer gifts in his name, which he did very generously.

For three or four years the marriage ceremonies were performed only for those who were brought up in the house of God. All the others lived with whatever women they pleased. There were some who had as many as two hundred; from that number down each man had as many as he liked. In order to supply themselves with wives, the lords and principal men stole all the women, so that when one of the common Indians wanted to marry it was almost impossible to find a wife. The lords had most of the women and would not give them up, nor could the others take them away from them. Neither entreaties, threats, or sermons or anything else sufficed to make them give up all these women and marry one with the sanction of the Church. They would answer that the Spaniards too had many women, and if we told them that the Spaniards had them as servants, they would say that they too had them for the same purpose. Although these Indians had many women to whom they were married, according to their custom, they also had them as a source of income, for they made them all weave, make blankets, and practice other similar crafts.[4] This continued until at last it pleased Our Lord that of their own volition some of them began, five or six years ago, to give up their multiplicity of wives and content themselves with one, marrying her as the Church ordains. These, together with the young men who are marrying for the first time, are now so many that they fill the churches.

There are days when they marry a hundred couples, and other days

3. See Gómara, p. 343. The dance called *netotelizth* is a dance of pleasure and rejoicing. It is danced by from 400 to 1000 persons, all nobles, holding each other by the hand. They dance to the music of two drums, one small and one large, and sing as they dance. The songs are gay and merry.

4. See Gómara, p. 439: "They give four reasons for having so many wives: the first is the lust of the flesh; the second is that they may have many children; the third, that they may be thought well of and be well served; the fourth, that they may have a source of income, for they make their wives work like slaves, spinning and weaving blankets for sale."

two, three, or even five hundred, and as the priests are so few it gives them a great deal of work, for it happens that one priest may have many to confess, baptize, betroth and marry, and besides he has to preach and say Mass and do other things that cannot be neglected. Elsewhere I have seen some examining candidates for marriage, others teaching those who are to be baptized, others who know different languages and serve as interpreters and explain to the priests the needs of the Indians who come, others who have charge of the sick, others of the new-born children, and others who provide for the celebration of festivals in the neighboring parishes and towns. In order to remove and uproot the old feasts, they celebrate the Christian festivals with great pomp, not only in the services and the administration of the sacraments, but also with dances and entertainment; all of this is necessary to wean them away from the evil customs into which they were born. But to return to the point and to make you understand the amount of work that the priests had to do, I shall tell you how one priest spent his time.

While he was writing this account he was sent for from a town called Santa Ana de Chiautempan, one league from Tlaxcallan, to come out and hear the confessions of some sick persons and also to baptize. When he arrived he found thirty sick people to confess, two hundred couples to betroth, many to baptize, and one dead man to bury, and he also had to preach to the town, which had assembled to hear him. On that day this friar baptized fifteen hundred persons, children and adults, giving them all oil and chrism; during the same day he heard fifteen confessions, although it was an hour after nightfall and he had not finished. This happened not to this priest alone, but to all who are here and wish to give themselves to the service of God and to the conversion and saving of the souls of the Indians, and it happens very commonly.

In Tzompantzinco, which is a town of a good many inhabitants with a well-populated district for a league around it, they all assembled one Sunday to hear Mass, and some four hundred and fifty couples were betrothed, some before and some after Mass during the whole day, and more than seven hundred children and five hundred adults were baptized. At the Sunday Mass two hundred couples were married and the Monday following one hundred and fifty couples were betrothed; most of them had followed the friars to Tecoac to be married. All of these do it now of their own volition and apparently without its causing them any difficulty or regret. In Tecoac five hundred more were baptized and two hundred and forty couples were betrothed, and then on Tuesday they baptized one hundred more and betrothed one hundred couples. They returned by way of other towns where they baptized many; and there were days when they betrothed over seven hundred and fifty couples. In this monastery of Tlaxcallan and in another they betrothed in one day over a thousand couples; it was the same in other towns, for at this time the natives were eager to marry a single wife, and they took the one whom, in their pagan state, they had married first.

In order to make no mistakes and to deprive no one of his legitimate wife, and to avoid giving anyone a concubine rather than a wife, there was in each parish a person who knew all the inhabitants, and those who wished to get married came to him with all their relatives and all their wives, so that all of them might have a chance to state their claims and the man might take his legitimate wife and satisfy the demands of the others by making them an allowance for their support and that of their children. It was a strange sight to see them come, for many of them brought a flock of wives and children like a flock of sheep. When these had been heard and sent away there came other Indians, well versed in the regulations concerning marriage and in the tracing of relationships. These men were called by the Spaniards *licenciados*[5] because they knew their subject as well as if they had studied it for many years. They discussed with the friars any impediments that might exist. The serious difficulties, after being examined and understood, were referred to the bishops and their advisers for decision. All this was very necessary because of the objections that have been made, no less serious or numerous than in the case of baptism.

Many of these Indians determined, by choice and in fact, to have nothing to do with any woman except the one whom they legitimately married after their conversion. They also gave up the vice of drunkenness and gave themselves so heartily to virtue and to the service of God that in this past year of 1536 two Indian youths, having made their confession and received communion, left this city of Tlaxcallan and, without saying anything to anybody, went more than fifty leagues into the interior to convert and teach other Indians. There they went about, suffering many hardships and doing very fruitful work, for they taught the people all that

5. Licentiates, *i.e.*, men who have taken their first university degree.

they knew and left them in a propitious state for receiving the Word of God. After this they returned and today are in this city of Tlaxcallan.

Some others have done likewise in many remote provinces and towns where, moved just by their word, the people destroyed their idols and erected crosses and set up images before which they recite the few prayers that these men taught them. This I saw in this same year when I went out to visit the towns toward the north coast,[6] about fifty leagues from here, that is, from Tlaxcallan.

We went through such rough country and such lofty mountains that my companions and I got into some places where, in order to get out, we had to climb a mountain three leagues high. One league of the distance was up a corner of a mountain which at times we climbed by means of holes in the rock where we put our toes and by grasping vines or ropes with our hands. Places like this were not a mere ten or twelve paces—we climbed one that was as high as a high tower. Other very rough places we climbed by means of ladders. There were some nine or ten of these, and one that had nineteen steps. These ladders were just one pole with some hollows cut a little into the wood into which you could get half of your foot, and there were ropes to hold on to. We were terrified to look down as we climbed because the height was so great that it made one dizzy. Even though we would have liked to return by a different road, we could not do so, for after we entered that country it rained very hard and the rivers, of which there were many very large ones, had risen. There was no lack of rivers in this country either, but the Indians used to take us across, sometimes on rafts, and sometimes they stretched a long rope from bank to bank and, holding on to it, half waded and half swam across.

One of these rivers is the one that the Spaniards called the Almería,[7] a very big stream. At this time of year the grass is very high and the roads are so overgrown that there was scarcely a narrow path visible, and even this was usually covered by the overhanging grass on the two sides, so that one's feet went along under the grass, without one's being able to see the ground. And there were very terrible vipers; for, though all over New Spain there were more and bigger vipers than in Castile, those of the cold country are less poisonous and the Indians have many remedies for their bite. In the country of which I am speaking, however, they are so poison-

6. The coast of the Gulf of Mexico.
7. The name given by the earliest explorers to what is now the Río de Nautla.

ous that the man whom they bite does not live twenty-four hours. As we went along, the Indians would keep telling us: "Here a man died of snake-bite, and there another, and over there still another," and all the members of our group were travelling barefoot! But God brought us all through without any injury or trouble. All this land of which I have spoken is everywhere habitable, both the high part and the low, though it was much more thickly populated in the past, for it is very much destroyed nowadays.

In this same year the lords of Tepantitla came to the monastery of Santa María de la Concepción in Tehuacán, a distance of twenty-five leagues. They came of their own volition and brought the idols of all their land which were so numerous that they aroused the wonder of both Spaniards and natives; it was amazing too to think where they had come from and by what road.

Chapter VIII

Of the many superstitions and magic practices that the Indians used to have; and of how they have progressed in the Faith.

The devil was not content with the service that this people did him by adoring him in the idols, but he also held them blinded by a thousand kinds of witchcraft and superstitious ceremonies.[1] They believed in a thousand omens and signs and were especially superstitious about the horned owl; if they heard it croak or hoot over the house on which it perched, they said that some one in that house would soon die. They had almost the same beliefs about barn owls and red owls and other nocturnal birds. Also if they heard the croaking of a creature that they call *cuzatli,* they took it as an omen of death for some one.

They were also superstitious about meeting snakes and scorpions and many other sorts of reptiles that crawl about the ground. They also believed that if a woman had twins, which happens frequently in this country, one of the parents would die; and the remedy that their cruel devil gave them was to kill one of the twins, in which case neither parent

1. This account of Indian superstitions, as far as the middle of page 154, is so closely paralleled by the passage in Las Casas, p. 376, that it is obvious that he was using Motolinía as a source. Torquemada's account (vol. II, pp. 82-84) is very close to Motolinía's at some points.

would die; and they often did this. When an earthquake occurred in any place where there was a pregnant woman they quickly covered up the jars or broke them, to keep it from moving;[2] and they said that the trembling of the earth was a sign that the corn in the granaries would soon be used up and give out. In many parts of this country earthquakes are frequent, as in Tecoatepec[3] for instance, where there were many during the half year that I spent there. They tell me that there are many more in Cuauhtemallan. If anyone fell ill with violent fever, the remedy was to make a little dog of cornmeal dough and put it on a leaf of maguey, and then in the morning put it out in a road; and they say that the illness will cling to the heels of the first person who passes and be carried away, and by this means the patient is much relieved.[4]

They also had books about dreams and their meaning, all expressed in figures and characters, and there were experts who interpreted them. They also had them for marriages.

When anyone lost anything, they made certain charms with grains of corn and looked into a bowl or vessel of water and said that in it they could see the person who had it and the house where he was. They also claimed to see in the water whether an absent person was dead or alive. To find out whether sick people would live they would take a handful of corn, the biggest kernels that they could get, and throw it as one throws dice. If any grain stood up on end, they were certain that the sick man would die.

They had many other forms of witchcraft and illusions with which the devil deceived them, all of which they have now given up so completely that no one who had not seen this change would believe the great Christianity and devotion of these natives. As if their lives were at stake each one strives to be better than his neighbor or acquaintance; and really there is so much to say and so much to tell about the fine Christianity of these Indians that one could make a good-sized book of that alone. May it please Our Lord to preserve them and give them grace to persevere in His service and in the good and holy works that they have begun.

The Indians have built many almshouses where they care for the sick and the poor, for out of their own poverty they provide abundantly for

2. The Earth? The reference is completely ambiguous.

3. Tehuantepec.

4. See Frazer, VI, p. 47 ff. Stones, twigs, or other objects touched by a diseased person and left at a cross road or in a gateway are supposed to transfer the disease to the first person who touches them.

them. As there are many Indians, even though they give very little "many littles make a mickle," and all the more if the giving is continuous, so that the hospitals are well provided for. Since they know how to serve as if they were born to it, they lack nothing; and from time to time they go through the whole province in search of sick people. They have their own doctors, experienced natives who know how to apply many herbs and medicines, and this suffices for them. Some of these doctors are so experienced that they have cured many serious and long-standing illnesses which Spaniards had suffered for many days without finding a remedy.

In this city of Tlaxcallan, in the year 1537, they built a fine almshouse, with its brotherhood dedicated to serving and burying the poor and celebrating the feasts. It is called the Hospital of the Incarnation because it was finished and equipped by that day. They opened and inaugurated it by going there in solemn procession and taking in one hundred and forty sick and poor, and on the following day, which was Easter, the people made a very large offering of corn, beans, and chili as well as sheep and pigs and native fowl,[5] which are so good that they give three or four Spanish fowl for one native bird. They gave a hundred and forty of the latter and an infinite number of Spanish ones. They also gave a great deal of clothing, and every day they continue to give offerings and alms, so much that although the hospital has been open not over seven months, its holdings in land and cattle are worth nearly one thousand pesos in gold; and it will increase greatly, for as the Indians have recently come into the Faith they give alms generously. In this matter I shall tell what I myself have seen—that last year in this province of Tlaxcallan alone the Indians freed over twenty thousand slaves and imposed heavy penalties so that no one should take slaves or buy or sell them, because God's law forbids it.

Every third day after Mass and on Sundays and feast days the catechism is recited, so that almost all of them, old and young, know not only the commandments but all the articles that they are under obligation to believe and to observe. This is so much of a custom with them that it leads to frequent confession, and there are even many of them who will not go to bed with a mortal sin on their conscience without first telling their confessor. Some of them make vows of chastity and others vow themselves to the religious life, although in this we restrain them very much because they are still very new in the Faith and we do not wish to let them

5. That is, turkeys.

take the habit. This is because we do not wish to put them to the test too soon; in the year 1527 they did give the habit to three or four youths, and they could not live up to it. They are now alive and married and live like Christians and say that at the time they did not realize what they were doing, but that if they were to do it now they would not go back on their vows, even if they died in the attempt. In this connection I shall tell about one Indian who last year made a vow to become a friar.

A youth named Juan, of high rank and native of a town in the province of Michoacán, which is called in their language Turecato and in Mexican, Tepeoacán, upon reading a life of St. Francis which had been translated into his language, was inspired with such devotion that he made a vow to become a friar. In order that his vow might not be supposed to have been lightly made he persisted in his purpose, dressed in a coarse robe, freed many slaves whom he owned and preached to them and taught them the commandments and what else he knew, and told them that if he had sooner known God and himself, he would sooner have given them their liberty. From then on they were to know that they were free; he begged them to love one another and be good Christians, and said that if they did so, he would consider them his brothers. Having done this, he divided up his jewels and furniture and renounced his title and estates and repeatedly requested to be received as a friar in Michoacán, which is forty leagues from Mexico. As they refused to grant his request in Michoacán, he came to Mexico and repeated it there, and when it was refused there also, he went to the Bishop of Mexico, who, seeing his cleverness and his good intention, would have granted the request, if he could. He became very fond of him and treated him well. The young man kept on wearing his coarse robe, and when Lent came he went back to his own land to hear the sermons in his own language and to make his confession. After Easter he returned to Mexico for the Chapter meeting that was held there and persisted in his request. What they did grant him was that he might live with the friars wearing the same coarse garment that he ordinarily wore, and they said that if they thought that his manner of life warranted it, they might give him the habit of the Order. This youth, as he was of high rank and well known, has been a great example in the whole province of Michoacán, which is very large and populous and has had big mines of all kinds of metals.

Some of the natives, at the Elevation of the Consecrated Host, have seen the radiant figure of a child, others have seen our Redeemer on the Cross in a blaze of splendor, and this has happened many times. When they see these visions they cannot refrain from falling upon their faces and are much comforted. They have also seen a beautiful crown about the head of a friar preaching to them. Once it seemed to be a crown of gold, and once of fire. Others have seen during Mass a ball or a flame of fire hovering over the Blessed Sacrament.

One person, who used to come to the church very early, one morning found the door shut, and raising his eyes to heaven saw that the heavens opened and through the opening he could see something very beautiful within; and he saw this on two days. All these things I learned from people whose word is to be trusted, and the persons who saw these visions were of exemplary character and frequented the sacraments. I do not know to what to attribute it except that God manifests Himself to these simple creatures—as He Himself promises to do—because they seek Him sincerely and in purity of soul.[6]

Chapter IX

Of the grief of these Indians when the friars were taken away from them; of their efforts to have friars sent to them; and of the honor which they pay to the sign of the cross.

At the Chapter which the Friars Minor held in Mexico in the year 1538 on May 19, the fourth Sunday after Easter, it was decided that, because of the scarcity of friars, certain monasteries situated near others should not be maintained as convents, but should be visited and supplied from others. The Indians learned at once of this decision, but in a garbled form. The report reached them that they were going to be left entirely without friars. When the decisions made by the Chapter were read, there were waiting to hear it the Indians who had been sent by their lords and stationed in relays to bring the news as to who was to be their guardian or preacher. For some houses no friars were named in the published list, but they were to be supplied from other convents. Among the former was Xochimilco, a big town on the fresh-water lake, four leagues from Mexico.

6. Matthew 5.8. "Blessed are the pure in heart, for they shall see God."

Although the list was read very late one day the news was known the following morning to all the people in that town, which had three friars in its monastery. Almost the entire population assembled and entered the monastery and church, which is not small. Many others who could not get into the church stayed out in the churchyard—for they say that there were more than ten thousand souls—and they all knelt before the Blessed Sacrament and began to call upon God and beseech Him not to allow them to be abandoned, since He had done them so great a favor in bringing them to a knowledge of Him. Many other sad and piteous words they spoke, each one using the best that his desire and need dictated, all this in a very loud voice; and the people in the courtyard did the same.

When the friars saw this great assembly and that the people all surrounded them and wept, they also wept without knowing why, for they did not as yet know what the Chapter had decided. Although they tried hard to console the Indians, the noise was so great that neither party could understand the other. This went on all of the day, Thursday, with the crowd continually increasing. While things were in this state some people decided to go to Mexico; neither those who went nor those who stayed behind remembered to eat. Those who went to Mexico arrived at the time of the celebration of Mass and rushed into the church of St. Francis so impetuously that they frightened the people there and, falling on their knees before the Blessed Sacrament, each one said what seemed best to him, some calling upon Our Lady for help, some upon St. Francis, and some upon other saints, weeping so bitterly the while that two or three times when I went into the chapel and heard the cause of their agitation, I was beside myself with amazement. They made me weep too when I saw them so sad. Although some of the friars and I tried to console them, they would not listen to us but said:

"Our fathers, why are you abandoning us now after baptizing us and marrying us? Remember the many times that you told us that it was for us that you came from Castile, and that God sent you. If you leave us now, to whom shall we turn? For the devils will try to deceive us again as they used to do and make us return to our idolatrous worship." We could not answer them because of the noise they were making but having finally imposed comparative silence, we told them the truth of what was happening, as it had been decided in the Chapter. We consoled them as best we could and promised never to leave them until our death. Many

Spaniards who were present were filled with amazement; others who heard what was going on came later and saw what they had not believed, and went away marveling at the affection that those poor people had for God and His mother and the saints.

Many of the Spaniards are incredulous in this matter of the conversion of the Indians, and others, as if they were a thousand leagues away from them, neither know nor see anything because they are too much absorbed and involved in acquiring the gold that they came to get, intending to return to Spain as soon as they have obtained it. Their attitude is revealed by their usual form of oath: "As I hope to get back to Spain."[1] However, the nobles and the virtuous and Christian gentlemen are very much edified to see the fine conversion of these native Indians.

The Indians continued in the state which I have described until we came out to return thanks after eating; then the Father Provincial comforted them and gave them two friars to go with them; and they went away as content and joyful with these two friars as if they had been given the whole world.

Chololtan was also one of the houses from which they removed the friars, and though it is nearly twenty leagues from Mexico they heard the news very quickly and in the same way as in Xochimilco. The first thing they did was to assemble and go to the monastery of St. Francis with the same tears and excitement as elsewhere, and not content with this they set out for Mexico—and not just three or four of them, but eight hundred, and some people even say that there were more than a thousand. They reached the church of St. Francis in Mexico very excited and more than a little wet, for it was raining very hard. They began to weep and beg the friars to "have pity on them and on all those who had stayed in Chololtan and not to take away the friars," saying that "if they, being sinners, did not deserve to have them leave the friars in their town, let them do it for the sake of the many innocent children whose souls would be lost if they had no one to train them and teach them the law of God." Besides this they said many very good words which sufficed to get them what they asked for.

That the mercy of God should not fail to reach, as it has always done, now does, and still shall do, to all parts of the world, and more abundantly where more is needed, He brought it about that, when things were in the

1. Compare the common formula: *así me salve Dios;* as I hope to be saved.

state I have described, there arrived from Spain twenty-five friars, who were sufficient to supply the deficiencies in those houses. More than this, when the Minister General of the Order of Friars Minor did not wish to send friars, and all the Provincials of the Order were preventing any friar from coming here, and the door of all human hope seemed closed[2] God worked upon the Empress Doña Isabel, who is now in Glory. She gave orders that more than a hundred friars should come out from Spain—although only forty of them came—and they did very fruitful work in the conversion of these natives.

In Mexico, in the year 1528, the Law took a man by force from the monastery of St. Francis for so trivial a cause that even if he had been arrested in the public square, he would have been released if they had been willing to hear his case with an attorney and counsel. His offenses were old and he was no longer liable for them; but, as they would not hear him, he was executed. Before this the Law had, with great violence, taken three or four others from the same monastery, violating its sanctuary.[3] The offenses of these men did not deserve the death penalty, and yet they were executed without trial, almost without giving them a chance to make their confession, which was contrary to all law, both human and divine.

Neither for these deaths nor for the one first mentioned did the Law ever do penance or give satisfaction to the Church or to the dead, yet the representatives of the Law were given absolution *ad reincidentiam*—or something of the sort. But I have observed that some of them God has not allowed to go unpunished, and He will do likewise with the rest unless they humble themselves, for they were absolved by an idiot without any penance for so enormous and public a sin. For this reason, and for others of the same kind, the prelate of the friars removed them from the monastery of St. Francis in Mexico, and they consumed the Most Blessed Sacrament and dismantled the altars, without the Spanish residents of Mexico doing anything about it, or showing any regret. They had no reason for this attitude, however, for the Franciscans were their chaplains and preachers during the Conquest, and three friars of very good and exemplary life died in Tetzcoco before the Spaniards came to live in Mexico, and those who were left continued always in their company.

2. At this point there is a blank in the manuscript which must be filled by some such word as *influyó*.

3. See above, Introduction, p. 5 and note 16.

The church of St. Francis was the first church in all this land and the one in which the Blessed Sacrament was first placed. These friars have always preached to the Spaniards and their Indians, and they are the ones who keep the Spaniards' consciences clear, for it is on this condition that the king gives them the Indians.[4] With all this the church of St. Francis in Mexico was, for over three months, without friars or sacrament, and there was scarcely any regret among the old Christians—or if there was, they kept silent about it for fear of the Law. Meanwhile the recent converts did what I have already told in order to keep themselves from being deprived of this sacrament and of their masters who taught and instructed them.

The symbol of the cross is so honored in this land in all the towns and along all the roads that they say that in no part of the world is it more honored, nor is there any place where there are such crosses or so many and such tall ones. Especially in the courtyards of the churches they are very impressive. On every Sunday and Feast Day they are adorned with quantities of roses and flowers and rushes and branches. In the churches and on the altar they have crosses of gold and silver and feathers —not solid, but gold leaf and feathers on wood. Many others have been and are still made of turquoises, of which there are many in this land, although they are mostly flat, for they get very few rounded ones.[5] After they have made or carved in wood the shape of the cross and covered it with a strong resin or glue and shaped the stones, they delicately soften the glue little by little with fire and set the turquoises until they have covered the whole cross; between the turquoises they set other stones of other colors. These crosses are very showy; lapidaries prize them highly and say that they are of great value. There is also a white stone that is clear and transparent of which they make very well carved crosses with pedestals.[6] Some of these are used as osculatories on the altars, for they make them about one span in height, or slightly larger.

On almost all the altar-pieces they paint a representation of the crucifix in the middle. Up till now, when they had no beaten gold they used

4. That is, on condition that they Christianize them. As the Spaniards mostly do not bother about it, the friars, who do it for them, relieve their consciences.

5. Spanish: *de tumba, i.e.,* vaulted, rounded. These are evidently the *xiuhtomolli* which Sahagún (vol. III, p. 280) describes as being like a hazelnut cut in two.

6. Possibly rock crystal, which however is very hard and difficult to carve, or transparent calcite, which would be easier to work. Eduard Seler (*Orfebrería,* p. 195 ff.) in speaking of rock crystal (quartz), says that apparently other colorless, transparent stones were designated by the same Aztec term.

to put diadems of gold leaf on the images on the altar-pieces, of which there are many. They make other crucifixes carved out of wood or other materials, so made that even though the crucifix may be the size of a man, a child could raise it from the ground with one hand.[7] Before this symbol of the cross some miracles have occurred which, for the sake of brevity, I shall omit, but I do say that the Indians hold it in such veneration that out of devotion and reverence for it many of them fast on Fridays and refrain from intercourse with their wives.

Those who, with great misgivings and only because they were obliged to, sent their children to be trained and taught in the house of God now come begging that they be received and instructed in the catechism and other matters relating to the Faith. There are now so many being taught that some monasteries have three, four or seven hundred pupils, or even as many as one thousand, depending on the population of the towns and provinces. They are so gentle and docile that ten Spanish children make more noise than a thousand Indians. Besides the children of the upper class, who are taught separately in the hall of the monastery, there are many other children of the common and low-class people whom they teach out in the courtyards.[8] The friars have accustomed them to hear Mass every day early in the morning; after Mass they teach them for a while, and then the children go to serve and assist their parents. Many of these children become servers in the churches, and later they marry and help Christianity all over the country.

It is a general custom here that as soon as a baby is born they make it a tiny cradle of slender rods, like a birdcage. Immediately after birth the child is placed in this cradle and as soon as the mother gets up she carries it on her back to the church or wherever she goes. When the baby is five or six months old the mother puts it, naked, into a blanket which covers the child, leaving out only its head. Then she arranges the blanket so that the child rests between her shoulders, knots the corners of the blanket across her chest, and thus she carries it along the roads and through the country, wherever she goes, and the child travels about sleeping as if in a comfortable bed. Some children are brought in this way to be baptized from the towns which are visited only infrequently by the

7. Torquemada (vol. III, p. 209) speaks of "hollow crucifixes made of reed, which, though they are the size of a very large man, weigh so little that a child can carry them."

8. This practice was continued. See Torquemada, vol. III, p. 111: "The catechism was, and still is, taught to the children of the common people out in the churchyard, and after the lesson they go off to help their parents."

friars. Others are brought shortly after birth, or in a few days, and often they bring them as soon as they are born, so that the first thing the child tastes is the salt which is put into its mouth at baptism. It is washed in the water of the Holy Spirit before it tastes its mother's milk or any other, for in this country it is the custom to keep babies for a day without food. After that they put them to the breast, and as they are hungry and want to nurse they do so without anyone's having to induce them to, or to use honey to make them suck. They wrap the child in very harsh and poor little swaddling clothes, introducing hardship at once to the exiled son of Eve, who is born into this vale of tears and comes to weep.

CHAPTER X

Of some Spaniards who have ill-treated the Indians, and the end to which they came. Conclusion of the second part.

EXPERIENCE has shown frequently, in many cases, that the Spaniards who have been cruel to the Indians have died evil and violent deaths, so much so that it has become a proverb that "God will be cruel to him who is cruel to the Indians." I do not wish to relate cruelties—although I know of many, some which I have seen and others which have been told me—but I do wish to tell of the punishments which God has inflicted upon some of those who abused their Indians. One Spaniard who was cruel to the Indians, as he was traveling along a road with laden Indians, at mid-day reached a wooded place. He was beating the Indians who were carrying the loads and calling them dogs. The beating never ceased and the epithets came thick and fast. At that moment a tiger appeared and seized the Spaniard! Carrying the man in his jaws he went into the wood and ate him up. And so the cruel animal freed the gentle Indians from him who treated them so cruelly.

Another Spaniard, who was coming from Peru—that land where gold has been well won—and had with him many *tlamemes,* or Indian porters, was to pass through a wilderness. They said to him:[1] ". . . . . do not sleep at such and such a place, for there are fierce lions and tigers

1. There is a blank in the manuscript at this point.

there." But as he thought more of his greed and of making the Indians march too much, and how he could use them to shield himself, they were forced to spend the night in the open. He began to call the Indians dogs, made them all surround him, and he lay down in the middle. At midnight came the lion—or the tiger—leapt into the middle of the group, snatched out the Spaniard and ate him right near there. The same thing happened to another steward or overseer who was traveling with one hundred and fifty Indians, treating them very badly and beating them. They stopped one night to sleep in the open and the tiger came and took him from the midst of the Indians and ate him; later I was near the place where he was eaten.

These Indians have great reverence for the sacred name of Jesus as a protection against the temptations of the devil, for there have been many occasions when the devil laid hands upon them, wishing to kill them, but when they speak the name of Jesus they are freed. To many of them the devil has appeared in very terrifying form and said with great fury: "Why do you not serve me? Why do you not call upon me? Why do you not honor me as you used to do? Why have you left me? Why have you been baptized?" etc. The Indians, by crying out and saying: "Jesus! Jesus! Jesus!", are freed and have escaped from his hands. Some of them have come out of the conflict maltreated and wounded by the devil so that they have had much to tell of their experience. Thus, the name of Jesus is a consolation and a defense against all the wiles of our adversary, the devil, and God has magnified His most blessed name in the hearts of these people. They show it with outward signs, for whenever in the Gospel the name of Jesus is mentioned many Indians fall on their knees upon the ground; they are adopting this as a custom, doing as St. Paul says. God also so spread abroad the virtue of the most holy name of Jesus that even in places as yet unconquered, where no priest or friar or Spaniard has ever been, this most holy name is depicted and reverenced.[2] It is very common in this land, both written and painted in the temples and churches in gold and in silver, in feathers and gold, and there are many examples of all these different manners. In the people's houses and in

2. The cross appears occasionally in pre-Spanish paintings and carvings, and there are references in some of the early accounts to crosses discovered in places where no Spaniard had been before. This may be what Motolinía is referring to.

many other places they have it carved in wood with an ornamental border. Every Sunday and every feast day they garland and adorn it with many kinds of roses and flowers.

Well, to conclude this second part, I say: Who can fail to be astonished on seeing the new marvels and mercies that God has shown this people? Why do not the men of the earth rejoice before whose eyes God does these things, and especially those who came with good intentions and conquered such great provinces as these that God might in them be known and worshipped? Though they may occasionally have been covetous of acquiring riches, it is to be believed that it was only incidentally and remotely. Who will not believe that the men whom God endowed with reason and who found themselves so often in great hardship and danger of death, who, I say, will not believe that these men would form and reform their consciences and intentions and offer themselves to die for the Faith and to exalt it among the heathen, and that this should be their sole and principal quest? All the conquerors and all Christians and friends of God must rejoice greatly to see so great a part of the population so completely Christianized in so short a time, and so inclined to all virtue and goodness. Wherefore I beseech all those who read this to praise and glorify God in their inmost hearts. Let them use the following praises, for, according to St. Bonaventure, in them are contained and to be found all the ways of praising God that exist in the Holy Scripture: "Praise and blessing, magnification and confession, thanks and glorification, exaltation, adoration, and satisfaction be to Thee, O God, our Lord most High, for the mercies shown to these Indians newly converted to Thy Holy Faith. Amen, Amen, Amen."

In this New Spain there were always great and continuous wars, the men of some provinces against those of others, and many died either in battle or as captives taken to be sacrificed to their demons. Now, by the goodness of God they have been converted and brought into such peace and quiet and are all so lawful that a Spaniard or an Indian porter can go for three or four hundred leagues laden with bars of gold, through woods and over mountains, through towns and wilderness, without any more fear than if he were going along the street of Benavente. And it is true that at the end of this month of February, 1541, in a town called Zapotitlán, it happened that an Indian left over one hundred loads of merchandise in a place in the middle of the market, and it remained there both through the night and during the day, and not a thing was missing.[3] On market-day, which is every five days, each person stands by the merchandise that he has to sell. In the middle of the five-day period there is another small market, and for this reason the merchandise is always left in the tianquizco or market-place, except during the rainy season. But this simplicity has not reached Mexico or its vicinity.

3. Torquemada (vol. III, pp. 336-337) quotes Motolinía to the effect that the friars who were sent out in 1537 to the Gulf coast observed that the Indians of those regions always spoke the truth and "never took other people's property, even if it lay around on the road for many days." Both this and Motolinía's concluding remarks in this chapter seem to destroy the value of his previous contention that the good behaviour of the Indians is due to their conversion.

BOOK THREE

CHAPTER I

Of how the Indians noted the year in which the Spaniards came and also the year of arrival of the friars. Of certain marvelous things which occurred in the country.

THE year in which the Spaniards came and entered this land was noted particularly by these Indians in the accounts of their years as a very remarkable thing which at first caused them great fear and wonder. They were astounded to see a people come over the water—which they had never seen and never heard that it was possible—in a dress so different from theirs, so intrepid and courageous, such a small number entering all the provinces of this land with such authority and boldness,[1] as if all the natives were their vassals. They were also filled with wonder and astonishment to see the horses and what the Spaniards did when mounted on them; some of them thought that men and horses were all one, although this was only at the beginning in the first towns, for afterwards they realized that the man had a separate existence and the horse was an animal, for these people observe and notice things. When they saw the men dismount they

1. No one who reads the accounts of the conquest can fail to be as astonished as the Indians.

called the horses Castilian *mazatl,* which means Castilian 'stags,' because there was no other animal here to which they could better compare them. They called the Spaniards *teteuh,* which means 'gods,' and the Spaniards, corrupting the word, said *teules.* This name was used for more than three years, until we gave the Indians to understand that there was only one God and that they should call the Spaniards Christians. Some foolish Spaniards took offense at this and complained. Filled with indignation against us, they said that we were depriving them of their name. The fools did this in all seriousness, not considering that they were usurping a name that belongs to God alone. After many of the Indians were baptized they then called the conquerors Spaniards.

The Indians also noted and marked the year when the twelve friars arrived together. Although some Franciscan friars came among the Spaniards in the beginning, the Indians paid no particular attention to them, either because they were few and scattered or because of the wars in which the Indians were involved. This year—that of the coming of the twelve Franciscans—they noted and considered more important than others, for they began to reckon from that time, as if it were the year of the coming or advent of God; and so they commonly say: "The year that Our Lord came; the year that the Faith came." For as soon as the friars reached Mexico, within a fortnight they held a Chapter meeting and assigned the twelve friars and the other five who were already in Mexico. All these seventeen were divided among the principal provinces of this land [2] and we began at once to learn the language and to preach with interpreters. There were also in Mexico two or three other priests and not many Spaniards, for in the course of about one year Pedro de Alvarado left there with a good-sized squadron of infantry and a fair number of mounted men bound for Cuauhtemallan. Then another troop went with Cristóbal de Olid to Las Higueras, and immediately after him Francisco de las Casas went with another. Not many days afterwards the Marquis Hernando Cortés set out with all the finest men and most of the horses that he had, so that I should say that there might be left in Mexico as many as fifty horses and approximately two hundred Spanish foot soldiers.

At this time all the native rulers of the lands were united and conspiring to rise and kill all the Christians, and many of the old lords were

2. Father Martín de Valencia with four companions stayed in Mexico, the remaining twelve were sent, in groups of four, to Texcoco, Tlaxcala, and Huejotzingo. See Torquemada, vol. III, p. 28.

still living. When the Spaniards came all the rulers and all the provinces differed greatly and were continually involved in wars against each other; but at this time of which I am speaking, when all those people left Mexico, I saw all the rulers so united and bound together and so prepared for war that they were very certain of victory if they undertook it. It would have been so in fact had not God miraculously blinded and confused them. The friars also played an important part, both by their prayers and preaching and also by the trouble that they took to pacify the quarrelsome factions among the Spaniards which were at that time very bitter and so hostile that they came to blows. There was no one to reconcile them or stand between their swords and lances except the friars, to whom God gave grace to bring about a reconciliation. Passions were as violently hostile as they say that they are now among the Spaniards in Peru. (God send them someone to pacify them, although they say that they want neither peace nor friars.) I could easily write more at length in this matter of the factions in Mexico, because I was present at everything that happened, but it seems to me that that would involve me in writing a history of men.

At this same time there were discovered some very rich silver mines[3] to which many of the Spaniards went, leaving very few in Mexico, where there were already so few. Those who wanted to go ran an even greater risk of losing their lives, for they were blinded by their covetousness and did not realize the dangers of the situation. Influenced by the reproofs, preaching, and advice of the friars, given in general as well as to individuals, they stationed guards, kept watch in the city, silenced the talk about mines, and ordered the people who were in outlying estates to be brought into the city. A few days later God Himself remedied the trouble by closing those mines with a great mountain which he threw upon them, so that they have never been found since. On the other hand, the friars, working with the Indians who by this time knew them and listened to their advice, checked the Indians in many ways and manners that it would take too long to tell. The reward which they received for this was to have

3. In the province of Michoacán, in the year 1525, according to Torquemada (bk. III, chap. XLIV, p. 336). In this passage, Torquemada gives alternative explanations of the disappearance of the mine: "Some say that a mountain fell upon it and choked it, others that the Indians blocked it up so skillfully that no trace of it has ever been found." In book XV, chapter XXII, he brings the subject up again and explains the disappearance as Motolinía does: "But God arranged it better by throwing a great mountain upon the mines, so that they were concealed from the eyes of men and never more were seen."

people say: "These friars are destroying us and preventing our being rich and making slaves of the Indians. They bring about the lowering of the tributes and defend the Indians and favor them against us. They are a set of old so and sos." The Spaniards fail to consider that if it were not for the friars, they would have no servants, either in their houses or on their farms, for they would have killed them all off, as is proved by experience in Santo Domingo and the other islands, where the Indians have been exterminated.

As for the rest, these native Indians are so timid and silent that, for this reason, people do not know of the many great miracles that God performs among them. Wherever there is a house of our Father St. Francis I see many sick Indians who come there with all kinds of diseases, many of them very dangerous, and then I see them restored and well, returning with great joy to their homes and lands. I know that they have a particular devotion to the habit and cord of St. Francis. This cord has saved many pregnant women from dangerous births, and this has happened many times and in many towns. Here in Tlaxcallan it is very common and was well demonstrated not many days ago. The doorkeeper of the monastery therefore has a cord to give to those who come to ask for it, though I really believe that the devotion which they have for the cord is as effective as the virtue of the cord itself, although I also believe that its virtue is not small, as will be clearly shown by what I am now going to tell.

In a town called Atlacuihuaya, a league from Mexico and near Chapultepec, the source of the water that runs to Mexico, there fell ill the son of a man named Domingo, who was by profession a *tezozonqui,* that is to say a carpenter or stoneworker. This man and his wife and children are devoted followers of St. Francis and his friars. One of the children fell ill, a boy of seven or eight years named Ascensio. In this country it is the custom to give a child the name of the day on which it is born. Those who are baptized as adults take the name of the day on which they are baptized. This boy was called Ascensio because he was born on Ascension day. When he was taken sick they came to the monastery, invoking the name of St. Francis, and as the child's illness increased the parents came more and more importunately to seek the help and favor of the saint. As God had ordained what was to be, He permitted the child Ascensio to die. He died one day in the morning about two hours after sunrise, but his death did not stop his parents, who, weeping bitterly, continued to call upon St. Francis, in whom they had great confidence. After midday they wrapped the child in his shroud, and before they did so many people saw that the child was dead, cold and stiff, and the grave was dug. Even though they were ready to carry him to the church, his parents say today that they always hoped that St. Francis would succeed in obtaining from God the favor of the child's life and would resuscitate him for them. At the hour when they were about to carry him to be buried, as his parents began once more to pray and call upon St. Francis, the child began to move. They quickly untied and unwound the shroud, and the child who was dead came back to life.

This happened at about vesper time, and all those who were present —and there were many of them—were astounded and greatly comforted. They reported the matter to the friars of St. Francis, and there came to the house the friar who was responsible for teaching them. His name was Fray Pedro de Gante. When he arrived with his companion he saw the child alive and well. Having had the facts vouched for by the child's parents and by all of those present, who were trustworthy, they called together the whole town and before them all the child's father gave testimony that it was true that his son had died and had been resuscitated. This miracle was published and spread abroad through all the towns of the neighborhood, and because of it many were strengthened in the Faith and began to believe the other marvels and miracles of Our Redeemer and of His saints, about which the friars preach to them. This miracle, just as I write it here, I received from the above-mentioned Fray Pedro de Gante, who was teacher of the children of Mexico and its surrounding territory, and was, for more than eleven years, responsible for visiting and teaching those towns.

In this land the devotion of both Spaniards and natives to St. Francis is so great, and God has in his name performed so many miracles and marvels, and so openly, that it may truly be said that God had reserved for him the conversion of those Indians, as He gave to his other apostles the conversion of other Indies and distant lands. From what I say here and from what I have seen, I suspect and even believe that one of the secret things that passed between Christ and Saint Francis in that seraphic conversation on Mount Averna [4]—which Saint Francis never told as long

4. The retreat in the Apennines in which St. Francis beheld the seraphic vision and received the stigmata. This name is variously given in English: *Mt. Alverno,* according to the Encyclopedia Britannica, and *LaVerna,* according to the Catholic Encyclopedia.

as he lived—was the subject of these riches which God had in reserve for him here where His holy religion must spread and extend greatly. I maintain that Saint Francis, the father of many peoples, foresaw and knew about this day.

Chapter II

Of the friars who have died in the conversion of the Indians of New Spain. Account of the life of Fray Martín de Valencia, which is very worthy of being noted and remembered.

More than thirty Friars Minor have now died in New Spain where they persevered and labored faithfully in the conversion of the Indians. They ended their days full of the obedience of their profession, exercised in the love of God and of their neighbor and in the confession of our holy Faith, and receiving the sacraments. Some of them were adorned with many virtues, but the one amongst them all who gave the greatest example of holiness and wisdom, both in Old Spain and in New Spain, was Fray Martín de Valencia, of blessed memory, first prelate and custodian in New Spain. He was the first whom God sent to this New World with apostolic authority.

I would not wish to have anyone give greater value than human and divine laws permit and reason demands to the things that I shall here relate. Let Him be judge Who is judge of the living and the dead, in Whose sight all mortal lives are clear and manifest, and leave the decision to His Holy Church at whose feet this whole work is laid. For men may be deceived in their judgments and opinions. God is always upright in the weighing of His judgment, but men are not; wherefore St. Augustine says that the Church venerates many who are in hell, that is to say, many of those who are not canonized by the Roman Church under the inspiration of the Holy Spirit. With this reservation I shall begin to write as briefly as I can the life of that servant of God, Fray Martín de Valencia, although I know that another friar and follower of his has already written of it at greater length.[1]

1. Fray Francisco Ximénez, one of Fray Martín de Valencia's eleven companions. See Torquemada, vol. III, p. 393.

This good man was born in the town called Valencia de Don Juan, which lies between the city of León and the town of Benavente, on the bank of the river Esla. It is in the bishopric of Oviedo. There exists in New Spain no account of his youth, only the story of the life that he led during his middle and last years. He took the habit in the town of Mayorga, which belongs to the Conde de Benavente, in a convent of the province of Santiago, one of the most ancient houses in Spain.

He had as his teacher Fray Juan de Argumanes, who was later Provincial of the Province of Santiago. By Fray Juan's teaching and his own diligent study the young man's understanding was enlightened to imitate the life of Our Redeemer, Jesus Christ. Wherefore, after he had taken his vows, when they took him to the town of Valencia, which is very near Mayorga, feeling that his mind was distracted by being among his relatives and friends he begged his companions to allow him to leave that town quickly. Then, taking off his habit, he hung it around his neck so that it covered his chest, threw the cord around his neck like a criminal and, naked except for his underclothes, he went out in broad daylight through the middle of the town and in sight of his friends and relatives, his companions leading him by the cord.

After he began to say Mass he grew continually from virtue to virtue, for besides what I myself saw in him—and I knew him for more than twenty years—I have heard many good religious say that in their time they had known no other who performed such penances or persevered always with such firmness in taking upon himself the burden of the Cross of Christ. When he went to Chapter meetings in other convents or provinces his self-discipline, humility, and poverty seemed to be a reproof to all. As he was much given to prayer and contemplation he asked permission from his Provincial to go to live in certain oratories of the province of Santiago called Los Angeles and El Hoyo. They are not very far from Ciudad Rodrigo and are houses removed from intercourse with the world, planned for contemplation and prayer.

When this servant of God had obtained permission to go and live at Santa María del Hoyo, and tried in that place to retire within himself and to give himself to God, the Enemy arranged many sorts of temptations for him, God permitting it for the good of his soul. He began to feel a great dryness and hardness of spirit and indifference in prayer. He abhorred the solitude. The trees seemed to him to be demons. He could not look upon the friars with love and charity. He took no pleasure in anything spiritual, and when he tried to pray he did it with great heaviness of spirit. He lived in torment.

There came to him a terrible temptation, which he could not throw off, to blaspheme against the Faith. It also seemed to him that when he celebrated and said Mass he did not consecrate, and he received Communion most unwillingly, as if he were forcing himself. This idea troubled him so much that he did not want to celebrate Mass and was unable to eat. With all these temptations he had grown so thin that he seemed to be nothing but skin and bones, and yet he thought that he was well and strong. This subtle temptation Satan was using to overthrow him in this way: when he should see that his victim was entirely deprived of natural strength he would leave him and so the good friar would collapse and not be able to recover himself, and would lose his mind. For this purpose Satan also kept Fray Martín awake at night, which is a great cause of madness. But as Our Lord never abandons His own, nor wishes them to fall, nor exposes anyone to more temptation than he can endure, He allowed him to suffer the temptation as long as he could without damage to his soul and then turned it to his advantage by allowing a poor woman to awaken him and give him a remedy for his temptation. This is no small evidence of the greatness of God; for He chooses, not the wise, but the simple-minded and humble to be instruments of His mercy, and so He did with this simple woman of whom I speak.

As this man of God went to ask for bread in a village called Robleda, four leagues from El Hoyo, the sister of the friars[2] of that village, seeing him so thin and weakened, said to him: "Oh Father, what is the matter with you? Why are you going about looking as if you were about to die of emaciation? Why don't you take care of yourself? For it looks as if you were going to die." These words penetrated the heart of that servant of God as if they had been spoken by an angel and, like one who awakens from a heavy sleep, he began to open the eyes of his understanding and to think how he was eating practically nothing. And he said to himself: "Truly, this is a temptation of the devil," and commending himself to God that He might enlighten him and deliver him from the blindness in which the devil held him, he changed his manner of life. Satan, seeing himself discovered, left him and the temptation ceased. Then the

2. Spanish: *la hermana de los frailes.* I do not know what this means.

man of God began to feel so great a weakness and faintness that he could scarcely stand. From then on he began to eat.

This experience taught him to perceive the wiles and snares of the devil. After he had been freed from those temptations, he enjoyed great peace and serenity of spirit. He delighted in the solitude, and the trees that he had formerly abhorred, with the birds that sang in them, now appeared to him a paradise. After that, wherever he was, he immediately planted a grove of trees; and when he became a prelate he asked everyone to plant trees, not only fruit trees but forest trees as well, so that the friars might go to pray amongst them.

God comforted him also in the celebration of Mass, which he now said with great devotion and after much preparation, for after matins he slept not at all, or very little, the better to prepare himself. He almost always said Mass very early, and with many heartfelt tears which bathed and adorned his face like pearls. He celebrated almost every day and usually confessed every third day.

Also from then on he felt a great love for the other friars, and when one arrived from outside the community he received him with such joy and love that he seemed to wish to take him into his heart. He delighted in the possessions and virtues of others as if they were his own. And so, as he persevered in this spirit of charity, God brought him to a profound love of his neighbor, so great that from his general love for the souls of men there grew the desire to suffer martyrdom and to go among the heathen to convert them and preach to them. That desire and holy zeal this servant of God achieved with much toil and many penitential practices, fasts, scourgings, vigils and very continuous prayers.

As he persevered in his holy desires the Lord was pleased to visit and console him in this way: One night in Advent when he was at matins, as soon as the office commenced he began to experience a new kind of devotion and great spiritual consolation and there came to his memory the conversion of the heathen. As he meditated on this he found in many passages of the psalms which he was reciting devout allusions to this, especially in that psalm which begins: "Eripe me de inimicis meis,"[3] This servant of God said to himself: "Oh, when shall this be? When shall this prophecy be fulfilled? Would I not be worthy to see this conversion, since we are now in the evening and end of our days and in the last age of the world?"

3. "Deliver me from mine enemies, O my God." Ps. 59.

All during the psalms the holy man was occupied with these pious desires, full of charity and love of his neighbor; by divine dispensation, although he was neither cantor in the choir nor a reader for that week, they gave him the duty of reading the lessons. He arose and began to read them. The lessons themselves, which were from the prophet Isaiah and appropriate to his purpose, excited his spirit more and more, to such an extent that as he stood reading from the pulpit he saw in the spirit a very great multitude of heathen souls that were converted and came to the Faith and to baptism. So great was the delight and joy that his soul felt within itself that he could neither repress nor contain himself, and, praising and blessing God, he said aloud three times: "Praised be Christ; praised be Christ; praised be Christ!" He said this in a very loud voice because it was not in his power to do otherwise. The friars, seeing that he appeared to be beside himself and not knowing the mystery, thought that he was going mad, and they took him and carried him to a cell and, nailing up the windows and locking the door, they went back to finish matins. He stayed in prison in a dazed condition until the day was fairly advanced, when he came to and, as he found himself shut up and in the dark, he tried to open the window, for he had not perceived that they had nailed it up. When he could not open it they say that he smiled, realizing the friars' fears that, being mad, he might throw himself out of the window. When he found himself thus imprisoned he began to think again and to contemplate the vision that he had seen and to beseech God to permit him to see it with his physical eyes. From that time on his desire increased to go among the heathen and preach to them and convert them to the Faith of Christ.

This vision Our Lord willed that His servant should see fulfilled in this New Spain. The first year that he came to this land, when he visited seven or eight towns near Mexico and many Indians gathered together to be taught and many came to the Faith and were baptized, seeing such evidence of Christianity in them and believing that it would go on increasing (as it did), he said to his companion: "Now I see fulfilled what the Lord showed me in the spirit"! Then he told him the vision that he had had in Spain in the monastery of Santa María del Hoyo in Estremadura.

Before that, not knowing when or how the vision that God had shown him was to be realized, he began to wish to go to heathen lands and to ask this from God with many prayers. He began also to mortify the flesh and bring it into subjection with fastings and scourgings. He was in the habit of scourging himself twice in addition to the times that the community did, so that, by the grace of God, he might by his exercise prepare himself to suffer martyrdom. As the rule of the Friars Minor says: "If any friar be moved by divine inspiration to wish to go among the Moors or other heathen, let him ask his Provincial for permission to carry out his wishes," so this servant of God three times asked for this permission. On one of these occasions he had to cross a river which was deep and so swift that he had enough to do to get himself across and was obliged to drop some books that he was carrying, among which was a Bible. The stream carried them a good distance while Fray Martín was commending them to God and praying Him to keep them from harm and beseeching Our Lady not to let him lose his books, in which he had noted many things for his own spiritual consolation. Quite a distance downstream he got them out of the river without their having suffered any damage from the water. On none of these occasions did his Provincial grant the permission that he asked, but he never ceased to beg God for it with very constant prayers, praying also to the Mother of God that by her intercession he might achieve and win it. For her he had a very special devotion and celebrated her feasts and festivals and octaves with all the solemnity he could and with such great joy that it was clearly evident that it came from his inmost heart.

At this time Fray Juan de Guadalupe of blessed memory was in the custodia of La Piedad, living, with other companions, in the greatest poverty. Fray Martín de Valencia made every effort to go there and join his company, and much trouble it cost him to achieve this. When, with great difficulty, he had obtained permission he dwelt with Fray Juan for some time. But as that province, which at that time was only a custodia, still aroused much opposition and had many opponents in other provinces as well—perhaps because its extreme poverty and harsh life were intolerable, perhaps because many good friars tried to join the company of the aforesaid Fray Juan de Guadalupe, who had been given permission from the Pope to receive them—its opponents tried to enlist against it the favor of the Catholic Sovereigns and of the King of Portugal, so that those friars might be driven out of their kingdoms. This persecution increased to such an extent that there came a time when the houses and monasteries were seized and some of them torn down and the friars, persecuted on all sides, took refuge on an island between two rivers which is neither in Castile nor in Portugal. The two rivers are the Tagus and the Guadiana. There they lived for some days under great difficulties until this persecution died out and, God helping those who were so zealous and so eager to keep their vows perfectly, they rebuilt their monasteries and added others. Of these monasteries they formed the province of La Pieded in Portugal, and four other houses were left in Castile.

At this time the friars of the province of Santiago besought Fray Martín de Valencia to come back to his own province, promising that they would give him a house such as he desired, in which he could maintain all the perfection and strictness that he wished. He accepted and built a house near Belvis and there established a monastery called Santa María del Berrocal, where he lived for some years, giving such a good example and such instruction both in the town of Belvis and in all the district that people looked upon him as an apostle, and all loved and obeyed him as a father.

While he was living in this monastery people were talking a great deal about a certain servant of God, the pious woman of Barco de Avila, to whom God communicated many secrets. As Fray Martín always kept in his memory the vision he had seen and in his soul the assurance of seeing it realized, he decided to go and visit this holy woman to ask her opinion and advice about the accomplishment of his desire, which was to go among the heathen. She, when she had heard his errand and commended him to God, replied that it was not the will of God that he should try to go at that time, but when the hour came God would call him, and he might be quite sure of that.

After some time the custodia of San Gabriel was formed from those four houses[4] which I said belonged to the followers of Fray Juan de Guadalupe plus seven others given by the province of Santiago, one of which was the monastery of Belvis which Fray Martín himself had built. All of them fell within the boundaries of the province of Santiago. The friars of all eleven houses met in the year of Our Lord 1516, on the eve of the feast of the Conception of Our Lady, and Fray Miguel de Córdoba, a man of lofty contemplation, was elected first custodian. At this same Chapter meeting the Count of Feria entreated them to assign the servant

4. The manuscript reads: *Pasado algún tiempo hízosele custodia de San Gabriel provincia de aquellas cuatro casas . . .* which makes no sense. Ramírez emends as follows: *Pasado algún tiempo hízose la custodia de San Gabriel de aquellas cuatro casas . . .* using as a guide Torquemada's account, which is based on Motolinía. See Torquemada vol. III, p. 395.

of God, Fray Martín de Valencia, to the monastery of San Onofre de la Lapa, one of the seven mentioned above. It is two leagues from Zafra and lies within the territory of the Count. This request was made because of the fame of Fray Martín's saintliness and for the consolation of the Count. God took the friar there that he might make peace and harmony between the two houses which had shortly before been united, that is to say, the houses of Priego and Feria. For though the Marquis and Marchioness were a good married couple and very Catholic Christians, the knights and servants of those two houses were very hostile. Then the Marquis sent for Fray Martín, who stayed with him in Montillo during one Lent, preaching and hearing confessions, and also acting as confessor to the Marquis. He brought about such peace and harmony between the two houses that he seemed to them more like an angel of the Lord than an earthly being, and all attributed to his prayers the harmony of the two houses.

His work was also very fruitful among the people of that town, and they were all much edified and comforted by the great example which he gave them during that Lent. It was the same wherever he lived, both within the monasteries and outside in the district, because everyone considered him a model of wisdom and saintliness.

Afterward, in the year 1518, on the eve of the Assumption of Our Lady that custodia of San Gabriel was made into a province and Fray Martín de Valencia was elected as first Provincial. In this capacity he set a great example of humility and penance, preaching and exhorting his friars more by example than by words, and though he was always increasing his penitential practices he made a special effort during that time, though he always wore a hair shirt and fasted on many days besides those indicated by the Church and by the Rule of the Order. He carried with him ashes to put in his food and sometimes in the soup, and if what he was eating had a pleasant taste, he would pour some water on it as a sauce, remembering the gall and vinegar that they gave to Christ.

Many friars and many good religious came to the province because of his fine reputation, and the servant of God received them lovingly. Often when he wanted to hold a Chapter meeting of the friars and hear the faults of the others, he first accused himself before them all, not so much on his own account as to give an example of humility, for he considered himself unworthy that another person should tell his faults to him. Thus in the presence of them all he scourged himself and then, rising, he kissed the feet of his friars. With such an example there was no subordinate who did not humble himself to the earth. When he had finished this he would begin his duties as prelate and, when he was seated in his place with pastoral authority, all the subordinates would recount their faults, as is the custom in religious orders, and the servant of God would reprove them charitably. Afterward he would speak to them from the heart, now about the virtue of poverty, now about obedience and humility, now about prayer. He talked more at length and more frequently concerning the latter, as he always practiced it himself.

Having governed the province of San Gabriel, and possessed always by his continual desire to go among the heathen, at the moment when he least expected it God called him in this manner. When the most reverend Fray Francisco de los Angeles was General of the Order and was making a round of visits, he came to the province of San Gabriel and held a Chapter meeting at the monastery of Belvis on St. Francis' day of the year 1523, two years after this land had been conquered by Hernando Cortés and his companions. At this chapter the general called Fray Martín de Valencia and talked long and seriously with him, telling him how the land of New Spain was newly discovered and conquered and how, judging by the news of the great numbers of native people and their character, he believed and hoped that a rich spiritual harvest would be gathered if there were laborers like Fray Martín. He said that he, Fray Francisco, had decided to go himself just at the time that they elected him Minister General, an office which interfered with the journey that he so greatly desired to make. Therefore he was asking Fray Martín to go with twelve companions, for if he would do it, Fray Francisco's confidence in the Divine Goodness assured him that the harvest and the conversions that they hoped for from Fray Martín's going would be very great.

This man of God had for so long a time been hoping that the Lord would fulfill his desires that one can well imagine what joy and gladness must have filled his soul at this news and what thanks he must have given to Our Lord. Like an obedient son he at once agreed to come, and then he remembered what the pious woman of Barco de Avila had said to him. Then, as quickly as he could, he chose his twelve companions and, having received the blessing of their Superior and General, they set out from the harbor of San Lúcar de Barrameda on the day of the Conversion of St. Paul, which in that year fell on a Tuesday. They reached la Gomera[5] on

5. One of the smaller of the Canary Islands.

the fourth of February and there said Mass in the church of Santa María del Paso and very devoutly received the Body of Our Redeemer and then reëmbarked. They reached the Island of San Juan and disembarked in Puerto Rico after twenty-seven days of sailing, on the third day of March, which in that year was mid-Lent. They stayed there in the Island of San Juan for ten days and left on Passion Sunday; the following Wednesday they entered Santo Domingo. They stayed in the Island of Española for six weeks and then embarked and came to the Island of Cuba, where they landed on the last day of April. They stayed only three days in Trinidad. They reëmbarked and came to San Juan de Ulúa on the twelfth of May, which that year was the eve of Pentecost, and stayed ten days in Medellín From there, having first given thanks to Our Lord for the good voyage that He had granted them, they came to Mexico and at once divided themselves among the principal provinces.

During all this trip Father Martín suffered great hardship, for as he was elderly and always went on foot and barefoot and the Lord often visited him with infirmities, he became very much exhausted. In order, like a good leader, to set an example, he always went ahead and would not take, to satisfy his needs, anything more than his companions did, nor even as much, not wishing to give any occasion for slackness where he had come to make a new planting. And so he suffered great toil, for in addition to his usual penance and abstinence, which was very great, and to the great amount of time that he spent in prayer, he worked hard to learn the language; but as he was already fifty years old and also because he did not wish to give up what God had communicated to him, he never did succeed with the language, although he tried three or four times to learn it. He did master some of the common words in order to teach the children to read, at which he worked very hard.

Because he could not preach in the language of the Indians, he took great pleasure in hearing others preach, and he would place himself beside them and engage in mental prayer, beseeching God to send his grace to the preacher and to those who heard him. In his old age also he increased his penitential practices, following the example of the holy Abbot Hilarion who ordinarily fasted four days during the week, eating nothing but bread and vegetables. In his time many of his subordinates, seeing that in spite of his age he set them such an example, imitated him. He also adopted the practice of kneeling frequently during the day and remaining each time on his knees for a quarter of an hour, which appeared to cause him a great deal of difficulty, for at the end of this exercise he would be panting and exhausted. In this practice he apparently imitated the glorious apostles St. James the younger and St. Bartholomew, for of both of them we read that they practiced this penance.

From Passion Sunday to Easter Sunday he meditated so much more intensely than at other times upon the Passion of the Son of God that the physical effect of his meditation was very apparent. Once in the season of which I speak a certain friar, a good religious, seeing him very thin and weak, asked him: "Father, are you ill? You certainly seem very thin and very weak. If it is not illness, will your Reverence tell me the cause of your debility?" He answered: "Believe me, Brother, since you compel me to tell you the truth, during the two weeks from Passion Sunday, which is commonly called Lazarus' Sunday, till Easter my spirit suffers so much that I cannot endure it without my body's also feeling it and showing it as you see." At Easter he recovered his strength again. These things this man of God did not tell to everyone, but only to those friars who were his most intimate friends, to whom he felt that it was right and suitable to tell them, for he was much averse to telling his secrets to anyone. That this is the truth will be proved by what I shall now relate. While he was in Spain at the monastery of Belvis preaching the Passion, when he reached the point at which Our Lord was nailed to the Cross his suffering was so great that his spirit left him and he went into a trance and became as rigid as a stick until they took him out of the pulpit. Twice again the same thing happened to him, although once, when he was living in the monastery of La Lapa, he revived sooner and tried to finish his sermon on the Passion, but the people had already left the monastery.

However much he fled from the world and from the friars to concentrate upon God alone, at times it was useless to hide himself, for so many affairs depended on him, both in connection with his office and with the cases of conscience about which he was consulted that they would not let him be. Very often those who went in search of him found him so far away in spirit than when they spoke to him he answered like a person waking from a heavy sleep. At other times, although he talked and communicated with the friars, it seemed as if he neither heard nor saw because his spirit was occupied with God. He was so harsh with his body that he scarcely allowed it to take the necessary amount of either food or sleep. In his illnesses, when he was an old man, he would have no bed but a pallet or a plank, nor would he drink even a little wine or take any other medicine. Although he was often ill we never saw him treated by a doctor nor did he bother with any medicines except the one which brought health to his soul.

This servant of God, Fray Martín de Valencia, lived in New Spain for ten years; when he came here he was fifty, which makes sixty in all. Of the ten years that I said he lived in New Spain he was Provincial of his Order for six years, and for four, Guardian in Tlaxcallan. He built that monastery and named it 'The Mother of God.' While he lived in that house he taught the children from their A B C's up to reading Latin, made them at times practice mental prayer and, after matins, sang hymns with them. He also taught them to stand with arms outstretched in the form of the Cross while reciting seven Pater Nosters and seven Ave María's, which he was in the habit of doing himself. He taught all the Indians, big and little, by example and by word, and therefore always had an interpreter. It is worth noting that three interpreters that he had all became friars and turned out to be very good religious.

The last year, when of his own will he held no office, he chose to live in a town called Tlalmanalco, which is eight leagues from Mexico. Near this monastery is another which is visited from Tlalmanalco, in a town called Amaquemecan. It is a very quiet house very well adapted for prayer, for it stands on the side of a little terrace and is a very devout hermitage. Near this house is a holy cave, very suitable for this servant of God to retire to at times for prayer. He used at times to come out of the cave into a grove in which there was one very big tree under which he went to pray in the morning, and they assure me that when he prayed there the tree used to be filled with birds whose song made a sweet harmony that comforted him greatly, so that he praised and blessed the Lord. When he left, the birds also went away, and after his death the birds never gathered there again in that manner. Both these things were noticed by many who had some conversation there with this servant of God: both the fact of their coming together and flying away on his account and the fact that they never appeared again after his death. I have been informed by a religious of goodly life that in that hermitage of Amaquemecan Saint Francis and Saint Anthony appeared to the man of God and departed from his presence leaving him greatly comforted.

While he was very much at peace leading this kind of life, Death came to him, the debt we all must pay. On the day of Saint Gabriel, being then in good health, he said to a companion: "The end is coming." His companion answered: "The end of what?" He kept silent and a while later said: "My head is aching." From then on his illness increased. He went with his companion to the convent of San Luis in Tlalmanalco, and as his illness grew worse, after he had received the Sacraments, they were going to take him, at the command of the Guardian, to Mexico to be treated, although this was much against his will. Placing him in a chair they carried him to the wharf, which is two leagues from Tlalmanalco, intending to put him into a boat to take him to Mexico by water. There were three friars with him. When they reached the wharf he felt that death was near and commending his soul to God who had made it, he died there in that field or river-bank.

He himself had said many years before that he was not to die in the house or in a bed, but out in the country, and so it apparently was fulfilled. He was ill only four days. He died on the eve of Passion Sunday, that is on Saturday, the day of San Benito, which is the twenty-first of March, in the year of Our Lord 1534. They took his body back to bury it in the monastery of San Luis in Tlalmanalco.

When the news of this good man's death was heard by the provincial or custodian who was eight leagues away, he came at once, and though Fray Martín had been buried four days before, he ordered him to be disinterred and placed in a coffin and said for him the Mass of Saint Gabriel because he knew that the dead man had a special devotion for that saint. At this Mass a certain trustworthy person (trustworthy, to judge by his manner and at the time at which he said it), said that he saw this servant of God, Fray Martín de Valencia, standing in front of his own tomb, dressed in habit and cord, with his hands crossed inside his sleeves and eyes cast down, and that he stood thus from the beginning of the Gloria until after the Communion. It is no marvel that this good man should have needed some prayers for his soul, for we read that men of great saintliness have needed them and have been kept a while in purgatory, though this has not prevented their performing miracles. They have told me that a dead man, commended to him, was brought back to life and that a sick woman who called upon him with devotion was cured; that a friar who was assailed by violent temptation was delivered from it by him, and many other things which, because I have not sufficient certainty about them, I neither believe nor disbelieve; but I call upon him as upon a friend of God whom I piously believe to be with God in His Glory, and I invoke his aid and intercession.

The names of the friars who came from Spain with this holy man are: Fray Francisco de Soto, Fray Martín de la Coruña, Fray Antonio de Ciudad Rodrigo, Fray García de Cisneros, Fray Juan de Ribas, Fray Francisco Jiménez, Fray Juan Juárez, Fray Luis de Fuensalida, and Fray Toribio Motolinía. These ten were priests and there were two lay brothers, Fray Juan de Palos and Fray Andrés de Córdoba.[6] All of the priests had taken the habit in the province of Santiago. Others came later who have worked and are still working hard at this holy task of converting the Indians. Their names I believe that God has written in His Book of Life rather than those of some who also came from Spain and, though they seemed to be good religious, have not persevered, and of others who devote themselves to preaching only to the Spaniards. Although for a time these find great comfort as long as their preaching is watered with the water of human praise, as soon as this lure fails they find themselves as dry as a stick and finally return to Castile. I think that this comes upon them as a judgment from God because He does not wish that those who come here should content themselves with preaching only to the Spaniards, for there was better opportunity for that in Spain. He wants them also to be of service to the Indians, as to people who are in greater need, and for whom they were called and sent. It is true that God has punished in many ways those who hate or abuse this people. Even those friars who are indifferent to these Indians or have a sort of dislike for them God makes unhappy, and they live here as if in torment until the country throws them off and casts them aside as dead and useless bodies. For this reason some of them have said in Spain things which are far from the truth, thinking perhaps that they were true, because while they were here God kept them blinded.

God also permits the Indians to scorn these friars, not receiving them into their towns and sometimes going elsewhere in search of the sacraments because they feel that the friars do not love them as they should. It

6. See above, bk. I, ch. I. The ten priests include Fray Martín de Valencia. As originally constituted the group consisted of twelve friars besides Fray Martín. However, one of them, Fray Joseph de la Coruña, was left in Spain to attend to certain business connected with the mission. Also, the lay brother Fray Juan de Palos took the place of a Fray Bernardino de la Torre, who left the group before they sailed. See Torquemada, vol. III, p. 17.

has happened that when such friars came to the towns the Indians fled from them. In particular in a town called Yeticlatlan a friar of a certain order which has not been very favorable to the Indians in word or deed came to this town and wished to baptize the children. The Spaniard to whom the people of this town had been entrusted took great pains to assemble the children and all the rest of the population, because it was a long time since any friar had visited the town and they were longing for the arrival of a priest. In the morning, when the friar went with the Spaniard from his rooms to the church where the people were assembled and the Indians saw the friar in some unfavorable light, they were instantly in a turmoil and fled in all directions saying: *Amo, amo,* which means: 'No, no, we do not want this man to baptize us or our children.' And neither the Spaniard nor the friars could make them assemble until later there came to the town the friars whom they wanted. This caused no little astonishment to the Spaniard who was in charge of them, and he used to tell it as a remarkable thing.

Although this was one particular instance, I say in general of all friars of all orders who come here that those of them who do not work faithfully here and those who go back to Castile will be asked by God for a strict account of how they employed the talent that he entrusted to them. What then shall I say of the Spanish laity, who have been and are cruel and tyrannous to the Indians, who consider only their own interests and the greed which blinds them, wanting to hold the Indians as slaves and enrich themselves with their sweat and toil? I have often heard that the Spaniards who were cruel to the Indians died at the hands of these same Indians, or died very miserable deaths, and I have heard many of them named. Since I have been in this country I have often seen it myself and observed it in the cases of persons whom I knew and had reproved for their treatment of the Indians.

CHAPTER III

Of the fact that no one should be praised in this life; of the difficulty that they experienced in getting away from the Indians their many wives; of how this land has been governed since the royal audiencia was established.

ACCORDING to the counsel of the sage, no man in this poor life should be unreservedly praised because he is still sailing upon this great and perilous sea and does not know whether the day will come when he can make a safe harbor. He alone can rightly be praised whom God has guided so that he is in safety and has reached the port of salvation; for the Gloria is sung only at the end. And this is my intention: to praise no living man in particular, but to sing the praise of the good life and example of the Friars Minor in this land. Obeying God, they departed from their own land, leaving their relatives and parents, leaving the houses and monasteries where they dwelt, practicing great abstinence and even greater penitential exercises. All of these houses are set apart from the towns and many of them built in the mountains and given over to prayer and contemplation.

Many of these men came desirous of martyrdom, had tried for a long time to achieve it, and had sought permission to go out among the heathen, although up to the present God has not willed that they should suffer the martyrdom of blood. But He brought them to this land of Canaan that they might build Him a new altar amongst this gentile and heathen people, and propagate and spread abroad His holy Name and Faith. This appears in many chapters of this book in the accounts of the towns and provinces that they converted and baptized at the beginning of the conversion when the multitude came to be baptized, and those who came were so many that it often happened that the priests could not lift the jar which they used, because their arms were so tired. Even though they changed from the right arm to the left, both arms got tired and they had calluses and even sores on their hands from holding the jar. It happened to one friar, who had recently shaved his head and his beard, that as he was baptizing many Indians in a big courtyard—for at that time there were as yet no churches—and the sun was blazing, it burned all his head and face so that the skin peeled off. At that time it would happen that a single priest would baptize in one day four, five or six thousand, and in

Xochimilco two priests together baptized in one day over fifteen thousand. One of them helped at times and then rested; he baptized not many over five thousand; the other, who bore the brunt of the work, baptized over ten thousand by actual count. Because those who sought baptism were so many the friars would visit and baptize three and four towns in a day and perform the rite many times daily.

The Indians would come out to receive them and meet them along the roads and give them many roses and flowers and sometimes cocoa, which is a drink very much used in this country, especially in the hot season. This respect and welcome that they give to the friars is the result of the commands of the Marquis of the Valley, Don Hernando Cortés, for from the beginning he ordered them to be very reverent and respectful to the priests, just as they used to be to the ministers of their idols. At that time they used also to give formal welcome to the Spaniards, which not all are now willing to allow and they have ordered the Indians not to do it, but all this has not sufficed to prevent it in some places.

Within six months after the friars came to this country, they began to preach, sometimes by using interpreters and sometimes by writing;[1] but since they began to speak the language they preach very frequently on Sundays and feast days and often on weekdays. On one day they would make the rounds and visit many parishes and towns. There are days when they preach two or three times, and when they have finished preaching there are always some people to be baptized. They thought up a thousand ways and means of bringing the Indians to the knowledge of the one true God, and used many kinds of teaching to wean them away from the error of idolatry. At first, to make their instruction attractive, they taught them the Per Signum Crucis, Pater Noster, Ave María, Credo, and Salve, all sung to a very simple and pleasing melody. They made for them in their own Anáhuac language metrical versions of the commandments, the articles of faith, and the sacraments, also set to music. The Indians sing them even today in many parts of New Spain. They also preached to the natives in many tongues and translated into their languages catechisms and sermons. In some monasteries there are two or three different

1. Torquemada describes this method (vol. III, p. 69). Making use of the Indians' own custom of picture writing, the friars had painted on one large sheet the Articles of Faith, on another the Ten Commandments, on another the Seven Sacraments, and whatever else they wished to teach the natives. When expounding any one of these subjects the preacher would hang up the appropriate chart where he could reach it with a pointer. These charts were used in all the schools for the Indian children even within the early years of Torquemada's experience.

tongues, and there are friars who preach in three totally different languages; and so they go traveling about and teaching in many places which had never heard or received the Word of God.

They had no little difficulty in removing and taking away from these natives their multitude of wives.[2] This was a matter of great difficulty because it was hard for the Indians to give up this old habit of the flesh, a thing to which sensuality is so prone. No human force or skill was sufficient to accomplish this had not the Merciful Father given His divine grace, for, leaving out of consideration the honor and the alliances which they contracted with many through their wives and the favor they obtained in this way, their wives were a great source of profit to them and wove and made clothing for them and served them well, for the principal wives brought with them others who were servants. After the Indians had been brought to contract real marriages, the friars had great difficulties and many scruples before they could give to each his real and lawful wife.

By the very difficult and strange cases and extremely intricate contracts which are to be found in this country the natives had contracted alliances with the daughters of men[3]—or of the demon—whence came giants, which are the great and terrible sins; they were not content with one wife, for one sin brings with it another, so that there is formed a chain of many links of sin with which the devil keeps them bound. But now they all accept matrimony and the law of God, although in some provinces they still have not given up all their mistresses and concubines.

The most continuous and the hardest work that was done among these Indians was in the matter of confessions, for they are so continuous that the whole year is a Lenten season and one has to hear them at any hour of the day and in any place, both in the churches and on the streets. The confessions of the sick are especially frequent and are very difficult, for as they are oppressed with illness and many of them have never made a confession, charity demands that one should help and prepare them, like one who is at the point of death, and set them upon the way of salvation. Many of them are deaf, others are covered with sores, so that certainly the confessors of this country cannot be nice or squeamish if they

2. See above, bk. II, ch. VII.

3. The reference is to Genesis 6.2 and 4: "the sons of God saw the daughters of men that they were fair; and they took them wives of all that they chose. . . . There were giants in the earth in those days; and also after that, when the sons of God came in unto the daughters of men and they bare children to them, the same became mighty men . . ."

are to endure their burden. Often the sick are so numerous that the confessors are like Joshua, beseeching God to stop the sun and lengthen the day so that they may finish hearing the confessions of the sick. I certainly believe that those who practice and persevere faithfully in this work suffer a form of martyrdom and perform a service very acceptable to God, for they are like the angels who sealed with the *Tau* those who moaned and grieved,[4] for what else is baptizing, marrying, and confessing but sealing the servants of God so that they may not be wounded by the angel with the sharp sword;[5] and those who are thus sealed they should strive to defend and preserve from the enemy, that they be not consumed and annihilated.

There was a time—and it lasted for some years—when those who by reason of their office should have defended and preserved the Indians treated them in such a manner that great bands of slaves were brought to Mexico, acquired God alone knows how.[6] What with the far from small tributes that the Indians paid, the many construction jobs that, in addition to all this, were laid upon them—with material provided at their expense—things were going in such a way that the Indians were in a fair way to be eaten up as one eats an apple. But their shepherd, to whom, by virtue of his office, they principally belonged, Fray Juan de Zumárraga, first bishop of Mexico, together with those of whom I am speaking—who are merely the dregs and off-scourings of the world[7]—so opposed the Spaniards' eating the apple without the peel and so embittered the peel for them that the Indians were not swallowed and exterminated. For God Who has predestined to His Glory many of these Indians and many of their sons and grandsons prevented it; and the Emperor, as soon as he was informed, provided such officials that since then the condition of the Indians has been steadily improving. Those who so well remedied the evils of this land are certainly deserving of perpetual remembrance. They were: the bishop Don Sebastian Ramírez, president of the royal audiencia, who had a special love for these Indians and wisely defended and preserved them and ruled the land in great peace with his good assistants. They, the judges who were appointed with him, deserve no less thanks than he. There is much that might be said about this audiencia and how it helped

4. Revelations 7. 2 and 3.

5. Spanish: *el ángel percuciente*. See Revelations 14.17.

6. See above, bk. I, ch. I.

7. Spanish: *y aquellos de quien al presente hablo, que son escorias y heces del mundo*. This must refer to the friars, and the relative clause must mean: "who are the humblest of the humble."

this land, for they found the country almost at the last gasp so that had they been much later they could have dug its grave—as in the case of the Islands. I feel more strongly about this than I speak. I believe that they are worthy of a great crown before the heavenly king and the earthly one as well. To complete the good work God brought Don Antonio de Mendoza, viceroy and governor, who put the seal upon the work, and in his office has proceeded prudently and always with great love for this land, keeping it well governed both in civil and religious matters. The judges were the licentiates Juan de Salmerón, Alonso Maldonado, Ceynos, and Quiroga.

CHAPTER IV

Of the humility of the friars of Saint Francis in their conversion of the Indians, and of their patience in adversities.

So great was the humility and mildness of the Friars Minor in their intercourse and dealings with the Indians that on some occasions when friars of other orders wanted to enter the Indian towns to settle and establish monasteries, the Indians themselves went and besought His Majesty's representative who ruled the land—who was at that time the bishop Don Sebastian Ramírez—asking him not to give them any other friars than those of Saint Francis, because they knew and loved them and were beloved by them. When the president [1] asked them the reason why they liked these friars better than the others, the Indians answered: "Because these go about poorly dressed and barefooted like us; they eat what we eat, they settle down among us, and their intercourse with us is gentle." On other occasions when the Franciscans wished to leave certain towns so that friars of other orders might go there, the Indians came in tears to say that if the Franciscans went away and left them, they would leave their houses and follow them; and they actually did it and followed the friars. This I saw with my own eyes. Because of this attitude of humility of the friars toward the Indians, all the officials of the royal audiencia treated them with great consideration, although in the beginning they had come from Castile filled with indignation against them and with the

1. Of the audiencia, *i. e.*, Don Sebastián Ramírez de Fuenleal.

intention of reproving and repressing them, because they had been informed that the friars ruled the Indians with a high hand and lorded it over them. After they saw that the opposite was true they became very fond of them and realized that what was said about the friars in Spain was the result of spite.

Some of the friars knew and associated with persons who could have helped them get bishoprics, but they would not allow it; others were actually elected to bishoprics and, when the news of the election came, humbly renounced the honor, saying that they were not worthy or deserving of so high a dignity. There is a difference of opinion as to whether or not they were right in refusing, for in this new land and among these humble people it was very desirable that the bishops should be, as in the primitive church, poor and humble, seeking not for wealth but for souls, and should not need to carry with them anything but their pontifical. It was much better that the Indians should not see luxurious bishops, dressed in delicate shirts, sleeping with sheets and mattresses and wearing soft garments, for those who have the cure of souls should imitate Christ in humility and poverty, bear his cross on their shoulders and wish to die on it. However, as these friars refused the honor simply and for the sake of humility, I believe that in God's judgment they will not be condemned for it.

One of the good things that the friars have in this land is humility, for many of the Spaniards humiliate them with insults and slanders; among the Indians there is nothing to make them vainglorious, for the Indians exceed them in penance and in being scorned of men. And so when there comes fresh from Castile some friar who was there considered to lead a life of great penance and to surpass the others, when he reaches here he is like a river flowing into the sea, for here the whole community lives very poorly and keeps every rule that can be kept. If they look at the Indians, they will see them miserably dressed and barefooted, their beds and dwellings exceedingly poor and their food more meager than that of the strictest penitent, so that these newcomers will find nothing on which to pride themselves. Much less is this so if they are ruled by reason, for everything belongs to God, and he blasphemes who says that any good thing is his own, for he is trying to make himself God. It is therefore madness for man to glory in things that do not belong to him, for one needs patience to await and receive the glory which Christ has promised us, to endure and bear the burden of all tribulations, and to suffer the blows of enemies without injury to the soul. Just as against savage discharges of artillery men set up soft and yielding things on which the shots may wreak their fury, so against the tribulations of the world, the flesh and the devil, one should set up a barrier of patience, for, if not, one's soul will quickly be disturbed and overcome.

In this manner the friars used patience as a shield against the insults of the Spaniards; when the latter very indignantly declared that the friars were destroying the country by favoring the Indians against them, the friars, to mitigate their anger, answered patiently: "If we did not defend the Indians, you would no longer have anyone to serve you; if we favor them, it is for the purpose of preserving them and so that you may have servants, and in defending and teaching them we are serving you and taking the burden from your consciences. When you took charge of them it was with the obligation of teaching them, and you think of nothing but making them serve you and give you all that they have or can get. Since they have little or nothing, if you exhaust them, then who will serve you?" And so, many of the Spaniards—at least the noble and virtuous ones—said, and still say, frequently, that if it were not for the friars of Saint Francis New Spain would be like the Islands, where there is no Indian left to be taught the law of God or to serve the Spaniards.

The latter also complained and spoke ill of the friars because they appeared to love the Indians better than they did the Spaniards and reproved the Spaniards harshly. For this reason many failed to give alms and felt a certain abhorrence of the friars. To this the friars replied that they had always considered the Spaniards as of the family of the Faith and that if any of them ever had any special spiritual or physical need, the friars attended to them rather than to the Indians; but as the Spaniards are very few in comparison to the natives and know better where to seek help—both physical and spiritual—and as the Indians have none to help them except those who have learned the language—the chief and in fact almost all of whom are of the Friars Minor—it is right that the friars should turn to help the Indians who are so numerous and so much in need of help. Even with them the friars cannot do all that they should because the Indians are so numerous. It is very right for the friars to do as they do, for the souls of these Indians did not cost Christ less than those of the Spaniards and Romans, and the law of God obliges one to help and encourage those upon whose lips the milk of the Faith is not yet dry rather than those who have already absorbed it and are accustomed to it.

Because the friars defended the Indians and tried to gain for them some time in which they could be taught the elements of the Faith, and to prevent their being made to work on Sundays and feast days, and because they tried to get them some reduction of the tributes, the Spaniards became so angry with the friars that they were determined to kill some of them, for it seemed to them that because of the friars they were losing the profit that they got out of the poor Indians. The tributes demanded of the Indians were so great that many towns, unable to pay, would sell to the money-lenders among them the lands and the children of the poor, and as the tributes were very frequent and they could not meet them by selling all that they had, some towns became entirely depopulated and others were losing their population when the situation was saved by decreasing the tribute. Because of this friction with the Spaniards the friars were on the point of leaving this land entirely and returning to Castile,[2] but God, who helps us in times of the greatest tribulation and necessity, did not permit it, for when His Catholic Majesty, the Emperor Don Carlos, was informed of the truth he obtained a license from the Pope for one hundred and fifty friars to come from Old Spain to this land.

CHAPTER V

Of how Fray Martín de Valencia tried to go on to convert new peoples and was unable to do it and other friars did it later.

AFTER Fray Martín de Valencia had preached and taught with his companions for eight years in Mexico and the neighboring provinces he wanted to go on and make an entrance into the more remote country in performance of his duty of preaching the Gospel. As he was prelate at that time, he left a deputy in his place; taking eight companions with him, he went to Tecoantepec, a harbor on the South Sea over a hundred leagues from Mexico, intending to take a ship there to go on further, for he had always been of the opinion that along the South Sea there were still many people to be discovered. Don Hernando Cortés, Marquis of

2. In 1526 the Franciscans held a meeting in Huejotzingo to decide whether or not they would return to Spain.

the Valley, had promised him ships to make this voyage and to take him where he so greatly desired to be so that he might there preach the Gospel and the Word of God without any previous military conquest. He stayed for seven months in the port of Tecoantepec, waiting for the ships, the shipbuilders having promised to have them finished by that time. The better to carry out his promise the Marquis himself went from Cuauhnahuac—a town in his marquisate where he usually resides, eleven leagues distant from Mexico—to Tecoantepec to hurry the completion of the ships and hand them over to Fray Martín, but with all that he could do they were not finished, for in this country it is only with great difficulty and a great expenditure of time and money that ships can be launched. The servant of God, seeing that he had no ships, went back to Mexico, leaving three of his companions to go in the ships, when they should be finished, and to make discoveries.

During the seven months that Fray Martín de Valencia was in Tecoantepec, he and his companions worked continually, teaching and instructing the people of that country, giving them the elements of the Faith in their language, which is that of the Zapotecs. They did it not only among these people, but in all the languages; and in all the towns through which they passed they preached and baptized.

Then they passed through a town called Mictlan, which in this language means hell, where they found some buildings more remarkable than those in any other part of New Spain. Among them was a temple of the devil and the dwelling of his ministers which were very handsome, especially a hall done in carved and recessed panels.[1] The work was done in stone with much ornamentation in intricate patterns. There were many doorways, each built of three great stones, two at the sides and one across the top, all of them very thick and broad. There was in this group of buildings another hall with round pillars, each of a single piece of stone and so big around that two men putting their arms around one could scarcely touch the tips of their fingers. They must have been about thirty feet high.

Fray Martín said that they would discover along the coast tribes that were handsomer and cleverer than these in New Spain, and that if God

1. Spanish: *una sala como de artesones. Artesonado* is the term used for the caisson paneling that was familiar to these Spaniards as a form of ceiling ornamentation. In the case of the "palace" of Mitla this paneling is used on the walls.

gave him life, he would spend it with those people as he had with these. It was not God's pleasure, however, that what Fray Martín so much desired should be discovered by him, although He did permit it to be discovered by Friars Minor. For one of the companions of the above-mentioned Fray Martín de Valencia, by name Fray Antonio de Ciudad Rodrigo, when he was Provincial in the year 1537, sent five friars to the coast of the North Sea. They went along preaching and teaching through the towns of Coatzacoalco and Puitel (this town, which is in the province of Tabasco, is settled by Spaniards and is called Santa María de la Victoria) and on to Xicalanco, where there was formerly a great deal of trading, and traders went there from Mexico—as some do even now. Passing along the coast the friars reached Champotón and Campech. This Campech was called by the Spaniards Yucatan. They spent two years in this journey and among these people and found in these Indians cleverness and a natural disposition for good, because they willingly listened to the teaching and the word of God. Two things the friars noticed in those Indians: that they were a very veracious people, and that they would not take the property of others even though it had been lying around for a long time. The friars left this country because of certain differences which arose between the Spaniards and the natives.[2]

In the year 1538 Fray Antonio de Ciudad Rodrigo sent three other friars in some ships belonging to the Marquis of the Valley to explore the South Sea. Although there were rumors and reports that these men had found a very rich and populous country, the report is not well authenticated, nor up to the present—that is, the beginning of the year 1540—has there come any reliable news.[3] This same year the same Provincial, Fray Antonio de Ciudad Rodrigo, sent two friars along the coast of the South Sea toward the North,[4] through Xalisco and New Galicia, with a captain who was going to explore. When they passed the land along that coast which is already discovered, known and conquered, they found two well-defined roads. The captain chose the right-hand one which bore inland and in a very few days it brought him to a mountain range so rough

2. Torquemada (vol. III, pp. 336-337) makes no reference to any trouble. He says simply that the friars went back to Mexico at the end of two years because they had no instructions to remain.

3. Torquemada, writing considerably later, ends the sentence thus: "afterwards it turned out to be very poor and scantily populated and for this reason they left it." Torquemada, vol. III, p. 357. This was the expedition of Francisco de Ulloa in 1539-40.

4. This refers to the expedition of Fray Marcos de Niza. It is curious that Motolinía, in speaking of these explorations which were actually going on while he was writing, should mention neither Fray Marcos de Niza nor Coronado by name.

that he could not cross it, and so he was obliged to return by the way he had come.

Of the two friars, one fell ill [5] and the other, with two interpreters, took the left-hand road which went close to the coast, and found it open and well marked all the way. In a few days he came to a country populated by poor people who came out to meet him, calling him a messenger from heaven, and all touching him and kissing his habit as if he really were. Some three or four hundred persons, and sometimes more, followed him from one day's journey to the next, and at mealtimes some of them would go hunting—for there was much game, especially hares, rabbits and deer—and, being very skillful, they quickly got as much as they wanted. First giving some to the friar, they shared what there was among themselves. In this way he travelled over three hundred leagues. Almost all the way along the road he heard of a land very thickly populated with people who wear clothes and have houses with flat roofs and of many stories.[6] These people, they said, were settled along the bank of a great river [7] where there are many walled towns, and at times the lords of the towns carry on wars against the others.

They also say that across that river there are other towns even larger and richer. In those on the first or nearer bank [8] they say that there are cows, smaller than those in Spain, and other animals very different from those of Castile; good clothing, not only of cotton but also of wool, and sheep from which they got the wool. I do not know what these sheep are like. These people wear shirts and garments which cover their bodies. They have shoes—not sandals—which cover the whole foot, something that has not been seen in any of the country so far discovered. They also bring from that land a great many turquoises. These and all the rest of the things that I have mentioned were to be found among the poor people whom the friar reached—not that they originated in their land, but were brought from those big towns where these people went at times to work and earn their living as day-laborers do in Spain.

Many expeditions had already gone out, both by sea and by land, in

5. Fray Marcos de Niza mentions leaving his companion, Fray Onorato, behind in Petatlán because he fell ill. Castañeda's account does not entirely agree with either. Castañeda, of course, wrote a good many years after the event.

6. The supposedly great and rich land of Cíbola.

7. The Río Grande. Motolinía has confused Fray Marcos de Niza's expedition with Coronado's.

8. That is, the western bank. If the reference is to buffalo (which the Spaniards called *vacas*, cows) this account seems to have them in the wrong place. The buffalo plains were east of the pueblo settlements on the Río Grande.

search of this country, and from all of them God had concealed it and willed that it should be discovered by a poor barefooted friar. When this friar brought the news, at the time that he told it they promised him that they would not conquer the land by fire and sword, as almost everything so far discovered on this mainland had been conquered, but would preach the Gospel to the natives. As the news was disseminated it spread rapidly to all parts of the country and many people wanted to go out and conquer this land, as if it were already discovered. Fortunately the lead was taken by the viceroy of this New Spain, Don Antonio de Mendoza,[9] with the best of intentions and an excellent desire to serve God as far as in him lay, without doing harm to his neighbors.

In the year 1539 two friars went through the province of Michuacán to some people called Chichimecas, who had already, on other occasions, allowed Friars Minor to enter their land and had received them peacefully and affectionately, but had always defended themselves against the Spaniards and prevented them from entering the country, both because they (*i. e.,* the Chichimecas) are warlike people who have little besides their bows and arrows, and because the Spaniards see little of interest in them.[10] Here these two friars that I have mentioned discovered about thirty small towns, the largest of which would not have six hundred inhabitants. These people very willingly received the Christian teaching and brought their children to be baptized, but so as to have more peace and a better disposition for receiving the Faith they asked for some years of exemption, saying that later they would pay a moderate tribute from what they raise and gather in their lands. Under such conditions they would give obedience to the King of Castile. All of this the Viceroy Don Antonio de Mendoza granted to them and gave them ten years of freedom in which they would pay no tribute.

Beyond these towns there are some plains, the most extensive in all New Spain. They are of very sterile soil, but entirely populated by very poor people who go about naked except for a breech clout. In cold weather

9. The expedition sent out in 1540 under the command of Francisco Vásquez Coronado.

10. Spanish: *de los españoles siempre se han defendido y vedádoles la entrada, así por ser gente belicosa y que poco más poseen de un arco con sus flechas, como porque los españoles ven poco interés en ellos.* A very unsatisfactory sentence. Torquemada (vol. III, p. 360), who follows Motolinía very closely at this point, has a much better reading: *de los españoles siempre se habían defendido y vedádoles la entrada, por ser gente belicosa; y tampoco a los españoles se les daba mucho, viendo el poco interese que podían sacar de ellos, pues poseen poco más que un buen arco con sus flechas.*

they cover themselves with deerskins, for there are many deer in all those plains, and also hares, rabbits, snakes, and vipers. They eat these roasted, for they have no stewed food nor do they have huts or houses or homes, but merely take shelter under trees.

Even of these there are not many except the *tunal,*[11] which is a tree with leaves as thick as two fingers, more or less, and as long as a man's foot and a span in width. One plants one leaf of these and it keeps on growing from one leaf to another and also sending out leaves at the sides and making a tree of them. The leaves at the base become very thick and strong until they are like the foot or trunk of a tree. The word tunal, or tuna for the fruit, is the name used in the Islands, for there are many of these trees there, although the fruit is not so abundant or so good as it is in this country. In this New Spain they call the tree *nopal* and the fruit *nochtli.* There are many species of the genus nochtli; some are called *montesinas,* and these are eaten only by the poor people; others are yellow and good; others are called *picadillas* and are half way between yellow and white, and they too are good, but best of all are the white ones. In their season they are abundant and last a long time, and the Spaniards are very fond of them, particularly in summer and on a hot journey, for they are very refreshing. Some are so good that they taste like pears, and others like grapes. Others are very red and are not prized at all. If anyone eats them, it is only because they ripen earlier than any of the others. They stain so much that they even color the urine of those who eat them so that it looks almost like blood. In fact some of the first conquistadores who came with Hernando Cortés, coming one day to a place where there were a great many of these trees, ate a great deal of the fruit without knowing what it was. Later when they all saw that they were passing blood, they were very much frightened, thinking that they had eaten some poisonous fruit and that they would all die. They were reassured by the Indians.

The cochineal insect, called in this language *nocheztli,* lives on these red tunas.[12] It is highly prized because it gives a very intense bright red, called *carmesí* (crimson) by the Spaniards. Because this dry country at

11. Cactus opuntia, Cactus tuna, or Cactus ficus indica.

12. According to Humboldt (vol. II, p. 460) there are two kinds of cochineal: the *grana fina* and the *grana silvestre,* which breed on different kinds of cactus. He quotes Clavigero (*Storia antica del Messico,* vol. I, p. 115) to the effect that the *grana fina* insect is raised on a kind of *Nopal* whose fruit is small, rather tasteless and white.

times has no water these Indians I speak of[13] drink the sap of these nopal leaves. There are also in those plains many *turmas de tierra,*[14] which so far as I know have not been found anywhere in New Spain except here.

CHAPTER VI

Of the very high mountains that surround all this land, and its great riches and fertility, and the many excellencies which the city of Mexico has.

No less fruitful and profitable are the trips and visitations that are continually made from the monasteries where the aforementioned friars reside; besides the neighboring towns which they visit frequently, they go out to other towns and lands fifty and a hundred leagues away. Before they finish one of these visits and return to their monasteries they have gone a hundred and fifty leagues and at times two hundred, for it is true that where the friars do not go there is no real Christianity. Because all the Spaniards are looking out for their own interests they make no effort to teach and instruct the Indians, nor is there anyone to tell them about the faith and belief of Christ, true God and universal Lord, or to try to destroy their superstitions and ceremonies and witchcraft, all very closely bound up with idolatry. It is therefore necessary for the friars to go about into all parts of the country.

New Spain is all so full of mountain ranges that if one stands in the biggest plain or level area and looks around, he will find on every side of him a mountain range, or ranges, at a distance of six or seven leagues—except in the plains that I mentioned in the last chapter and on some parts of the seacoast. There is one chain of mountains[1] especially, on the North Sea, that is to say on the ocean, which is the sea crossed by those who come from Spain. These mountains run for many leagues, the whole length of the territory that has been explored, now more than five thousand leagues, and people are still going on discovering new country. This land narrows

13. The Chichimecas.

14. Does he mean potato, or the white truffle (Tubar Cibarium)? The expressions *turma de tierra* and *criadilla de tierra* are apparently interchangeable and both mean truffle, but *criadilla de tierra* is also given as meaning potato. We know that when potatoes were first introduced into Italy they were called truffles. At the time of the discovery the potato was cultivated in South America but was *unknown in Mexico,* according to Humboldt, vol. II, p. 397.

1. The words *sierra, montaña* and *monte* seem to be used interchangeably.

so that it is only fifteen leagues across from sea to sea, from Nombre de Dios, a town on the coast of the North Sea, to Panamá, another town on the coast of the South Sea.

These ranges that I speak of, after passing this narrow part of the country, form two legs, one following the shore of the North Sea and the other going in the direction of Peru in very lofty and rugged mountains, incomparably greater than the Alps or the Pyrenees. I believe that on the whole surface of the globe there are no other mountains so high or so rugged. They can without mistake be called the biggest and richest in the world, for of this chain of ranges—not to mention the one that runs down to Peru—they have already discovered over five thousand leagues, as I said, and have not yet reached the end. The most remarkable thing, and one which causes very great wonder, is that so many and such great mountains should have been unknown for such a multitude of years as have passed since the great general deluge, when they are right on the ocean where so many ships sail and the violent winds and great storms and tempests have thrown and scattered so many ships far off the course and route that they were following. Although the ships have been so numerous and this has gone on for so many years, no one has ever come upon these ranges and the mountains have never been seen. The cause of this we must leave to Him who is the cause of all causes, believing that, since it has pleased Him that they should not be seen or discovered until our day, that has been best and most advantageous for the Christian faith and religion. The highest part of New Spain and the highest mountains—because they rise from the highest ground—seem to be those around Mexico. Mexico is entirely surrounded by mountains and has a very beautiful crown of ranges around her, and the city itself is situated in the middle. This gives it great beauty and adornment and great security and strength. Mexico also draws great profit from those ranges, as will be told later.[2] There are very beautiful hills which surround the city like a wall.

The divine presence in the Blessed Sacrament dwells in Mexico, not only in the cathedral church, but also in three monasteries of Augustinians, Dominicans, and Franciscans. There are also many other churches. In the main church the bishop has his seat, with his dignitaries, canons, priests, and chaplains. The church is well served and much adorned with vessels and ornaments for divine worship, as well as with musical instruments. In the monasteries there are many very devout religious. From among

2. See below, bk. III, ch. VIII.

them come many preachers who preach to the Indians and convert them to the true faith of Christ, using not only the Spanish language, but the many other languages that are found in the Indian provinces. In Mexico also resides the viceroy, representing the person of the Emperor and great monarch, Charles the Fifth; also the royal audiencia which rules and governs the land and administers justice. This city also has its very honorable municipal council, or government, which governs it and maintains excellent order. It has very noble gentlemen and very virtuous husbands, most liberal in alms-giving. There are many excellent confraternities which honor and celebrate the principal feasts, console and relieve many poor sick people, and give honorable burial to the dead. The city has a very fine almshouse called the Hospital de la Concepción de Nuestra Señora, endowed with great indulgences and pardons obtained for it by its patron, Don Hernando Cortés, Marquis of the Valley. This almshouse also has much property and a large income.

The city of Mexico, or Tenochtitlán, is as full of merchants and craftsmen as one of the largest in Spain. It is well laid out and better built, with good, large, strong houses, and is well provided and supplied with all things necessary, both native products and things brought from Spain. Ordinarily one hundred mule trains or convoys are on the road between here and the port of Vera Cruz, carrying goods for the city; and many carts are engaged in the same business. Every day crowds of Indians come into the city laden with supplies and tributes. They come both by land and by water in skiffs or boats which in the Indian language are called canoas. All of these provisions are used in Mexico, which causes some wonder, for one can see clearly that this city of Mexico alone consumes more than two or three cities of its size in Spain. The reason for this is that all the houses are very full of people, and also, as they are all in easy circumstances and without poverty, they spend freely.

The city has many very handsome horses, made so by the corn and continual green fodder which they eat all the year round—both the cornstalks, which are much better than green barley and last a long time, and later a very good kind of little reed which is always growing green in the water that surrounds the city. There is a great deal of livestock: cows, mares, sheep, goats, and pigs. Along one causeway a big pipe comes into the city, bringing very fine water that is carried to many streets. Along this same causeway there is on one side a very beautiful pleasure ground, and on the other side the land is full of market gardens for the distance of a league.

O Mexico, encircled and crowned by such mountains! Now your fame will rightly fly abroad, for in you there shines the faith and gospel of Christ! You who were once mistress of sins are now a teacher of the truth, and you who once stood in darkness and shadows now glow with the light of Christian teaching! You are more exalted and magnified by your present subjection to the most unconquered Caesar, Don Carlos, than you were by the tyrannical power with which you once sought to subjugate all men. Then you were a Babylon, full of confusion and evil; now you are another Jerusalem, mother of provinces and kingdoms. Then you went and wandered where you pleased, guided by the will of a heathen fool who ruled you with barbaric laws; now many watch over you that you may live according to laws both human and divine. Once, with the authority of the Prince of Darkness, you eagerly threatened, captured, and sacrificed both men and women and, on bits of card or paper, offered their blood to the devil; now, with prayers and just and holy sacrifices you adore and confess the Lord of lords. O Mexico, if you would raise your eyes to the mountains which surround you, you would see that there are more good angels helping and defending you than there were devils in former days attacking you to make you fall into sin and error!

Certainly there is not little, but very much, to say about the country and surroundings of Mexico—I mean the watersheds of that crown of ranges that is visible all around. All the slopes and environs of the ranges are thickly populated. Within that territory there are over forty large- and medium-sized towns, not counting many other small ones subject to them. Just in the district of which I am speaking there are nine or ten well-built monasteries full of friars, and all of them well occupied with the conversion and improvement of the Indians. In the towns there are many churches, for some of the towns that have no monastery have over ten churches, and all well equipped and each with its very good bell or bells. The exterior of all the churches is very handsome and ornamented with battlements, and the country, in itself gay and brilliant, because of the coolness of the mountains above and the water in the lowlands, makes a pleasing appearance all around, greatly to the adornment of the city.

Part of the slopes and the summits of the hills are among the best mountains in the world, for they bear cedars and many large cypresses—in fact many houses and churches are built of cypress wood. There are very many pine trees, extremely tall and straight, and others which the Spaniards also call pines or beeches. There are a great many very large liveoaks and *madroños* and some deciduous oaks. From these mountains flow streams and rivers, and on the slopes and in the valleys are many large springs. All this water augmented by the rainwater forms a great lake, and the city of Mexico is situated partly in the lake and partly on the shore. On the west a causeway divides the lake. One part is of very bad water, and the other is fresh water; the fresh water flows into the salt because it is on a higher level. This causeway has four or five openings, each with its bridge, through which a great deal of water flows from the fresh-water lake into the body of salt water. Originally Mexico was founded lower than it now stands. The greater part of the city was surrounded by fresh water and contained many cool groves of cedars, cypresses, willows, and other flowering trees. The Indian lords do not try to raise fruit-trees, because fruit is brought to them by their vassals, but rather forest trees from which they can pluck flowers and where they raise birds, both to enjoy their song and to shoot them with blowguns which they use very skillfully.

When Mexico was thus built in the lake, some two leagues away to the east a great opening was formed through which there came so much water that in the few days that it continued to flow it raised the level of the whole lake so much that the water covered the low buildings,[3] or rose more than half a man's height[4] above the first story. At that time most of the inhabitants retreated to the west, which was terra firma. The Indians say that many fish, some as big and thick as a man's thigh, came through the opening. This caused a great deal of astonishment because no fish live in the salt water of the lake, and in the fresh water part they are so small that the largest are the size of a man's palm. This water that burst out in this way must be from some river that runs somewhere through those mountains, for it has burst out on two other occasions from between two snow-covered mountains that can be seen from Mexico to the west and south. Once was since the Christians have been in the land, and the other time was a few years before. The first time the stream of water

3. Torquemada (vol. I, p. 292) says: "two leagues from the city to the *south*," and tells us that the spring (*manantial*) was opened up by order of the Mexican king Ahuitzotl.

4. Motolinía says *más de medio estado;* Torquemada (vol. I, p. 292) says *un estado*. The *estado* is reckoned as 1.67 meters.

was so great that the Indians indicate that it was twice the size of the big river of the city of Los Angeles,[5] which in most places is always crossed by bridges. That time too there appeared the same big fish as when the stream came out into the lake. The water then flowed down the other slope of the range, toward Huexotzinco, and I have been near where this stream appeared and have verified the matter by questioning all the Indians of that country.

Between these snow-capped mountains is the pass which they originally crossed when going from the city of Los Angeles to Mexico. It is no longer used because the Spaniards have discovered other better roads. One of these mountains the Indians call the White Mountain,[6] because it is always snow-covered; the other they call the Smoking Mountain,[7] and though both are very high, I think the Smoking Mountain is the higher. It is rounded in shape from the bottom, though the base comes down and spreads out much more. The land around this mountain is very beautiful and of a mild climate, especially on the southern slope. Up at the top of the mountain this volcano has a great crater from which a huge burst of smoke used to come up, on some days three or four times. From Mexico to the summit of the crater is a distance of twelve leagues, and when the smoke came out it was as clear as if it were very near, for it seemed to come out in a great burst and very thick. After rising upward in a column as high and as thick as the tower of the great church of Seville, its fury slackened and it sank down in whatever direction the wind carried it. These eruptions of smoke ceased after the year 1528, a fact much commented upon by both Spaniards and Indians. Some claimed that it was the mouth of hell.

5. The Atoyac. See Torquemada, vol. 1, p. 293.
6. Iztaccihuatl.
7. Popocatepetl.

CHAPTER VII

Of the names of Mexico, its founders, and the state and greatness of its lord, Moteuczoma.

ACCORDING to the etymology of this language some people interpret the name Mexico as meaning spring or fountain, and it is true that there are a great many springs round about the city which makes that interpretation seem not inappropriate. The natives say, however, that the name Mexico was brought by the first founders[1] of the city who were called Mexiti; even some time later the inhabitants of the city were called Mexitis. This name they took from their principal god or idol.[2] The place in which they settled they called Tenochtitlán because of a tree called nochtli[3] that they found there growing out of a stone, which they called *tetl;* so the name would mean 'the fruit which comes out of a stone.'

Afterward, as time went on and the people increased and the settlement grew, the city was divided into two sections, or two cities. The principal section they called Mexico and its inhabitants Mexicans. These Mexicans were, in this land, like the Romans of old. In this section called Mexico there resided the great lord of this land whose name was Moteuczoma. When named with more refinement and courtesy and greater respect they called him Moteuczomatzin, which means 'a man who is angered or serious.' It was in this part as being the most aristocratic that the Spaniards built their city; and this section alone is very large and has also a great many Indian houses, but all of them are outside of the part laid out by the Spaniards. The other section is called Tlaltilolco, which in their language means 'a small island,'[4] because there was a piece of land there higher and drier than all the rest, which was merely springs and canebrakes. All of this section is inhabited by Indians. There are a great many houses and many more inhabitants.

In each of these two cities or sections there is a very large square in

1. See above, Introductory Letter, p. 27 ff., and below p. 213.

2. Mexitli. According to Torquemada (vol. I, p. 293) this was another name of Huitzilopuchtli. Sahagún (vol. III, p. 136) says that Mecitli was a much respected priest, whose name the people took.

3. See above, bk. III, ch. V, where Motolinía says that the plant is called *nopal,* and the fruit, *nochtli.*

4. Compare Torquemada, vol. I, p. 295. *Tlatelulco* means an artificial mound of earth. The original name was *Xlatilulco,* which means a mound of sand.

which they usually hold a big market every day where an enormous number of people meet to buy and sell. In these markets, which the Indians call tianquizco, they sell everything that the land produces, from gold and silver to reeds and kindling wood. The Indians call this section 'San Francisco de Mexico,' because San Francisco was the first church in this city and in all New Spain. The other section they call 'Santiago de Tlaltilolco;' and though the section has many churches, the principal one is that of Santiago because it is a church with three naves. At the Mass which is said for the Indians in the morning the church is crowded with them, and however early they open the doors, the Indians are already waiting; for as they have not much to do to dress or adorn themselves, they set out for the church as soon as it gets light. Here in this church is the Indian school, with friars to teach and train them in what they have to do. In this whole country the Indians name first the saint of their principal church and then the town; thus they say 'Santa María de Tlaxcallan,' 'San Miguel de Huexotzinco,' 'San Antonio de Tetzcoco,' and so on.

Let no one think that I have taken too long to tell the glory of Mexico, because, in truth, I have touched only very briefly upon a small part of the much that might be said about her, for I believe that in all of Europe there are few cities that have such a situation and such surroundings, with so many and such well-situated towns round about them. I will go further and assert that I doubt if there is anything so good and so rich as Tenochtitlán, and so full of people; for this great city of Tenochtitlán has opposite it, to the east and on the other side of the lake, the town of Tetzcoco. It must be four or five leagues across the width of the lake, which is eight leagues long. This is the salt lake, and the fresh water one must be almost as long again.

This city of Tetzcoco was the second leading town of the country, and likewise its lord was the second ranking lord of the land. He had under him fifteen provinces, reaching as far as that of Tuzapan, which is on the coast of the North Sea. In Tetzcoco there were very great temples of the devil and very handsome houses and dwellings of the nobles. Especially notable among these was the house of the principal lord: both the old one with its garden surrounded by over a thousand very large and beautiful cedars—most of which are still standing although the house has been razed—and his other house in which a whole army could be lodged, with many gardens and a very large pool which was entered in boats through an underground passage. The town of Tetzcoco is so large that it covers more than a league in breadth and over six in length, and has many different parishes and innumerable inhabitants.

One league from Mexico-Tenochtitlán to the east is the city or town of Tlacopán, in which resided the third lord of the land who had ten provinces under him. These two lords that I have mentioned might well be called kings, for they lacked none of the attributes of royalty. To the north, four leagues from Tenochtitlán, is the town of Cuautitlán, residence of the fourth lord of the land, who was lord of many other towns. Between this town and Mexico there are other big towns which I will not name, both for the sake of brevity and because the names are strange.

Two leagues to the south of Mexico is the town of Coyoacán. Its lord was fifth in rank and had many vassals. It is a very cool town. It was here that the Spaniards stayed after they had conquered Tenochtitlán until they had built houses to live in in Mexico—for the conquest had destroyed all the best and biggest part of the city. Two leagues farther on, also to the south, that is, four leagues from Mexico, is the large town of Xochimilco, and then toward the east lie the towns of the fresh-water lake, as they are called, and also Tlalmanalco, with its province of Chalco, where there are infinite numbers of people. On the other side of Tetzcoco, toward the north, is the very thickly populated country of Otompa and Tepepolco. These towns that I have mentioned, and many others, surround Mexico within that crown of mountain ranges, and there are very many others beyond the mountains; for across the widest part of the settled country toward Mexico it is six leagues to the towns on the outer slopes, and in all directions round about it is very populous and beautiful country.

The rulers of the provinces and principal towns were like lords,[5] and above them all were the two of highest rank, the lords of Tetzcoco and Tlacopán. These two and all the others resided most of the time in Mexico and formed the court of Moteuczoma, who acted as king and was much feared and implicitly obeyed. He celebrated his festivals with such solemnity and pomp that the Spaniards who were present at them were astounded not only at this, but also at the sight of the city and the temples and the surrounding towns. Upon seeing the service that he had and the pomp with which he was served, the sumptuous houses that he owned and those of the other lords, the solicitude and number of the servitors

5. Spanish: *eran como señores de salva o de ditado.* A *señor de salva* was one who had an official food taster; a *señor de ditado* was one who took his title from a place name, town, or estate.

and the crowds of people—innumerable as the grass of the fields—the Spaniards were so filled with astonishment that they said to each other: "What is this that we see? Is it an illusion or an enchantment? Such great and wonderful houses have been concealed all this time from men who thought that they knew all about the world!"

In this city Moteuczomatzin had all kinds of animals, both beasts and reptiles and birds of all varieties, even waterfowl that live on fish, and birds of the kind that eat flies, and for all of them he had attendants who gave them food and collected provisions for them. Moteuczoma was so much interested in this that if he saw flying through the air a bird that took his fancy, he would order it caught, and they would bring him that very bird. One Spaniard who is a trustworthy witness, being one day in the presence of Moteuczoma, saw that he had taken a fancy to a hawk that flew by—or perhaps it was to show off his power before the Spaniards—however that may be, he ordered his men to bring him the bird, and such was the diligence of those who went after it that they brought him that very same wild hawk and put it into his hands.

He had also many gardens and pleasure grounds with pavilions in them; and rocky islands with much game and enclosed woods and mountains with very fine houses and cool lodges, all very well swept and clean, for he had as many serving people as the greatest lord in the world.

The streets and highways of this great city were so clean and well swept that there was nothing to stumble over, and wherever Moteuczoma went, both in this city and anywhere else, the road was swept and the ground so firm and smooth that even if the sole of the foot were as delicate as the palm of the hand, it would not be hurt by going unshod. What can I say of the cleanliness of the temples of the devil, and of their steps and courtyards, and of the houses of Moteuczoma and the other lords, which were not only white-washed, but polished, and repainted and repolished for every festival.

In order to enter his palace, which they call tecpan, they all took off their shoes, and those who went in to transact business with him had to wear coarse blankets. If they were great lords, or it was in cold weather, they would put on a poor coarse blanket over the good ones which they wore. When they spoke to him they stood with their heads bowed low and without raising their eyes, and when he answered them it was in such a low voice and with such authority that he did not seem to move his lips. He rarely did this (*i. e.*, answer), for usually his answer was given through his intimates and familiars, who were always at his side for that purpose and served as secretaries, as it were. This custom belonged not only to Moteuczoma, but I myself at first saw it followed by others of the principal lords; and this gravity was more characteristic of the greater lords. What the lords said and the word that they most usually spoke at the end of the speeches or business that was addressed to them was *tlaa,* uttered in a low voice, which means 'yes' or 'all right.'

When Moteuczoma went out of his palace many lords and important personages went with him, and all the people in the streets along which he passed bowed low to him with great respect and without raising their eyes to look at him, but all standing until he had passed, like a friar bowed during the Gloria.

All his vassals, great and small, had great fear and respect for him, for he was cruel and very severe in his punishments. When the Marquis of the Valley entered the land, talking with the lord of the province, he asked him if he recognized the overlordship of Moteuczoma, or was bound to him as a vassal, and the Indian answered: "Who is there who is not the vassal and slave of Moteuczomatzin? Who is as great a lord as Moteuczomatzin?" This meant to imply that in all the land there was no one his superior or even his equal.

Moteuczoma had, in his palace, dwarfs and little hunchbacks who were purposely deformed when children. They broke and dislocated their bones because the lords in this land used them as servants just as the great Turk now uses eunuchs.

He also had royal eagles—these eagles of New Spain may justly be called 'royal' because they are extremely large. The cages in which they were kept were large and made of poles as big around as a man's thigh. When the eagle came near the net behind which it was imprisoned, people moved away and fled from it as if it were a lion or other wild beast. They have very strong claws, the foot and talons as big as a man's, as is also the leg. The body is very large and the beak very savage. For one meal they will eat a turkey,[6] which is as big and bigger than a good Spanish peacock. This fowl that I speak of is more like a peacock than any other bird, for it spreads its tail in the same way, although it has not so many or such beautiful feathers, and its voice is as ugly as the peacock's.

6. Spanish: *gallo de papada.*

In this country I have heard of griffins, which they say are to be found in some great mountains that are four or five leagues from a town called Tehuacán, which lies to the north. From there these griffins used to come down to a valley called Ahuacatlán which lies between two heavily wooded ranges. They would come down and carry men off in their claws to the mountains where they ate them; and it came about that everyone left the valley for fear of the griffins. The Indians say that they had very strong claws, like iron. They also say that there lives in these mountains an animal like a lion, which is covered with wool, but the wool or fleece is something like down. They are very savage and have such strong teeth that they eat even the bones of the deer that they catch. This animal is called *ocotochtli*.[7] I have seen one of these animals. The griffins have not been seen for over eighty years, nor does anyone remember them.

Let us now return to Tenochtitlán and its founding. The founders of the city were foreigners, for the first inhabitants of the land were called Chichimecas and Otomíes. These had no idols or houses of stone or wood, but only straw huts. They lived on game, not always roasted, but raw or dried in the sun. They ate some little fruit that the earth produced without cultivation, also roots and herbs—in short they lived like brute beasts.

They became masters of this land as the Spaniards now have, for they took possession of the land, not—to be sure—in the manner in which the Spaniards did, but very gradually and over a period of years; and just as the Spaniards have brought with them many things belonging to Spain, such as horses, cows, flocks, dresses, garments, birds, wheat, plants and many kinds of seeds both of flowers and of vegetables, etc., so in their own way the Mexicans brought in many things that were not here before and enriched the land by their skill and industry. They cleared and cultivated it, when previously it had been merely wild mountain country and those who inhabited it lived like savages. These Mexicans brought in the first idols and articles of clothing and footwear and cotton and some birds. They began to construct buildings both of adobe and of stone, and so

7. Sahagún (vol. III, p. 153) describes the *ocotochtli* as follows: It lives in the woods and crags, is the size of a hound, low and big bodied; its coat is brownish gray on top and whitish underneath, with small black spots. Its fur is soft, its head round with small ears like a cat. It has a very rough tongue. It is very swift and a great jumper. Its cry is a thin soprano. Nicolás León (*Ensayo de nomenclatura e identificación de las láminas 98 a 138 del libro XI de la Historia de las cosas de la Nueva España escrita por Fray Bernardino de Sahagún*) gives *ocotochtla* as meaning 'the place of wildcats,' *lugar de gatos monteses,* which would indicate that an *ocotochtli* was a wildcat. See Sahagún, vol. III, pp. 320 and 331.

today almost all the stoneworkers of the land are from Tenochtitlán or Tetzcoco; and they go out all over the country to build and to cut stone for wages, just as the Asturians and the Basques come into Spain. Among all the Indians there are many different crafts and all of these they say were invented by the Mexicans.

CHAPTER VIII

Of the time when Mexico was founded, of the great riches in its mountains and surrounding country, and of its virtues and of many other things to be found in this land.

THE Mexicans came in to settle this land, as one can see by their books and by records which they have in certain very remarkable volumes of skillfully painted figures and characters.[1] These records were kept to preserve the memory of their ancient history, their lineages, wars, conquests, and other things of the sort which were worthy of being perpetuated.

By these books we find that the Mexicans came to New Spain four hundred and forty-eight years ago, counting back from this year of 1540, and that Tenochtitlán was built two hundred and forty years ago. Up to the present it has been impossible to learn or ascertain who these Mexicans were or where they had their origin. For some time it was considered most probable that they came from a place called Teocolhuacán, which the Spaniards call Culiacán. This town is two hundred leagues from Mexico. But since it has been discovered and conquered they find that it has a language very different from that spoken by the natives of Mexico; and besides the difference of language there was no tradition which would lead one to believe or even surmise that the Mexicans had come from Culiacán. The language of the Mexicans is that of the Nahua people.

Mexico, at the time of Moteuczoma and when the Spaniards came there, was all very much surrounded by water, which has been decreasing ever since the year 1524. At that time one could enter the city only by three causeways. By the one to the west they could reach the mainland in half a league, for on that side Mexico is very near the shore; the

1. See above, Introductory Letter, p. 24 ff., and note 1.

other two causeways are to the south and to the north; by the southern one they had to go a league to reach terra firma. To the east the city is entirely surrounded by water and there is no causeway at all.

Mexico was very strong and well arranged, for it had some wide streets of water, and other streets with houses, arranged alternately, a street with houses and a canal. Midway between the houses ran a lane or narrow street on to which the doors of the houses opened. Along the canals there were many bridges crossing from one side to the other. Besides this the city had its public squares and courtyards before the temples of the devils and the houses of the lords. There were a great many *acallis,* or boats, which served the houses, and many others belonging to dealers who came to the city with provisions. All the towns round about also were full of innumerable boats which were always going back and forth to the city. The causeways had bridges that were easy to raise, and for protection along the waterfront they had the boats that I have mentioned, which were innumerable and swarmed all over the water and along the canals. The number of inhabitants was incalculable. They could use as fortresses the temples of the devil and the houses of the chief lord, Moteuczoma, and of the other lords—for all the lords who were subject to Moteuczoma had houses in the city and resided there a great deal of the time. However great a lord might be he was glad to attend Moteuczoma in his palace, and if any lord was exempted from this, it was only the lord of Tetzcoco.

For Indians their provision for war was abundant and not bad, for they had many houses full of javelins with flint points and quantities of bows and arrows and long wooden swords made of a very strong wood and set with sharp flints, so that with one blow they could cut off a horse's head. They also had weapons like short, thick lances made of these same flints. Besides these they had many slings, so that when they opened fire with slings, arrows, and javelins all at once it seemed like a heavy rain. This city was so strong that it seemed that no human power would suffice to take it, for besides its armament and munitions, it was the capital and mistress of the whole land, and its lord, Moteuczoma, gloried in his residence and in the strength of his city and the multitude of his vassals. He would send out his messengers from the city through all the land and they were well obeyed and served. Others, from afar, hearing of his power and fame, came with gifts to offer him obedience. Against those who rebelled or did not obey his commands or his captains, whom he sent to many parts of the land, he showed himself as a very stern avenger.

No lord in this land had ever been heard of who was so feared and so well obeyed as Moteuczoma, nor had anyone so ennobled and strengthened the city of Mexico; indeed, his overconfidence betrayed him. Neither he nor any other of the native lords could ever have believed that there was sufficient strength in the world to take Mexico. Strong in this confidence they received the Spaniards into Mexico and let them enter in peace and stay in the city, saying: "Whenever we want to throw them out of our city, and out of the whole land, it will be within our power, and when we want to kill them we will kill them, for it will be only a question of our will and desire to do so.". But God delivered the great city into the hands of His people because of the great sins and abominations committed in it. Much was also due to the remarkable ingenuity and unheard of strategy of Don Hernando Cortés, Marquis of the Valley, in building the brigantines to take Mexico, for without them it would have been impossible—so well fortified was it. Certainly this and his determination and courage when he scuttled the ships in which he had come, and later when they drove him out of Mexico and he left the city in defeat but would not withdraw nor head toward the coast, in spite of the entreaties of the few companions he had left, and his wise and valiant behaviour in the whole conquest of New Spain are all things to justify placing him on the tablet of Fame, and putting him in equal comparison with any of the captains, kings, and emperors of the ancients, for there is so much to say about his prowess and his invincible spirit that that alone would suffice to make a big book.

Sometimes I have thought to write and say something about the things found in this New Spain, native and indigenous to it, as well as about those that have been brought from Castile, and how they have adapted themselves to this land. I see, however, that for lack of time even this that I have written is a mere patchwork, and that I cannot properly carry out my intention in what I have begun. Very often charity obliges me to succor my neighbors in time of need so that I am hourly compelled to minister to them.

Since I have begun, it will be only reasonable to say something about these mountains that I said were big and rich. Their size I have already discussed; I shall now tell of their richness and wealth and of what is to be found in the rivers that have their source in them, for they produce much gold and silver and all the metals, and many kinds of stones, especially turquoises, and others which the people here call chalchihuitl. The fine specimens of the latter are emeralds.[2] Off the coast from these mountains lies the Island of Pearls, although it is far from this New Spain, and it is one of the great riches of the world. There is also alum, and woad,[3] the seed of which was brought from Europe and grows extremely well in these mountains. It can be harvested oftener and gives more dye[4] than in any part of Europe. There is also abundant and very good brazilwood.

The land through which these mountains extend, especially the part that they call New Spain—or as far as the Golfo-Dulce[5]—is certainly very good, and would be more so if they had planted it with plants that would do very well in it, such as grapes and olives, for these mountains form valleys and slopes and ravines where one could make excellent vineyards and olive groves.

In this country there are many blackberry bushes and their fruit is larger than in Castile. In many places in the mountains there are big wild grapevines, and no one knows who planted them. They throw out very long shoots and bear many clusters and produce grapes which are eaten green. Some Spaniards make vinegar of them, and some have made wine, but only in small quantities. The land produces a great deal of very good cotton. There is much cocoa, for the land which produces cocoa must be very good. Since this cocoa is both food and drink and also currency in this land, I want to explain what it is and how it grows.

Cocoa is the fruit of a medium-sized tree beside which, as soon as

2. The Aztec-Spanish dictionaries give *chalchihuitl* as *esmeralda basta,* 'low grade emerald,' but Sahagún (vol. III, p. 279) describes it as green and non-transparent, mixed with white. Motolinía evidently uses this term to designate both the fine green stones, which he refers to as emeralds, and the less prized ones as well. Sahagún (*loc. cit.*) calls the fine ones *quetzalitztli,* and describes them as follows: "There are in this land very good emeralds, which are called *quetzalitztli;* they are precious . . . and are so called because *quetzalli* means certain very green feathers, and *itztli* means the stone from which knives are made (obsidian), which is very polished and without spots; and both these qualities are present in the good emerald, which is very green, has no spots, is very polished and transparent and brilliant." He also speaks of a kind called *quetzalchalchihuitl* "because it is very green and is like the *chalchihuitl.* The ones which are not good have spots and streaks." It is impossible, on the basis of these descriptions, to make any positive identification of the stones. Seler (Sahagún, vol. v, pp. 211-212) suggests for *chalchihuitl,* "chlorite, serpentine or other similar stones." *Quetzalitztli,* he says "very probably means fine varieties of stones of the class of jadeite." In view of the fact that jadeite is *not* transparent, or even translucent (except in excessively thin slices), this identification is impossible.

3. Spanish: *pastel.* Botanical name, Isatis tinctoria.

4. Spanish: *es de más paños.* Does it mean that one can dye *more* cloth with it or more *kinds* of cloth?

5. In Guatemala, opening into the bay of Honduras.

they plant the seed, they set another tree that grows tall and shades the cocoa tree and serves as a sort of mother to it.[6] The seeds are like the almonds of Castile, except that when well grown they are bigger. The fruit is borne in pods with sections marked in them, like little melons, and each of these pods usually has about thirty seeds or 'almonds' of cocoa. It is eaten green, as soon as the 'almonds' begin to harden, and is very good. They also eat it dried, but only a few grains and not often. Its most general use is as money, and it is current all through this country. One 'load' is made up of three 'numbers,' each containing eight thousand 'almonds,' or cocoa beans. This unit the Indians call *xiquipilli*. The 'load' is twenty-four thousand beans, and in the place where it is harvested the 'load' is worth five or six gold pesos, but as it is carried inland the price increases, and it also rises and falls according to the year, for in a good year the yield is abundant. Severe cold causes a small crop, for it is very delicate. This cocoa is a very generally used drink; ground up and mixed with corn and other grains, also ground, it is drunk all over the country, and it is for this that it is used. In some places they make it very well. It is good and is considered a very nourishing drink.

In these mountains there are pepper trees, different from the Malabar pepper, for it does not burn so much and is not so fine, but is a natural pepper, milder than the other.[7] There are also cinnamon trees. This cinnamon is lighter colored and thicker. Many mountains also are full of liquidambar trees. These are beautiful trees and many of them are very tall. Their leaf is like ivy. The sap that is drawn from them is called by the Spaniards liquidambar; it is sweet-smelling, has medicinal virtues, and is highly valued among the Indians. The Indians of New Spain mix it with its own bark to solidify it, for they do not want it liquid, and make it into cakes which they wrap in big leaves. They use it for perfume and also to cure certain diseases.

There are two kinds of trees from which they get balsam, and from both kinds they make great quantities. From one of these two kinds of trees, which is called *xiloxochitl*,[8] the Indians make balsam, and made it before the Spaniards came. This balsam has a somewhat stronger odor

6. Torquemada (vol. II, p. 620) says "beside it they plant a cutting of another tree, which they call *cacahuanantl*, that is to say, the mother of cocoa."

7. Spanish: *más doncel*. According to Ramírez in *Historia de los Indios* (vol. I, p. 190), this means 'less acrid or biting.'

8. Sahagún (vol. III, p. 276) mentions *xiloxóchitl* as a flower which grows on a plant (not a tree) called by the same name.

and does not get as dark as what the Spaniards make. These trees grow on the banks of the rivers which flow out of these mountains toward the North Sea, and not on the other side. The same is true of the trees from which they get the liquidambar and of the kind from which the Spaniards get balsam. They all grow toward the north, though the liquidambar trees and the tree from which the Spaniards make balsam are also found high up in the mountains. This balsam is very valuable, and they use it to treat and cure many diseases. It is made only in a few places, and I believe that the reason is that they have not yet recognized the trees, especially the xiloxochitl, which I think is the best, for it has already been tested by experience.

Of the genus palm there are ten or twelve species that I have seen. Some of them bear dates and I believe that if they cured and preserved them they would be good. The Indians, being poor, eat them green, without bothering to cure them, and find them good because they eat them with 'hunger sauce.' There are wild cassia trees which, if they were grafted, would be good, because the other cassia trees do well here. This tree was planted in Haiti by the Friars Minor before anyone else planted them, and here in New Spain these same friars have planted nearly all the fruit trees and have persuaded the Spaniards to plant them too. They also taught many people how to graft, which is the reason why there are today many very good orchards. There will be many more, for the Spaniards, seeing that the land produces a hundredfold what they plant, are doing a great deal of planting and grafting good fruit and valuable trees. Palms have also been grown from dates brought from Spain, and have borne fruit very quickly.

There is rampion in these mountains, and some say also rhubarb, but this has not been proved. There are many other medicinal roots and herbs with which the Indians cure themselves of different ailments and have experience of their virtue. There are medium-sized trees that have burrs like those of the chestnut, except that they are not so big or so rough. Inside they are full of red grains as large as coriander seeds. This red coloring matter the painters mix with nocheztli, which I said was very good[9] and of which there is also some in these mountains. There are a great many mulberry trees, both the dark and the white kinds. The berries they bear are very small.

9. See above, bk. III, ch. V.

They have recently taken to raising silkworms.[10] The crop is good and takes less time to raise than in Spain. There is provision for raising silk in great quantities as time goes on, and although they are just beginning to do it, there are people who harvest as much as three or four hundred pounds. I have even been told that in this year of 1540 some will get a thousand pounds. Of the silk that has been raised here some has been dyed, which improves its quality; when put into the bleach it does not fade because of the excellence of the colors. The best dyes in this country are red, blue, and yellow. The mineral yellow is the best. The Indians make many colors from flowers, and when the painters wish to change from one color to another they lick the brush clean, for the paints are made from the juice of flowers.

There is a great deal of wax and honey in these mountains, especially in Campech. They say that there is as much honey and wax there, and just as good, as in Safi, Africa. This land of Campech the Spaniards called Yucatan when they first came to the country, and from this name New Spain came to be called Yucatan. But no such name is to be found in all these lands. The Spaniards made a mistake when they reached it, for as they talked with the Indians of that coast, to all their questions the Indians answered: *"tectetan, tectetan,"* which means: "I don't understand you, I don't understand you," and the Spaniards, not understanding what the Indians were saying, said: "Yucatan is the name of this country." The same thing happened in the case of a cape that the land forms there, which they called Cape Cotoch; cotoch in that language means house.

10. See above, Introductory Letter, pp. 30-31, and below, ch. XVIII.

Chapter IX

Continuing the subject of the things to be found in New Spain and in the mountains which surround Mexico.

Such is the productivity and so great the wealth and fertility of this land of New Spain that it is beyond belief, but the very best of it and the part that surpasses all the other lands and provinces is that crown of ranges which, as I have said, encircles the city of Mexico, in which there is to be found in abundance all that I have mentioned and much more. Besides the many kinds of trees, plants and beneficial herbs that are found in them these mountains have, within themselves, three kinds or varieties of country. At the summit the country is cold, but not so cold as to be snow-covered except in a few very high ranges near the road that runs from Vera Cruz to Mexico, or on some other mountain tops where a little snow collects in severe and stormy years when it is very cold. In this high land there are great pine forests, and the wood is extremely good and so handsome that when cut it looks like orange wood or box. Coming down from the summit toward the coast of the North Sea it is all a temperate country, and the farther down and nearer the coast, the warmer it is.

This part toward the north is very green and fertile. Most of the year there is rain or mist, and fog high up in the mountains. There are many kinds of trees which the Spaniards had not known before, and as they are of different kinds and differ from each other in foliage they make these the most verdant and beautiful mountains in the world. It is a country very suitable for hermits and contemplatives, and I even believe that those who come here in the near future will see that, just as this land was a second Egypt in its idolatries and sins, and then flowered into great holiness, so also these mountains and this country will flower and be filled with hermits and contemplative penitents. There is even now beginning to be abundant evidence of this, as I shall tell later, in the fourth part of this narrative or history, if it please God to bring it into being.[1] Therefore let those who shall come take note, and we shall see how Christianity has come from Asia, which is in the east, to reach the utmost limit of Europe, which is our Spain, and from there is coming

1. Apparently it did not, for the account ends with part III.

with rapid strides to this land, which is the most remote part of the west. Does the ocean perchance present any obstacle to its passage? Certainly not, for to the will and desire of Him who created it, the sea can represent no division or separation. Shall not the will and grace of God go as far as ships can go? Yes, and much beyond, for in all the circumference of the earth shall the name of God be praised and glorified and exalted; as in the beginning the Church flourished in the east, which is the beginning of the world, just so it shall flourish now, at the end of the centuries, in the west, which is the end of the world.[2]

Well, to return to our purpose, I say that there are in this land mountains of gypsum of very good quality, especially in a town called Cozcatlán. It is to be found all over the country, but in the form of a white stone, from which it has been made very successfully, but this other that I am talking about is the "mirror gypsum"[3] and is very abundant and very good. There are also springs of living salt. It is a remarkable sight to see the white springs that are always forming very white veins. When the water is taken out and poured on to white-washed beds like small threshing floors and exposed to the sun it soon turns into salt.

Among the many fruits to be found in these mountains and in all of New Spain there is one called *ahuacatl*.[4] On the trees this fruit looks and hangs like big early figs, but in flavor it is rather like the piñon nut. There are four or five different kinds of these ahuacatl. The common and usual ones all through the country, which are available all the year, are the ones I have already mentioned which are like early figs. From these they have made an oil which is very good both to eat and to burn. There are others as big as very large pears, and they are so good that I believe them to be the best fruit in New Spain, both in flavor and in virtue. There are other bigger ones, like small squashes, and of these

2. Compare the much less optimistic attitude of Sahagún: "The Church militant started out from Palestine . . . and crossing the Ocean has come to this western land of India, where there were many different peoples and tongues, many of which have already died out and those that remain are on the road to extinction. . . But in the matter of the Catholic Faith its soil is sterile and very difficult to cultivate, and the Catholic Faith has very feeble roots and bears little fruit in return for excessive labor and very easily dries up and dies. It seems to me that the Catholic Faith cannot last long in this land. . . It has merely come to the Islands and New Spain and Peru in passing, on the way to China . . . where I believe that it will last for many years." See Sahagún, vol. III, pp. 302-3.

3. Spanish: *lo de los espejos*. The crystalized gypsum known as selenite and, in Spanish, as *espejuelo*.

4. The aguacate or avocado.

there are two kinds: one has a big seed and little flesh, and the other has more flesh and is good. All these three kinds of large ahuacatl grow in the hot country. There are others that are very small, scarcely larger than Cordovan olives, and the Indians when they first saw olives gave them this name and called them little ahuacatl. This fruit is so good that they give it to the sick; when the Indians fasted they used to abstain from it because it is a nourishing fruit. All these varieties of ahuacatl are eaten by dogs and cats in preference to chicken, for I have seen a dog who had had his fill of chicken offered ahuacatl and eat them eagerly, like a man who has had his fill of meat eating an olive. The tree is as big as a large pear tree; the leaf is broad and very green and has a pleasant odor; it is good for *agua de piernas* and better for *agua de barbas*.[5]

Many other things are to be found on the slopes of these mountains toward the North Coast. I have noticed and seen by experience that the mountains and the land that are toward the north and enjoy the north wind are greener and more fruitful. Inland, toward the south and west, in these same mountains the country is dry and it rains only in the rainy season, and even less than in the other parts of New Spain. So there is a great difference between one part and another. If one stands at the summit of the mountains on the northern side, where, as I have said, it rains or mists or is foggy most of the year, the peaks of the ranges are hidden; and on the other side, little more than a crossbow shot away, it is dry most of the time. It is indeed very remarkable that in such a short distance there should be two such great extremes.

In this dry country there are different trees from those of the other part, such as the *guayacán*,[6] a tree that cures those who suffer from pustules, which are here called *infinitas*.[7] I believe that this name was brought

5. I have been unable to make out the meaning of these two expressions.

6. Guaiacum or lignum vitae, various varieties of which grow in South America, Mexico, and the islands of the Caribbean.

7. Syphilis. In an anonymous work called *Times Store House* (Wm. Jaggard, London, 1619) the second chapter of the fourth book deals with "the Neapolitan disease or great pox or French pox" and the use of Guaiacum as a curative agent. According to the anonymous author Guaiacum loses its efficacy when brought to Europe. One must take the treatment where the tree grows, and one must be sure to get the right kind of Guaiacum. One uses only "the little loppings of a young tree, barely two years old," first bruised between the teeth and afterward boiled in an uncovered earthen vessel. A pint of this infusion taken every morning and every evening, and followed each time by two hours of exercise is reported to have cured a bad case completely in two weeks.

See also Oviedo y Valdés, ch. LXXV. He states positively that the disease originated in the West Indies. "Your Majesty can take it as fact that this disease came from the Indies and is very common among the Indians, but not so dangerous there as here. On the contrary, the Indians very easily cure themselves by the use of an infusion of Guyacan."

by soldiers and workmen[8] recently come from Castile. Just a short while ago they discovered an herb which they called sarsaparilla, of which there is a great deal, and many have been healed and cured of this same disease by a water made from this herb.

As it would be endless to explain and specify all the things that are to be found in these mountains, I shall merely say that on the coast, which is a hot country like the Islands, one finds all the same things as in Haiti and the other islands, and many others, both native and imported from Castile, which do not grow there. It is true that there have not been so many cassia trees or so much sugar cane raised here, although they could be raised in much greater quantities than there, for besides some sugar factories which have been built, the Indians are so fond of sugar cane, to eat in the cane, that they have planted a great deal and it produces very well and the Indians take to it even better and sell it all the year around in their markets like any other fruit. In the inland country, with what it originally had and what has been brought from Spain and can be produced and raised here, there is material enough to supply with fruit all of Asia, Africa, and Europe; wherefore this may well be called another New World.

What this country begs of God is that He give to its king a long life and many sons, so that he may give it a prince to rule and ennoble it and give it prosperity, both spiritual and temporal. This is a matter of vital importance; for a land so large and so remote and distant cannot be well governed from so far away, nor can a thing so far removed and divided from Castile endure, without suffering great desolation and many difficulties, and deteriorating from day to day because it lacks the personal presence of its principal lord and king to govern it and maintain it in justice and perpetual peace, and reward the good and loyal vassals, punishing the rebels and tyrants who would usurp the property of the crown.

8. Spanish: *gente plática.*

CHAPTER X

Of the great number of rivers and streams in these mountains, and especially two remarkable springs; of other peculiarities and characteristics of these mountains; and of how the lions and tigers have killed many people.

WHAT the soil needs most and what makes it good is abundant water, of which there is a great deal in these mountains, both rain water, by which the soil is frequently irrigated, and the water of fountains and springs in which the land abounds—I mean to the north and south. So great is the number of brooks and rivers that flow everywhere from these mountains that in truth I once counted in the space of two leagues twenty-five rivers and brooks, and that was not in the part of the country where there is the most water, but just that it happened to occur to me, as I was going on a trip, to count what rivers and brooks there might be in two leagues, so as to be able to make an accurate statement, and I found the twenty-five rivers and brooks that I have mentioned. In many other parts of these mountains one would find what I have said, and much more, for the land is very hilly.

Throughout New Spain there are very large and very beautiful springs, some of them so large that even at their source they form a river. I have seen this in many different places. Among them, two seem to me to be especially worthy of being recorded and to be reasons for glorifying and praising the Lord who made them. All the Spaniards who have seen them have found in them much cause for praising and blessing God, who created such things, and they all say and confess that in all the lands through which they travelled they never saw such a thing. Both these springs rise at the foot of these mountains and are of very fine, clear water. One the Spaniards call the spring of Ahuilizapán, because it rises in a town of that name, which in our tongue means 'white water;' it is very white and clear and rises with great force. The other is in a town called Aticpac. This is a round spring, so large that a person would have difficulty in shooting a crossbow bolt from one side to the other. It is very deep in the middle; at the edges it has thirty-eight to forty-three feet of water. In all parts of it the water is so clear that one can see the ground at the bottom—or rather, the stones, for it rises among great stones and rocks, and one can see everything as clearly as if it were only about three feet under water. From this pool there flows so much water that it forms a great, wide river full of fish, and there are many good fish in the pool itself.

This spring that I speak of rises at the foot of two mountains and has above it a very remarkable and most beautiful rocky hill covered with a pleasant grove, so that it could not be prettier or better modeled or proportioned if it were painted or, as they say, made of wax. At the bottom it is very round, and as it rises it narrows equally on all sides and must be between five and six hundred feet high. In the old days many sacrifices were offered both on the hill and at the spring, as being especially striking spots.

It is certainly a very noteworthy and wonderful thing to see from some distance mountains so high and so huge that it seems impossible that any river could pass through them, and to know that in their depths God gives the rivers their channels and their courses, now wide and clear, now narrow and remote.[1] In some places they flow very gently; in others they run with such violence that it inspires fear and terror in those who look at them to see them make their way between great lofty cliffs of precipitous rock and to see a mighty river running into a very narrow channel. At other times He makes the rivers fall from so great a height that one can scarcely see the bottom, and no one dares approach the edge to look. If a mountain is placed across its path, the river's violence mines and pierces it and makes a way by which it can insinuate itself and carry its fury to the other side, leaving above it a firm, safe bridge cut out of the mountain itself, over which one can pass without danger. High up on these mountains and also down below it is all inhabited country, and also along the river banks and on the slopes there are towns that show up from a distance and greatly adorn and beautify all that region.

When the friars go out from their monasteries to preach and baptize in the towns situated in these mountains, which are far away from the monasteries, as soon as the news of their coming is known, the lords of those towns come out to the road to meet them or send messengers from thirty or forty leagues away to beg them to come to their towns to

1. Spanish: *ya anchas, ya llanas, angostas y apartadas.* Something is wrong with this sentence. There is no feminine plural noun for these adjectives to agree with. Apparently they modify *canales y cursos,* and should be masculine. Also, I have translated it as if it read: *ya anchas y llanas, ya angostas y apartadas.*

baptize many people who are waiting for the friars to teach them the Word of God. Some of these towns are high up on the mountains, others are down in the depth of the valleys, and so the friars have to ascend into the clouds—for as the mountains are so high they are always covered with clouds—and at other times descend into the abyss. As the terrain is very uneven and, on account of the dampness, is in many places covered with mud and very slippery and treacherous, the poor friars cannot make these journeys without suffering great difficulties and hardships. I am sure that those who travel around this country will well remember what I say, and confess and admit that all this is true. In spite of all this the friars go to them and administer the sacraments and preach the word and gospel of Christ; for, seeing their faith and the urgency with which they demand it, what toil would one not undertake for God and for the souls which He created in His own image and likeness and redeemed with His precious blood, for whom He Himself says that He passed days of sorrow and of great toil?

The towns lower down on the coast, when they hear that the friars are making visits, go at once to receive them and take them in acallis, or boats, to their towns; for in the country toward the coast one has in many places to travel by the rivers, since the roads have fallen into disrepair because there are so few inhabitants. This part of the country, formerly thickly settled and filled with people, is now very much depopulated. Very few Indians are left: this is due to the heavy tributes and taxes that the Spaniards demanded and the houses that they had to build for the Spaniards far away from their own towns, and the many Indians that the Spaniards took as slaves although they were not rightfully of that class; and in some places because of wars and military raids; another reason is that the lions and tigers have eaten a great many people, which they did not do before the Spaniards came. The reason for this is supposed to be that when the population was large the lions and tigers did not dare to come out or to come down from the high mountains to the lowland, and later they preyed upon the Indians who died along the roads. Perhaps it was by permission of God, because when all the other towns in the land received the Faith and were baptized it would have been right for these also to awake and seek the true God, and they did not do it. The same fate overtook them as overtook the foreign gentiles who settled Samaria; for because they neither feared

God nor worshipped Him, God ordered the lions to descend from the mountains and kill and eat them. In this same manner, at the time I speak of, the lions and tigers here came out into the coast towns and killed and ate many Indians, and some Spaniards as well, so that many towns were almost entirely depopulated and the Indians were obliged to leave the land. Those who remained had to live close together and build enclosures and palisades, and even so they were not safe unless they kept watch at night.

I myself saw other towns where the inhabitants retired to sleep at night high up above the ground; for they build their straw huts on four wooden posts. In the space that is covered by the straw there is an attic or scaffold, closed on all sides, and every night they go up there to sleep and take their hens and dogs and cats up with them. If they forget to shut up anything, the tigers and lions are so unerring that they eat up anything that is forgotten and left down below. The dogs and cats and birds are so clever that at nightfall they all get into a place of safety, without any need of one's ringing the curfew, for they are all careful to take refuge in time, on pain of death and of being eaten by the lions and tigers. Since the natives have been baptized and come to confession and have built churches the cruelty of those animals has greatly decreased.

In order to defend and preserve their Indians, the Spaniards got good dogs, which they brought from Castile, and with them they have killed many tigers and lions. In one town called Chocamán they killed one hundred and ten tigers and lions by actual count, and in another named Amatlán the Indian lord of the town got two of the Spanish dogs, one of them very good, with which he killed one hundred and twenty lions and tigers. I saw many of the skins. When they kill these animals the men have to help the dogs, for here when the tigers and lions are attacked they at once climb up into the trees, and one has to shoot arrows at them to get them down, since they often cannot be reached even with a long lance, for they climb trees like a cat. When men are travelling in a group in this country and sleep out of doors, they build a great many fires around themselves, for the lions and tigers are very much afraid of fire and flee from it.

For these reasons that I have mentioned most of the intercourse and travelling of the Indians in that land is by acallis, or boats, on the water. Acalli in this language means 'a house built on water.' In these boats they navigate the big rivers, like those along the coast, and carry on their fishing and commerce. In these also they go out into the sea, and in the big ones they go from one island to another, or venture to cross some small gulf. These acallis, or boats, are made each of a single piece of a tree as big and as thick as the length demands and in proportion to the width that they can give it, which is the diameter of the tree of which it is made. They have master craftsmen who make these boats, just as in the Basque provinces there are master shipbuilders; and as the rivers grow larger as they approach the coast, so the acallis, or boats, are also bigger.

In all the big rivers of the coast, and even at a distance of a good many leagues upstream, there are sharks and lizards,[2] which are marine beasts. Some claim that these lizards are a kind of crocodile. Some of them are eighteen feet long, and I have even been told that in some places there are bigger ones, almost as thick through the body as a horse. There are others smaller. Where these beasts or the sharks are especially savage no one dares to put a hand out of the boat, for these creatures are very quick in the water and snap off whatever they can reach, and can carry off a man in their jaws. They also have killed many Indians and some few Spaniards. The lizards come out of the water and are very well armed by their own skin, which is so hard that striking it with a spear or an arrow is no more use than striking a rock. On nights when the Indians sleep on the water in those boats they have to be very careful for fear of the marine beasts; and for fear of the lions and tigers they do not dare to land.

The rivers also, before they empty into the sea, form very big estuaries and wide lagoons, so wide that one can scarcely see from one shore to the other, and out on the lagoon one almost loses sight of land. When there is a strong wind these lagoons form great waves, as does the sea, and so violent that if any Indians go out to fish in those acallis and are caught in the storm, it terrifies them and endangers their lives. So that, as Saint Paul says, all the world is full of pitfalls, dangers, snares and traps, from all of which God delivers those occupied and engaged in His service, as He does those who have to do with the conversion of

2. *Alligator mississipiensis* (length up to 12 ft.) is found in southern North America. *Crocodilus acutus* occurs throughout the West Indies and from the southern United States to Colombia. Which of the two is referred to in the text is hard to say.

these Indians; for up to the present we know of no friar who has been killed by wild beasts, although some have been among them; nor has any friar died in any ship that has come from Spain, nor has any ship been lost in which friars were travelling, for God protects them marvellously.

CHAPTER XI

Continuing the same subject, naming some great rivers that come down from the mountains, and telling of their riches; treats somewhat of Peru.

HAVING said something about the mountains, although very briefly, it will be only right to say something about the rivers that flow from them, which are very numerous and very great, as is shown by the navigation chart, in which one can clearly see that their size is such that from many of them one can get fresh water way out at sea, and one can sail up them for many leagues. All their banks used to be thickly settled by Indians, although now in many parts and provinces the conquests and raids made by our fleets have greatly depopulated the country and the remaining Indians have been frightened and have fled inland. I have seen some of these rivers that I shall speak of, but I shall tell here of only one, which is neither the largest nor the smallest; judging by it, one may understand what the size of the others must be and what they are like.

This river of which I speak is called in the Indian language Papaloapán,[1] which is a good name, for it swallows[2] and draws into itself many rivers. The land watered by this river is of the best and richest in all New Spain, and the Spaniards coveted it. Those who received allotments here got heavy tributes and sucked the land so dry that they left it poorer than any other, for it was so far from Mexico that it had no one to protect it. The Spaniards named it the River of Alvarado,[3] because when they came to conquer this land the Adelantado Pedro de

1. According to Torquemada (vol. II, p. 614) *Papaloapan* means butterfly.

2. Motolinía is playing on the first syllables of the name, *papa,* and the Spanish verb *papar,* which means to swallow.

3 Apparently the name Alvarado is now confined to the lagoon at the mouth of the river, and the river itself is called by the Indian name.

Alvarado went ahead with his ship and went inland up this river. It rises in the mountains of Tzonquilica, though its principal and largest spring is the one at Aticpac which I have mentioned.[4] Into this river of Papaloapán flow other large rivers, such as the Quimichtepec, Huitzila, Chinantla, Quauhquepaltepec, Tochtlan, and the Teuhziyuca.[5] There is no small quantity of gold in all these rivers, but the richest one is the Huitzila.

Each of these rivers, being large, is navigable by boat, and there is a great deal of very good fish in them. After all of these tributaries enter the main stream it becomes a very fine river, running between beautiful banks covered with great groves. When it is in flood it tears up the trees, and it is certainly a sight to see its violence and how it rises. Before it empties into the sea it overflows and fills great estuaries and forms great lagoons, and with all this it is at the lowest some thirteen or fourteen feet deep and forms three channels, one rocky, one muddy, and one sandy. This river has so many fish that all those estuaries and lagoons are crammed full, and the fish seem to swarm on all sides. I could say a great deal about this river and its riches, and so that you may have some idea of it, I shall tell about one single estuary seven or eight leagues long which is called 'God's Pool.'

This estuary or lagoon that I speak of forms the boundary between two towns, one called Quauhquepaltepec and the other Otlatitlán. Both were big and rich in inhabitants as in everything else. The lagoon is as wide as a good-sized river and is very deep, and, though it carries a good body of water, since it goes through very level country, it does not seem to have any current. Because of the abundant fish to be found there it is frequented by sharks, lizards, and *bufeos.*[6] There are shad as big as dolphins, and they travel in schools and leap out of the water like dolphins. There are also shad like the Spanish variety and of the same size. Both kinds resemble each other in scales, in nature, and in name. Manatees, or *malatis,* come up this estuary and breed here.

Many birds of many different kinds also feed here. There are royal herons, and others as big but darker and with shorter necks; there are

4. See above, bk. III, ch. x.

5. Ramírez, in *Historia de los Indios,* p. 202, says that the names of these rivers are very hard to decipher in the manuscript. Torquemada (vol. II, p. 614), who is following Motolinía closely, gives the names as Quiyotepec, Huitzilan, Chinantla, Quauhquetzpaltepec, Tuztlan, Teyuciyacan. These names do not appear on modern maps.

6. I have been unable to identify this fish.

other birds like storks but with a bigger bill, which is a very cruel weapon; there are night-herons, from many of which they make beautiful plumes, for the feathers are much larger than is the case with the Spanish night-heron, and there are innumerable pelicans and cormorants. Some of these and other birds catch many fish by diving under water. The other, smaller birds who do not know how to fish wait for the struggle between the big fish and the smaller ones, and between the medium-sized ones and the little ones, and when the school is broken up and some of the fish jump out of the water and others take refuge by the shore, then these birds feed on the fish that jump and on the ones that come to the edge of the water. Then, when least expected, hawks and falcons swoop down to feed upon the birds that are feeding upon the fish, and as there are so many of them they find plenty to feed upon. Both are so remarkable that it fills one with wonder to see how one set feeds upon the other, and the other upon still another, and each has its slayer.

Then, turning to the bank and the meadows, there are deer and rabbits and hares in abundance, especially deer, and the tigers and lions come here to feed upon them. On both sides of the lagoon, moreover, are very fine groves, and besides the birds that I have already mentioned, there is a sort of reptile which the Indians call *quaulitizpal,*[7] which means 'a wood serpent;'[8] the big lizards they call 'water serpents.' In the Islands they call the former iguanas. They live on land and also partly on land and partly in the water, and they seem very terrible to people who do not know them. They are marked with many different colors and are approximately four feet long. Others in the mountains and woods are duller colored and smaller. Both of these they eat on fish days, and their flesh and flavor is like rabbit. They come out into the sun and climb up into the trees, especially on clear days.

In this estuary and in the river there are many other kinds of birds, especially some very beautiful ones which the Indians call *teocacholli,*[9]

7. Quauhquetzpalin, according to Torquemada (vol. II, p. 615).

8. Spanish: *sierpe de monte.* Torquemada (*loc. cit.*) calls it *sierpe de árboles.*

9. Sahagún (vol. III, pp. 163-164) calls this bird *tlauhquechol* or *teoquechol,* and says of it "It lives in the water and is like a duck. Its feet are like those of a duck, broad and red (*colorados*); its beak also is red (*colorado*) and shaped like an apothecary's spatula; it has a little red (*colorado*) crest on its head; its breast, underparts, tail and wings are of a very fine red (*encarnado*); the back and wing joint very red (*colorado*), the beak and feet yellow. They say that this bird is the prince of the white herons, which flock to it wherever they see it." He seems to be undecided about the feet, which are once called red and once yellow! In reality they are yellow, and the plumage is a

which means 'god *cacholli*.' The Indians regard these birds as gods, both because of their beauty and because of their value. All their plumage is very fine for the work that the Indians do in gold and feathers. These birds are larger than Castilian cocks. Among many other species of ducks there are also some that are black with a little white on the wings which are neither exactly geese nor exactly wild ducks.[10] These also are valuable. From them they get the feathers used in weaving the rich feather mantles. Inland one of these birds was equivalent in value to a slave. Now the Indians have ducks from Castile, and wild ducks to pluck and get feathers for weaving, but the feathers of the Castilian ducks are not as good as those of the native ones.

In this river and its lagoons and estuaries they catch manatees, which, I believe, are the most valuable fish in the world. Some of them have as much flesh as an ox, and their mouth very much resembles that of an ox. The mouth is somewhat more hidden and the chin thicker and more fleshy than in the ox. They come out to feed along the banks, and know how to choose good pasturage, for they live on grass. They do not come more than half way out of the water, and raise themselves on their two hands, or rather wide stumps or flippers, on which one can see four nails, as in the case of the elephant, only these are much smaller. Their eyes and hide are like the elephant's. The rest of their appearance and characteristics are well described in the book of the *General History of the Indies*.[11] They are to be found in this estuary, and here the Indians harpoon them and catch them with nets.

Of the two occasions on which I was on the estuary that I speak of, one was in the afternoon of a clear, calm day, and in truth I went along open mouthed looking at that 'Pool of God.' I saw how trifling are man's affairs and the buildings and pools of the great princes and lords of Spain, and how everything is counterfeit among the princes of this world who work so hard to hunt birds in order to fly their falcons, and take such pride in them; and others strive to hoard silver and gold, and

---

deep pink, with crimson on the head, back, and wings. The bird has been identified as the roseate spoonbill (see Seler, *Feather Ornaments*, p. 68).

10. Spanish: *lavancos*. These birds which Fray Toribio describes as "neither exactly geese nor exactly wild ducks," are undoubtedly tree ducks (Dendrocygna). For this ornithological information I am indebted to Professor Samuel A. Elliot of Smith College.

11. Probably Oviedo y Valdés, *General y natural historia de las Indias*, of which the *Sumario* was published in Toledo in 1526. The manatí, and the method of harpooning it, are described in ch. LXXXIII.

build houses and gardens and pools, and on this they base their happiness. Let them consider, and come here, for here they will find it all together, made by the hand of God, without toil or trouble; all of which invites one to give thanks to Him who made the springs and brooks and everything else in the world, created with such beauty, and all for the service of man.

With all this they are discontented. From a land as rich and as distant as Spain many have come, discontented with what contented their parents—who, perchance, were better and more worth while than they—to seek that black gold of this land which costs so dear, and to enrich themselves and usurp, in alien territory, what belongs to the poor Indians and treat them and make use of them like slaves. For if one considers and observes, what have all the rivers of New Spain been but so many rivers of Babylon, by which so many have died and so many bodies and souls have perished? And, oh, how the widows and even the wives in Spain weep over this, mourning for those who were drowned in these rivers and killed in this land, and for those who are living here in forgetfulness and in sin, without thought of returning to their homes or where they left the wives given to them by the law and commandment of God. Others delay their departure, not wishing to go until they are very rich, and most of these God allows to end by dying in the poorhouse. There ought to be a judge for these men, to bring pressure to bear on them with penalties, for it would be better for them to be good for evil reasons than to let them persevere in their sin. Some part of the blame may rest upon the prelates and confessors, for if they did what they could and chastised and reproved these evildoers, they would go back to their homes and take care of their children. The inhabitants of the Islands, not content with the Indians whom they have exterminated, depopulating the Islands, seek out all kinds of ways and means of coming with their fleets to make raids on the mainland. Let them put as good a face upon this as they wish before men, for in the sight of God I know not how it will appear.

Oh, what a river of Babylon flowed in the land of Peru! And into what bitter tears was converted the accursed black gold, for greed of which many sold their patrimonies, on which they could have lived as well as their ancestors! Deceived by their vain fancies they came to weep in the land from which they thought to get the means of enjoyment;

for even before they reached Peru scarcely one out of ten, or ten out of a hundred, escaped, and those who did escape, when they reached Peru, died a thousand times of hunger and as often of thirst, not to mention many other innumerable difficulties; and that does not count the ones who died by the sword, who were not the smallest number. Because one out of a thousand has returned to Spain laden with riches, perchance ill-gotten, which will not, according to Saint Augustine, last to the third heir—and these men and their gold are all of the same color (*i.e.,* yellow) because along with the gold they have acquired a thousand diseases. Some are crippled with syphilis, others with colic, with diseases of the spleen, the kidneys, or with the 'stone' and a thousand other kinds and classes of ills, so that those who come to New Spain are recognized by their color and people say at once, "He's from Peru." But for each one, I say, who returns to Spain with all these diseases (not to mention the worst, which is that of the soul) as a rich man, a thousand other fools are moved to go in search of the death of both soul and body. And since you were not content to get along with what you had in Spain and live as your ancestors did, as a penalty for your error it is only right that you should suffer fatigues and troubles without number.

O land of Peru, river of Babylon, mountains of Gilboa, where so many Spaniards and so noble a people have perished and died, you were indeed included in the curse of David,[12] for on many parts of your land there falls no rain or dew. Ye nobles of Spain, weep over these accursed mountains! For those who, in the wars of Italy and Africa, fought like lions against their enemies and flew like eagles in pursuit of their adversaries, in Peru died not like valiant men nor as befitted them, but of hunger and thirst and cold, suffering innumerable other troubles, some on the sea, some in harbors, others on the roads and others in the mountains and wilds.

I have heard it stated as true that although the land of Peru was among the last to be discovered it has cost more Spanish lives than did the Islands and the Mainland and New Spain. Where in heathen countries have there been so recently so many battles as there have been between Christians in Peru, and such cruel ones, where so many men died? The field was well marked with the blood that was shed there.

12. II Samuel 1.21. "Ye mountains of Gilboa, let there be no dew, neither let there be rain, upon you, nor fields of offerings; for there the shield of the mighty is vilely cast away, the shield of Saul, as though he had not been anointed with oil."

What happened later shows the great horror of these cruel deaths; for as this battle[13] was fought in open fields where there are neither trees nor forests, on some nights many lights were seen and many fearful and horrible cries were heard, as of people engaged in battle, crying: "Down with them! Down with them! Kill them! Kill them! Have at them! Have at them! Catch him! Carry him off! Don't spare his life!" Etc. Many Spaniards who have come from Peru to New Spain have certified that this is true. This fact also bears witness to it, that the place where the battle was fought was thereafter so fearful that even in the daytime no one dared to pass through it, and those who are obliged by necessity to go that way appear to go in terror and their hair stands on end without their being able to prevent it.

More potent was the avarice of our Spaniards to destroy and depopulate this land than all the sacrifices and wars and assassinations that took place in its pagan days, even counting all those who were sacrificed everywhere—and they were numerous. Because some had the diabolical notion and idea that if they carried on their conquest with fire and blood, the Indians would serve them better and would always remain in subjection and fear, they laid waste all the towns to which they came. How much better would it have been in truth to win them by love so as to have them to use! The land, if populated, would have been rich and all of them would have been rich too and would not have had so much of which to give a strict accounting at the time of the final judgment, since God Himself says that for each soul of a fellow creature thou shalt give thine own, and nothing else; for Christ, as Sovereign Lord, takes what is good and is satisfied only with the best as well for the Indian who dies in your service because of the excessive work that you give him, or by your agency, and especially if by your fault he dies without baptism. For remember, you are their guardians and they are given to you as wards and as a trust and you have to give an account of them, and a very strict one, for the blood and the death of these whom you value so little will cry aloud before God, as well from the land of Peru as from the Islands and the Mainland.

So keep the pot well filled and don't bother about your will,[14] for he who does not do what he ought eats his death from his own pot.[15]

13. This seems to refer to one particular battle, which, however, he has not previously mentioned.

14. Spanish: *ande buena olla y mal testamento.*

15. Spanish: *su muerte come en la olla.*

Do not worry about knowing whence comes the hen that you have not paid for, nor why they bring the rabbits and quail and other gifts and tributes, for you wish your wants to be supplied without caring to know the damage that your cattle are doing in other people's fields and seeded ground—jewels which, when it comes time to pay the tributes, are excessive—and bid them furnish blankets and shoes for the men servants and the maids, and clothing and footgear for the slaves and honey and wax and salt and pottery and matting and whatever the ladies fancy. To demand all this of the blacks is an abuse which should be remedied and one should feel that this tribute is received with a bad conscience, for all these things shall be brought forward and presented at the day of your death, if you do not before that make restitution. Do not wait until the moment of accounting, when you cannot turn back and there is no opportunity to reform. Certainly God shows great mercy to those whom He withdraws from their sins on this side of death and gives them time for repentance and the light of knowledge. This is the object of writing such things as I have written, that he who sleeps may wake.

When the Spaniards embark for this land some are told and some imagine that they are going to the Island of Ophir, whence King Solomon brought very fine gold, and that all who go there will become rich. Others think that they are going to the Isles of Tarshish or to the great Cipango, where the gold is so plentiful everywhere that they gather it by the skirtful. Others say that they are going in search of the Seven Cities, which are so great and so rich that they will all be lords. O fools and worse than fools! If only God would let *one* of all those who have died in these parts rise from the dead and go about the world and disillusion men and bear witness to the truth and cry aloud so that men would cease to come to such places to seek death with their hands! They are like tickets in a lottery of which twenty are numbered and have prizes, while ten or twelve thousand come out blank.

CHAPTER XII

Of the intelligence and great skill of the Indians in learning everything that they are taught; everything that they see with their eyes they make very quickly.

HE who teaches men knowledge, that same One provided and gave to these Indians great intelligence and skill to learn all the subjects, arts, and crafts that have been taught them, and they have succeeded with all of them in so short a time because as soon as they see the crafts that in Castile men take many years to learn, just by looking at them and watching the craftsmen work many have become masters. Their understanding is keen, modest, and quiet, not proud or showy as in other nations.

They learned to read quickly, both in Spanish and in Latin, in print and in manuscript. There is scarcely a letter written in their own language out of the many which they write to each other, for as messengers are cheap the letters go thick and fast. And all know how to read them, even those who have recently begun to be taught.

They learned to write in a short time, for after writing only a few days they can at once make an exact copy of the material that their masters give them. If the masters change the form of writing—as it is a very common thing for different men to make the letters in different ways—they also change their writing at once and make it like what their master gives them.

In the second year after we began to teach them they gave a papal bull as a copy to a boy from Tetzcoco, and he copied it so exactly that his writing seemed to be the original itself, for the first line was in large letters and below he made the signature exactly as it was on the original, and a Christ with an image of Our Lady, all so exact that there seemed to be no difference between the model and the other writing. A Spaniard took it to Castile as a remarkable and first-class thing. Large letters, Greek letters, the lines of the pentagram and the musical notes—both for plain song and for organum—they do very freely and have made many books of them. They have also learned to bind books and illuminate them—some of them very well—and they have made woodcuts with very perfect figures, so much so that everyone who sees them is astonished, for they make them perfect the very first time. I have some very fine examples of these.

The third year we started to teach them singing and some people laughed and made fun of it, both because the Indians seemed to be singing out of tune and because they seemed to have weak voices—and in truth they do not have voices as strong or as sweet as the Spaniards. I think it is caused by their going about barefooted, with their chests ill-protected, and by their food being so poor. But as there are many of them to choose from, there are always fairly good choirs.

It was quite a sight to see the first man who began to teach them to sing. He was an old friar[1] who knew scarcely anything of the Indian language, only Castilian, and he talked with the boys as correctly and sensibly as if he were talking with intelligent Spaniards. Those of us who heard him were helpless with laughter, and the boys listening to him stood openmouthed to see what he meant. It was marvellous that, although at first they did not understand a thing and the old man had no interpreter, in a short time they understood him and learned to sing so that now there are many of them so skillful that they direct choirs. As they are quick-witted and have an excellent memory, most of what they sing they know by heart, so that if the pages get mixed up or the book falls while they are singing this does not prevent them from singing on without the slightest error. Also, if they lay the book on a table, the ones who see it upside down or from the side sing just as well as those who are in front of it. One of these Indian singers, an inhabitant of this city of Tlaxcallan, has composed unaided a whole Mass which has been approved by good Castilian singers who have seen it.

Instead of organs they have a music played upon harmonized flutes which sounds really like a pipe organ[2] because there are many flutes together. This music was taught to the Indians by some minstrels who came from Spain. As there was no one here who could receive and feed them all together, we asked them to divide themselves up among the Indian towns and teach them for pay, and so they taught them. The Indians also make *chirimías,*[3] though they do not know how to give them the proper tone.

1. Fray Juan Caro. See above, bk. II, ch. III.
2. Spanish: *órganos de palo.*
3. An instrument somewhat resembling the clarinet.

An Indian boy who played the flute taught other Indians in Tehuacán, and within a month they all knew how to play a Mass and vespers, hymns, the Magnificat and some motets, and in six months they were very good flutists. Here in Tlaxcallan there was a Spaniard who played the rebec, and an Indian made a rebec and asked the Spaniard to teach him. The Spaniard gave him only three lessons, in which he learned all that the Spaniard knew, and in less than ten days he was playing the rebec with the flutes, and they say that it sounded above them all. Just recently I have learned that there is in Mexico a maestro who plays the viol[4] and has already made viols of all four voices. I believe that within the year the Indians if they are any good will know as much as their teacher.

There were many different opinions, both among the friars and among other people, about beginning to teach them Latin or grammar, and certainly it was difficult enough to teach them; but, as we have succeeded very well with it, we consider the effort worth while, for many of them are good grammarians and compose long, correct sentences and verses in hexameter and pentameter.

What one should value most is the good discipline of the students, like that of novice friars, and costing little effort on the part of the teacher. These students and school-boys have their well-regulated school, where they are taught by themselves; after it was seen that they were making progress in their studies, those from the section of San Francisco de México were transferred to the other section which is called Santiago de Tlatilolco, where they are now, with two friars who teach them and an Indian instructor who expounds grammar to them.[5]

A very good thing happened to a priest, recently come from Castile who could not believe that the Indians knew the catechism or the Pater Noster or the Creed correctly. Other Spaniards told him that they did, but he was still incredulous. Just then the students came out of school and the priest, thinking that they were some of the other Indians, asked one of them if he knew the Pater Noster. They boy said that he did, and the priest made him repeat it and then made him say the Creed, and he said it correctly. The priest criticized a word which the boy had used correctly, and as the Indian insisted that he was right and the priest insisted that

4. Spanish: *vihuela de arco.*

5. Both Sahagún (vol. III, pp. 87-91) and Torquemada (vol. III, pp. 111-112.) discuss the work done by this school, its early success and later decline.

he was not, the student was obliged to prove why he was right, and he asked the priest in Latin: "Reverende Pater, cujus casus est?" Then as the priest knew no grammar he was confused and embarrassed.

CHAPTER XIII

Of the mechanical trades that the Indians have learned from the Spaniards; and of those which they knew before.

THE Indians have reached a high degree of perfection in the mechanical trades, both those which they originally knew and those which they learned for the first time from the Spaniards. They have become great painters since they saw the examples of Flemish and Italian art and the pictures of saints that the Spaniards brought. Some very fine pieces have come to this country, for everything comes where there is gold and silver. Especially fine are the painters in Mexico, for everything good that comes to this country ultimately reaches this city. Formerly they could paint nothing but a flower or a bird or a design, and if they painted a man or a horse, the figure was very badly formed; now they make good images. They also learned to beat gold, for a gold beater who came to this New Spain, although he tried to conceal his craft from the Indians, was unable to do so, for they watched all the details of the craft, counted the number of blows he struck with the hammer, and noticed how he kept turning the mold. Within a year they made gold leaf.

Some have also learned to make good tooled and gilded leather by stealing the craft from the master when he would not teach it to them, although they had considerable difficulty in giving it the gold and silver colors. They have also made some good bells with a good tone. This was one of the crafts in which they had the best success. To be good silversmiths all that they lack is the tools which they do not have, but by hammering with one stone upon another they can make a plain cup and a plate. In casting a piece and making it in a mold they surpass the Spanish silversmiths, for they can cast a bird whose tongue, head, and wings move, and they can mold a monkey or other monster which moves its head, tongue, hands and feet, and in its hands they put little implements, so that the figure seems to be dancing with them. What is even more remarkable, they can make a piece half in gold and half in silver and cast a fish with all its scales, in gold and silver, alternating.

They have learned to tan hides, to make blacksmith's bellows, and they are good shoemakers, who make shoes, housemaid's slippers, laced boots, slippers, clogs for women, and everything else that is made in Spain. This trade began in Michuacán because it is there that they tan good deerskins. They make all the necessary parts of a saddle.[1] It is true that they were not succeeding in making the tree, but as a saddlemaker had a tree at his door an Indian waited till the saddler went in to eat and stole the tree so as to make one by it. Then another day at the same hour, while the saddler was eating, the Indian put the tree back in its place, and six or seven days later he came along the streets selling saddletrees, and went to the saddlemaker's house and asked him if he wanted to buy some of those trees. This, I think, grieved the saddler, for as soon as the Indians learn a craft the Spaniards have to lower their prices. As there is only one man who practices each craft they sell at any price they choose to ask, and the skill and great cleverness of the Indians has interfered seriously with this.

There are Indian blacksmiths, weavers, stonecutters, carpenters, and carvers. The trade that they have taken up best and the one in which they have had the greatest success is tailoring, for they can make breeches, doublet, coat or waistcoat of whatever kind you ask for as well as in Castile, and all other garments, whose styles are innumerable—for they (*i. e.*, the Spaniards) do nothing but change their clothes and seek for new fashions. They also make gloves and hose of knitted silk, and silk caps, and they are also fairly good embroiderers. They fashion *bandurrias,*[2] *vihuelas,*[3] and harps, with all sorts of garlands and adornments. They have made so many armchairs that the Spaniards' houses are full of them. They also make very good flutes.

In Mexico there was a certain penitent and as he wore a sambenito,[4] the Indians seeing that this was a new style of garment, one of them thought that the Spaniards wore it in Lent as an act of devotion, and he went home at once and made sambenitos, very well made and brightly

1. The following parts are enumerated: *bastos y fuste, coraza y sobre-coraza.* The *fuste* is the saddle-tree; the others parts I have not been able to identify.

2. A flat-backed stringed instrument like the lower half of a guitar.

3. A guitar-like instrument whose strings were plucked with the fingers. The *vihuela de arco* (See above, bk. III, ch. XII) is a different instrument, belonging to the violin family.

4. A yellow scapular with a red Saint Andrew's cross on the front and back. The wearing of this garment was imposed as a penance by the Inquisition on repentant and reconciled heretics.

colored. Then he went about Mexico to sell his garment among the Spaniards, saying in the Indian language: "Tic cohuaznequi sambenito?" which means, "Will you buy a sambenito?" The incident provoked so much laughter all over the country that I think it even reached Spain, and in Mexico the phrase "Ti que quis benito" became a proverb.

CHAPTER XIV

Of the death of three children who were killed by the Indians because they preached to them and destroyed their idols, and of how the children killed one who said that he was the god of wine.

AT the beginning, when the Friars Minor came to seek the salvation of the souls of these Indians, it seemed best to them that the sons of the lords and principal personages should be collected in the monasteries. In this matter, as in everything else that had to do with the teaching of Christianity, they were much favored and aided by the Marquis of the Valley, who was governing at that time; and as the Indians loved and feared him greatly they willingly obeyed his command in everything, even in giving up their sons, which at first was so hard for them that some lords concealed them and instead adorned and dressed up the son of some servant, vassal, or slave and sent him, accompanied, as a further precaution, by others to serve him, so as not to have to give up their own son. Others gave up some of their sons and kept the eldest and the favorites. This was at first, until they saw that the children who were brought up in the house of God were well treated and well taught, for when they recognized the advantages, they themselves came to bring them to us and to pray with them. Then we found out about the children whom they had concealed. Since it comes in appropriately, I shall tell here about how the children killed an Indian who claimed to be a god, and then about the murder of one boy by his father and the deaths of two other Indian children who had become Christians.

When the Friars Minor, in their first year in the city of Tlaxcallan, took the sons of the lords and principal men to train them in the doctrine of our holy Faith, those who served in the temples of the devil were persisting in the service of the idols and in inducing the people not to give up their gods, who, they claimed, were truer than those that the friars preached, and they said that they would prove this. For this reason, there went out into the tianquizco, or market-place, one of the ministers of the devil, who, because he was dressed in certain insignia of an idol, or devil, called Ometochtli and because he was his minister, was called Ometoch Cotoya, as will be depicted here.[1] This devil Ometochtli was one of the principal Indian gods and was worshipped as the god of wine and very much feared and respected; for they were all in the habit of getting drunk and from their drunkenness came all their vices and sins.

These ministers, thus dressed in the garments of the devil, seldom came out of the temples or courtyards of the devil, and when they did come out they were treated with such respect and reverence that people scarcely dared to raise their eyes to look at them. Well, this minister, thus dressed, went out and walked about in the marketplace, eating and chewing certain sharp stones that they use here in place of knives. These stones are as black as jet, and by a special technique they cut them very thin and about six inches in length[2] with edges as sharp as a knife, which, however, break and chip very easily. This minister of the devil, to show how fierce he was and that he could do what others could not, was going about the marketplace chewing these blades. At that time the children who were being taught at the monastery were coming back from bathing in the river and had to cross the tianquizco, or marketplace, and when they saw so many people following the devil they asked what that was, and some Indians answered, saying: "Our god Ometochtli." The children said: "He is not a god, but a devil who lies to you and deceives you." In the middle of the marketplace stood a cross where the children used to go to pray as they passed. Here they stopped until all the people had gathered together, for as there were many of them they were scattered about the place.

While they were there the evil demon—or rather the man who wore his garments—came toward them and began to scold the children and show himself very savage, saying to them that they would all die very soon, for they had angered him and had left his house and gone to that of Saint Mary. To this the bigger children, who were bolder, answered that he was a liar and that they were not in the least afraid of him, for he was not God, but the devil and an evil deceiver. Meanwhile the minister of the

1. No description follows. Does this indicate that a sketch of the god Ometochtli with his insignia was to be inserted in the manuscript?

2. Spanish: *un jeme*. The distance from the tip of the thumb to the tip of the first finger.

devil continued to assert that he was a god and that he was going to kill them all, looking very angry in order to frighten them more. Then one of the boys said: "Let us see now who will die, we or this man," and stooped to pick up a stone and said to the others: "Let us drive this devil away, for God will help us." Saying this, he threw the stone at him, and then all the others came to his assistance. Although the devil stood up to them at first, he began to flee when so many boys attacked him and the children pursued him, yelling and throwing stones at him. He was about to escape, but since God permitted and his sins deserved it, he stumbled and fell, and scarcely had he fallen when they had him killed and buried under stones, and, full of glee, were saying: "We killed the devil who was trying to kill us. Now the macehuales (who are the common people) will see that he was no god, but only a liar, and that God and Saint Mary are good." The strife and the contest over, it seemed as if they had killed not a man, but the devil himself.

And just as when the battle is done those who remain in the field are joyful over their victory and the vanquished are dispirited and sad, so all those who believed in and served the idols were sad and dispirited; the people in the marketplace were astounded and the children very proud, saying: "Christ and Saint Mary have helped us to kill this devil." Meanwhile many of those ministers of the devil had come, all very fierce, and they wanted to lay hands upon the boys, but did not dare because God did not allow it nor give them courage to do so. Rather were they astounded to see the great daring of the boys.

The children went back very joyfully to the monastery and on entering told how they had killed the devil. The friars did not understand them very well until the interpreter told them that they had killed a man who wore the insignia of the devil. The friars were horrified, and wishing to punish and frighten them, asked who had done it. To which they all answered together: "We did it." Their teacher asked them again: "Who threw the first stone?" One boy answered and said: "I threw it," and then the master ordered him to be whipped, saying: "How had he come to do such a thing and to kill a man?" The boy answered that they had killed not a man, but a devil, and that if the friars did not believe it they should go and see. Then the friars went out to the marketplace and saw only a great heap of stones. As they removed some of them and uncovered what was underneath, they saw that the dead man was dressed in the pontifical robes of the devil and was as ugly as the devil himself. The affair was of no mean value, for by this one episode alone many Indians began to realize the deceits and lies of the devil and to give up their false ideas and come to be reconciled and ally themselves with God and hear His word.

In this city of Tlaxcallan a child was concealed by his father. In this city there are four heads, or principal lords, amongst whom is divided the whole province, which is pretty large and furnishes, they say, a hundred thousand fighting men. Besides these four principal lords there were many others who had and still have many vassals. One of the chief of these, Acxotecatl, had sixty wives, and by the principal ones he had four sons. Three of these he sent to the monastery to be taught, and the eldest and handsomest, whom he loved most, the son of his chief wife, he kept hidden in his house. After several days, and when the children who were already in this monastery were disclosing secrets, both about idolatrous practices and about the children whom the lords were concealing, those three brothers told the friars how their father had concealed their elder brother in his house. When the friars learned this, they demanded the boy of his father. The father brought him, and I am told that he was very handsome and some twelve or thirteen years old. After some days, when he had learned something of the Christian Faith he asked to be baptized. This was done and he was named Cristóbal.

This child, besides being among those of the highest social position and very handsome and clever and of a good disposition, showed the beginnings of being a very good Christian, for what he heard and learned he taught to his father's vassals, and even told his father to give up his idols and the sins in which he was living, especially the sin of drunkenness, because it was all, he said, a very great wickedness. He urged his father to turn from his evil ways and know the God of heaven and Jesus Christ, His son, for He would pardon him; and he said that this was true, for thus it was taught by the fathers who serve God.

The father was one of the savage and warlike Indians, grown old in sins and wickedness, as appeared later, and his hands were stained with murders and homicides. His son's words were unable to soften his hardened heart, and as the child Cristóbal saw in his father's house the jars full of the wine with which the latter and his vassals intoxicated themselves and also saw the idols, he broke and destroyed them all. The servants and vassals complained to the father, saying: "Your son Cristóbal is breaking your idols and ours and spilling all the wine that he can find. He is throwing you and us into shame and poverty." This is the Indian manner of speaking, as are other expressions used in this book which do not agree with the Spanish usage. Besides the servants and vassals who said this, one of his wives—a woman of high rank who had a son by this same Acxotecatl—roused his anger and urged him on to kill Cristóbal, so that, with him dead, another son, Bernardino, who was hers, would inherit; and so it was that Bernardino now possesses his father's estate.

This woman was called Xochipapalotzin, which means Butterfly-flower. She also said to her husband: "Your son Cristóbal is casting you into poverty and shame." The boy kept on admonishing the mother and the servants of the house and urging them to give up their idols and their sins together, and he kept removing and breaking them (*i. e.,* the idols). At last the woman so aroused her husband's anger and led him on that he, who was by nature very cruel, determined to kill his eldest son Cristóbal, and with this end in view he sent for all his sons, saying that he wished to have a festival and enjoy their company. When they reached their father's house he took them to some rooms within the house and took Cristóbal, whom he had determined to kill, and ordered the other brothers to go out, but the oldest of the three, named Luis (from whom I got the information, because he saw how it all happened), when he saw that he was being turned out and that his elder brother was crying bitterly, went up to a roof and from there saw through a window how the cruel father took Cristóbal by the hair and threw him on the ground and kicked him cruelly.

It was a wonder that he did not die (for the father was a man of great physical strength; and this is true, for I who write this knew him). As he did not succeed in killing him in this way, he took a thick oak club and struck him many times all over his body until he broke and crushed his arms and legs and his hands, with which the child was protecting his head. So violent were these blows that all his body was streaming with blood. Meanwhile the child was calling continually upon God, saying in his own language: "O Lord, my God, have mercy upon me, and if it be Thy will that I should die, let me die; and if it be Thy will that I should live, deliver me from this cruel father of mine."

By this time the father was tired, and they assert that the boy, in spite of the wounds that he had received, raised himself and was about to go out through the door, but that cruel woman whose name I said was Butterfly-flower stopped him at the door when his father, out of sheer weariness, would have let him go. At this point Cristóbal's mother, who was in another room some distance away, heard what was going on and came running, her mother's heart breaking, and did not stop until she entered the room where her son lay calling upon God. As she tried to take him in her arms to have pity on him as a mother would do, her cruel husband, or rather her enemy, prevented her. She exclaimed with tears and lamentations: "Why are you killing my son? How could your hands kill your own son? Would that you had first killed me—that I had not seen the only son I bore so cruelly tortured. Let me take away my son; kill me, if you wish, and spare this one who is a child and is your son and mine." Thereupon that evil man took his own wife by the hair and kicked her until he was tired. Then he called someone to remove her, and certain Indians came and carried away the sad mother, who felt more keenly the sufferings of her beloved son than her own.

The cruel father then, seeing that the boy was still conscious though very badly wounded and suffering, ordered him to be thrown into a big fire of very hot coals of dry live-oak bark, which is the kind of firewood used by the nobles in this land. It is a wood that lasts a long time and makes very hot coals. Into this fire he threw him and rolled him cruelly about, back and front, the boy continually calling upon God and upon Saint Mary. When they took him out of the fire, almost dead, some say that the father went in to get a sword and others say a dagger, and finally stabbed the child to death. But the truth, as I have ascertained, is that the faher went to look for his sword, but did not find it. When they took the child out of the fire they wrapped him in some blankets and he lived all one night, with great patience commending himself to God and enduring with great fortitude the pain caused by the fire and by the wounds, continually calling upon God and upon Saint Mary. In the morning he told them to call his father, who came; and when he had come the child said to him: "O Father, do not think that I am angry, for I am very happy and know that you have done me an honor greater than the value of your estate." Having said this, he asked for drink and they gave him a glass of cocoa, which is in this land what wine is in Spain—not intoxicating but nutritious—and as soon as he drank he died.

When the boy was dead his father ordered them to bury him in the corner of a room and frightened all the members of his household so that no one should tell of the child's death. Especially he spoke to the other three sons who were being brought up in the monastery, saying to them:

"Do not say anything, for if the Captain hears of it he will hang me." At first all the Indians called the Marquis of the Valley 'captain,' and had great fear of him.

Not content with this, but adding crime to crime, that wicked murderer became afraid of his wife, mother of the murdered boy, whose name was Tlapaxilotzin. (I have never been able to find out whether she was baptized or not, for as I write this now, in the month of March of the year 1539, it is nearly twelve years since the event.)[3] Because of his fear that she would disclose the death of her son, he had her taken to a country house or farm of his called Quimichocán, not far from the inn of Tecoac, which is on the highway from Mexico to the port of Vera Cruz. The son was buried in a town called Atlihuetzia, four leagues from there and within two leagues of Tlaxcallan. I came to this town to get information and I saw where the child died and where they buried him, and I am writing this now in that same town. Its name is Atlihuetzia, which means 'where the water falls,' for just here a river plunges over some cliffs and falls from a great height. He ordered those who carried off his wife to kill her and bury her very secretly. I have not been able to ascertain how she died.

The way in which the murders committed by this Acxotecatl came to be discovered was as follows: A Spaniard, passing through Acxotecatl's land, maltreated some of the latter's vassals, and they complained to him. He went with them to where the Spaniard was, and when he reached there treated the Spaniard very badly. When the latter escaped from Acxotecatl's hands, leaving behind him certain of his gold and clothing, he considered that God had showed him great mercy, and, not stopping much along the way, he reached Mexico and complained to the authorities of the ill treatment that he had suffered at the hands of that lord, and of how he had been robbed. An order arrived and a Spanish constable in Tlaxcallan arrested Acxotecatl, and, as the Indian was one of the principal lords of Tlaxcallan (after the four great lords) it was necessary for an examiner to come with authority from the one who governed Mexico. The examiner who came was Martín de Calahorra, a citizen of Mexico, one of the conquistadores and a person to whom one could well entrust any judicial office. When he had completed his investigation and returned to the Spaniard his gold and clothing, and Acxotecatl thought that he

3. Torquemada (vol. III, p. 88), in recounting the same story, says: "All this happened in the year 1527."

was free, certain indications of the murders of his son and wife began to come out, as may be seen in the official record of the trial drawn up by Martín de Calahorra. Some things, however, are more openly declared now than they were at that time, and others could be better ascertained at that time because the crimes were more recent, though I have gone to great pains not to offend against the truth in what I say.

After Acxotecatl was sentenced to death for these two crimes and many others that were brought up against him, Martín de Calahorra got together all the Spaniards that he could in order to carry out the sentence with security. He was afraid of what might happen, for Acxotecatl was a valiant man and related to many important people and, though he had been sentenced, he seemed to feel no fear. When they took him out and led him to be hanged, he kept saying: "Is this Tlaxcallan? How is it that you, Tlaxcaltecas, allow me to die, and haven't the courage to rescue me from these few Spaniards?" God knows how frightened the Spaniards were! But as justice comes from above, not all Acxotecatl's courage nor his many relatives nor the multitude of people availed him; those few Spaniards took him and left him on the gallows.

As soon as it was known where the father had buried his son, there went from this monastery a friar named Fray Andrés de Córdoba accompanied by many of the leading Indians to get the body of the child, who had already been buried for more than a year. Some of those who went with Fray Andrés de Córdoba assure me that the body was dried up but not decomposed.

Two years after the death of the child Cristóbal, there came here to Tlaxcallan a Dominican friar named Fray Bernardino Minaya, with a companion, on their way to the province of Oaxyecac. At that time the guardian of the monastery here in Tlaxcallan was our father Fray Martín de Valencia, of glorious memory, whom the Dominican fathers asked to give them some one of the boys whom we had taught to help them in the matter of teaching the elements of the Faith, if there was anyone who would, for God's sake, be willing to go to do that work. When the boys were asked, two volunteered, both very handsome children and sons of very important personages. One was called Antonio. He had with him a servant of his own age named Juan. The other was called Diego. At the time that they were about to start out, Father Martín de Valencia said to them; "My sons, consider that you are to go away from your own land

and that you are going among people who do not yet know God, and I believe that you will encounter many hardships. I feel your troubles as if you were my own sons and I am even afraid that they may kill you on your journeys. Therefore before you decide consider the matter well." To this both the boys together, guided by the Holy Spirit, replied: "Father, it is for this that you have taught us the obligations laid upon us by the true faith. How, then, should there fail to be some among us who would volunteer to undergo hardship in the service of God? We are ready to go with the fathers and to accept willingly any hardship for God's sake, and if He should be pleased to take our lives, why should we not give them for Him? Did they not kill Saint Peter by crucifying him and did they not behead Saint Paul and was not Saint Bartholomew flayed in God's service? Why, then, should we not die for Him, if that be His pleasure"? Then Fray Martín gave them his blessing and they went away with those two friars and reached Tepeyacac, which is almost ten leagues from Tlaxcallan.

In those days there was no monastery in Tepeyacac, as there is today, but the province was visited from Huexotzinco, which is another ten leagues from Tepeyacac, and the visits were very infrequent; therefore that town and all the province were very full of idols, although they were concealed. Then Father Bernardino Minaya sent those boys to seek for idols in all the Indians' houses and bring them to him. They spent three or four days doing this, during which time they brought him all the idols that they could find. Afterward they went more than a league from the town to see if there were more idols in other towns near there. One of these towns was called Cuauhtinchán,[4] and the other, because it has not a good name in Spanish, they call the town of Orduña, since it was given to a certain Francisco Orduña. From some houses in the latter town some idols were taken by the boy Antonio, who was accompanied by his page named Juan.

Meanwhile some lords and important men had—as appeared later—arranged to kill these children because they were breaking their idols and depriving them of their gods. Antonio came with the idols that he had collected in Orduña to see if there were any in the other town called Cuautitlán. When he entered one house there was no one in it but a child guarding the door. The other boy, Antonio's servant, remained with this

4. Below, the name is wrongly given as Cuautitlán; later it appears as Coatlinchan.

child, and while he was there two of the leading Indians came with clubs of live oak, and as soon as they arrived, without a word, they fell upon the boy Juan who had remained at the door. At the noise they made, the other boy, Antonio, came out at once, and when he saw the cruelty with which those brutes were treating his servant, instead of fleeing, he said to them with great spirit: "Why are you killing my companion; for it is not his fault, but mine? I am the one who is taking away your idols, because I know that they are devils and not gods. If you consider them gods, take them and leave that boy alone, for he has done you no harm." Saying this he threw on the ground some idols which he was carrying in his skirt. By the time he finished speaking these words, the Indians had killed the child Juan, and then they fell upon the other, Antonio, so that they also killed him.

As soon as it grew dark they took the bodies of the two boys, who according to those who knew them were of the same age as Cristóbal, and carried them to the town of Orduña and threw them into a deep ravine, thinking that if the bodies were thrown there no one would ever know of their wickedness. But when the boy Antonio did not appear he was sought with great diligence, and Fray Bernardino Minaya urgently requested the assistance of a constable called Alvaro de Sandoval who lived in Tepeyacac. He and the Dominican fathers searched very assiduously, for when the boys had been given to them in Tlaxcallan the lad Antonio had been especially commended to their care because he was the grandson of the greatest lord of Tlaxcallan, whose name was Xicotencatl. He was the principal lord to receive the Spaniards when they entered this land and helped and supported them with his own property. This Xicotencatl and Maxiscatzin[5] commanded the entire province of Tlaxcallan, and the boy Antonio was to have been his grandfather's heir. Now a younger brother of his, Don Luis Moscoso, has inherited the estate in his stead. The dead boys were found; for traces were quickly discovered which showed the way they had gone and where they had disappeared. It was soon learned who had killed them, and when the murderers were arrested, they never confessed at whose order they had killed the boys, but said that they had done it and knew very well the evil that they had done. They admitted that they deserved death and asked to be baptized before their execution. Then they went to get the bodies of the boys and

5. The second ranking lord of Tlaxcallan. See below, ch. XVI.

brought them back and buried them in a chapel where Mass used to be said, because at that time there was no church.

These Dominican fathers grieved greatly for the death of these children, but even more for the grief that Father Fray Martín de Valencia would feel, since he had so especially entrusted the boys to their care when he gave them leave to go. They felt that it would be well to send the murderers and assassins to him, and so they sent them in the care of some Indians to Tlaxcallan. When the lord and principal men of Coatlinchan heard of the affair, fearing that some part of the punishment might fall upon them, they sent jewels and gifts of gold to a Spaniard who was in Coatlinchan, asking him to prevent the prisoners' being taken to Tlaxcallan. The Spaniard communicated with another who was in charge of Tlaxcallan and divided the bribe with him, and the latter came out upon the road and prevented the departure of the prisoners. All this plotting turned out to the disadvantage of the men who had started it, because the constable went for the two Spaniards and handed them over to Fray Bernardino Minaya. One they fastened with his head in the stocks, the other they bound, and whipped them both cruelly. The gold they took from them. As for the murderers, as soon as the affair was known in Mexico the Law sent for them and they were hanged. The lord of Coatlinchan, as he did not mend his ways but added sin to sin, also died on the gallows with other leading men. When Fray Martín de Valencia learned of the death of the boys whom he had brought up like sons and who had gone with his permission, he grieved greatly and wept for them as for his own sons; on the other hand it was a consolation to him to see that there were now in this land those who would die confessing God. But he could not refrain from shedding many tears when he remembered what they had said to him at the time of their departure, that is: "Did they not kill Saint Peter and Saint Paul and flay Saint Bartholomew? Then if they kill us, is not God doing us a very great favor"?

CHAPTER XV

Of the help that the children gave in the conversion of the Indians, of how the Indian girls were put into school and how long it lasted, and of two notable events that occurred between two Indian women and two youths.

IF these children had not helped in the work of conversion, and if the interpreters alone had had to do it all, it seems to me that they would have been as the bishop of Tlaxcallan wrote to the Emperor: "We bishops, without the friars who interpret for us, are like moulting hawks." So the friars would have been without the children.[1] Almost the same service was rendered by the Indian girls who—at least the daughters of the lords—were in many provinces of this New Spain collected and put under the discipline of devout Spanish women whom the Empress sent to carry on this holy work, commanding and providing that houses should be built for them in which they might be collected and taught. This good work and instruction went on for some ten years and no longer, for these girls were taught only with a view to marriage and to be able to sew and embroider.

They all know how to weave and make cloth with many different designs. Their fabrics, whether intended for blankets for the men or shirts for the women—which they call *huipillis*—are many of them woven in colors. Although the Spaniards call these garments shirts, they are worn outside the other clothing, and for this reason they make them very elegant and of many colors, of dyed cotton or of rabbit fur, which is like the *sirgo* or silk of Castile. They also make bed coverings of this latter material which are more showy than costly. It is not damaged by washing, but the white part gets whiter and whiter because the colors are dyed in the wool and do not run. The silk which is made here, although there is as yet very little of it, is so fine that it does not deteriorate even if it is rinsed in a strong solution of lye. The embroidery done in cotton cannot be washed, for it stains everything it touches because the cotton is dyed in the thread. They do very good work with merino wool, and the Indians value it highly.

1. Not only the Indian children. They were greatly helped also by a little Spanish boy who had learned the language by playing with the Indian children. His family consented to his living with the friars and interpreting for them. He later entered the Franciscan Order and became Fray Alonso de Molina, author of an Aztec grammar and dictionary. See Torquemada, vol. III, pp. 32-33.

All these kinds of work were done by those girls. Later, when their parents came to be baptized, there was no necessity for them to be taught beyond the point of learning to be Christians and to live according to the law of marriage.[2] In the ten years that this teaching was carried on many girls who were nearly grown up when they entered got married and taught the others. During the time that they were in the school they learned the elements of Christianity and the office of Our Lady, which they always said at its appropriate time and season. Some of them even continued this good custom after they were married, until the care of their children and the responsibility of managing the house and family made them give it up. It was a sight worth seeing at one time in Huexotzinco when there were a great many recently married young women and a very holy shrine of Our Lady to which all or most of them used to go early in the morning to chant the Hours of Our Lady in very harmonious and orderly fashion, although none of them knew how to read music. Many of these girls, sometimes with their teachers and sometimes accompanied by some old Indian women—for there were also some devout women who acted as doorkeepers and as guardians of the younger ones—used to go out to teach, both in the churchyards and in the houses of the ladies, and they converted many women and brought them to be baptized and to be devout Christians and almsgivers. They have always been a great help in the teaching of the Faith.

A very noteworthy thing happened in Mexico to an Indian girl who was molested and made love to by a young bachelor. As she defended herself against him the devil incited another youth to try the same thing. As she defended herself against the second as well as against the first, the two youths joined forces and planned to take from the girl by force what they had not been able to make her give them willingly. With this object in view they waited for her for several days, and as she came out of the door of her house early in the evening they took her and carried her to an abandoned house where they tried to force her. She defended herself valiantly, however, calling upon God and Saint Mary, and neither of the youths could get at her. As the two separately could do nothing, they joined forces, but as they could accomplish nothing by entreaties, they began to maltreat her, slapping and striking her and threatening

2. Spanish: *más de cuanto supieron ser cristianas y vivir en la ley de matrimonio.* The *más* is a conjecture made by Ramírez. The text of Torquemada (vol. III, p. 108), which here follows Motolinía pretty closely, gives us the sense.

her cruelly, she meanwhile persisting in the defense of her honor. So they spent the whole night, during which the youths could accomplish nothing, for God, upon whom the girl kept calling with tears and with all her heart, delivered her from this peril. As they had her there all night and could not prevail against her, the maiden came out of the experience free and untouched. Then in the morning, to put herself in greater safety, she went to the girls' dormitory and told the mother superior what had happened to her, and although she was a poor girl, she was received into the company of the daughters of the lords because of the good example she had given and because God's hand supported her.

Elsewhere it happened that when a certain woman became a widow while still young, a married man made love to her and annoyed her and she could not defend herself from him. One day he was alone with the widow, burning with his evil desires, and she said to him: "How is it that you attempt to get such a thing from me? Do you think that because I have no husband to protect me, you can offend God with me? If for no other consideration but that we are both members of the guild of Our Lady and that by doing this we should greatly offend Her and She would be justly angry with us and we should not be worthy to call ourselves members of Her guild or to take Her blessed candles in our hands, for this reason it would be only right that you should leave me alone. Since, however, you will not leave me for this reason, let me tell you that I am determined to die rather than commit such a sin." These words were so forcible and so impressed themselves upon the man's heart and filled him with such compunction that he instantly answered the woman: "You have won my soul, which was blind and lost. You have acted like a good Christian and servant of Saint Mary. I promise you to give up this sin and to confess and do penance for it, remaining under great obligation to you for as long as I shall live."

CHAPTER XVI

Of what constitutes a province; of the size and extent of Tlaxcallan, and of the noteworthy things that are to be found in it.

TLAXCALLAN is a province in New Spain; the whole territory had the same name although there are many towns in it. This province is one of the principal ones in all New Spain, and from it, as I have said, they used to send out a hundred thousand warriors. The lord and people of this province always supported the Marquis of the Valley and the Spaniards who came with him at the beginning of the conquest until the whole country quieted down and was at peace. In this land it is customary to give the name of province to the big town which has other smaller towns subject to it; and many of these provinces have a small area and not many citizens. Tlaxcallan, which is the strongest and most populous province and is among those in this land which have the most territory, extends fifteen leagues in length (that is, going from Vera Cruz to Mexico) and ten leagues in breadth.

In Tlaxcallan there is a great spring which rises in the northern part of the province. It is five leagues from the principal city in a town called Atzompa, which in their language means 'head.' It is well named, for this spring is the head and source of the largest of the rivers that flow into the South Sea.[1] It flows into the sea at Zacatollan. This river rises above the inn of Atlancatepec, flows around above Tlaxcallan, and then turning again comes down a valley and passes through the city of Tlaxcallan. By the time it reaches the city it is very large, and it goes on and waters a great part of the province. Besides this river the province has many other springs, streams, and large lakes which have water in them all the year, and also small fish. It has many and very good pastures where the Spaniards and the natives are already pasturing large herds of cattle.

Tlaxcallan has also large mountains, especially one in the northern part which begins two leagues from the city and is two leagues more to the summit.[2] All this mountain is covered with pines and live oaks; in most years it has snow on the summit (there are few places in this New Spain where the snow collects, for the land is very warm). The mountain

1. Called, in various parts of its course, Atoyac, Las Balsas, and Mexcala.
2. Torquemada (vol. I, p. 276) places this mountain "east and slightly south."

is round; its base covers over fifteen leagues and almost all of it is Tlaxcaltec territory. It is here that the storm clouds gather, whence come the rain-laden clouds that water Tlaxcallan and the adjacent towns so that they consider it a certain sign of rain when they see clouds over this mountain. They usually gather from ten o'clock in the morning till noon. From noon till the hour of Vespers they begin to scatter and spread, some toward Tlaxcallan, others toward the city of Los Angeles, and others toward Huexotzinco. This is a very well attested and very noteworthy phenomenon, and because of it the Indians, before the coming of the Spaniards, had a great and idolatrous reverence for this mountain, and all the people of the territory would come to it to pray for water and perform many devilish sacrifices in honor of a goddess whom they called Matlalcueye, which in their language means 'blue tunic,' because that was the principal garment of this goddess. They considered her the goddess of water, and because water is blue they dressed her in a blue robe. This goddess and the god Tlaloc they held to be gods and lords of water. Tlaloc was the lord and patron of Tetzcoco, Mexico, and its surrounding country; and the goddess of Tlaxcallan and its province (this means that one was honored in one place and the other in the other), but throughout the land they prayed to both together for water when they needed it.

In order to destroy and wipe out this idolatry and the abominable sacrifices that were performed in the land, that good servant of God, Father Martín de Valencia, climbed to the summit of the mountain and burned all the idols and raised there the sign of the Cross and built a shrine which he called Saint Bartholomew's. He placed someone in it to keep the shrine; and that no one might again invoke the devil there, he labored hard to make the Indians understand that it is the true God alone who gives water, and that it is to Him that they must pray for it.

The soil of Tlaxcallan is fertile and yields a great deal of corn, beans, and red pepper. The people are strong and healthy and the most skilled in the practice of war of any in the land. The population is large and very poor, because with no resources but the corn that they grow they have to feed and clothe themselves and pay their tributes.

Tlaxcallan is situated in a good district, for to the west it has Mexico twenty leagues away, and to the south the city of Los Angeles at a distance of five leagues, and the harbour of Vera Cruz at forty leagues.

Tlaxcallan is divided into four principal centers or jurisdictions. The oldest lord, who founded the city, built on a high ridge called Tepeticpac, which means 'on a mountain,' for it is a league up to the top of the ridge from the lowland where the river flows and where the city now stands. The reason for building in high places was the many wars that they carried on with each other. In order to be in a safe and strong position, they sought high and open ground where they could sleep with less to worry about, since they had no walls nor doors in their houses—although in some towns there were enclosures and defenses—because the wars were sure to come every year. This first lord that I speak of and his people and jurisdiction were to the north.

After the people multiplied, the second lord built lower down on a slope or side hill nearer the river. This settlement is called Ocotelolco, which means 'pine grove in a dry country.' Here lived the chief captain of all Tlaxcallan, a brave and powerful man called Maxiscatzin, who received the Spaniards and showed them much friendship and helped them in their whole conquest of all New Spain. Here in this section was the densest population in Tlaxcallan and the place where many people came together because of a great market that was held there. This lord had large houses with many rooms, and in one hall in this house the friars of Saint Francis had their church for three years. After they moved into their monastery the first bishop of Tlaxcallan, Don Julián Garcés, took possession of the hall for his cathedral church and named it Santa María de la Concepción. This lord has his people and his jurisdiction toward the city of Los Angeles, which is to the south.

The third lord built on lower ground up the river. The place is called Tizatlan, which means 'a place where there is gypsum,' or 'a vein of gypsum,' and there is a great deal of it there of very good quality. Here lived that great old lord who was blind from old age. His name was Xicotencatl.[3] He gave many presents and supplies to the great captain, Hernando Cortés, and although he was so old and blind he had himself carried a long distance to receive the aforesaid captain. Later he provided him with many men for the war against the city of Mexico and its conquest, for he is lord of more people and more vassals than any other. His jurisdiction lies to the east.

The fourth lord of Tlaxcallan built down stream, on a slope called Quiahuiztlan. He also has a wide jurisdiction, to the west. He also helped by furnishing many men for the conquest of Mexico City. These Tlaxcal-

3. See above, bk. III, ch. XIV, p. 252.

tecas have always been faithful friends and companions of the Spaniards in everything that lay within their power, and so the conquistadores say that Tlaxcallan deserves to have His Majesty grant it many favors, and that if it had not been for Tlaxcallan all would have died when the Mexicans drove the Christians out of Mexico and the Tlaxcaltecas took them in.

There is in Tlaxcallan a fair-sized monastery of Franciscans. The church is large and good. The monasteries here in New Spain are sufficiently large for the friars who live in them, although they seem small to the Spaniards; and these houses are constantly being built smaller and poorer. The reason is that at first they built according to whether the province or town was large or small, hoping that more friars would come from Spain, as well as those, both Spaniards and natives who would be trained here; but as they have seen that few friars come and that the provinces and towns which want them are many and that they must divide themselves up among them all, a monastery of seven or eight cells seems big to them. Except in the Spanish towns there are not more than four or five friars in the other monasteries. To return to Tlaxcallan—it has a good almshouse and more than fifty churches, small and medium sized, and all well equipped.

Between the year of 1537 and this year of 1540 the city has been much beautified, for they are rich in labor for building and they have large quarries of very good stone. This city is destined to be very populous and to have very fine buildings, for they have begun to build on the level ground by the river, and it is well laid out. And as there are in Tlaxcallan many other lords of lower rank than the four principal ones, who all have vassals and are building in many streets, this will cause it to become very shortly a great city. Within the city and for two and three leagues around almost all the people are Nahuas and speak the main language of New Spain, which is Nahuatl. The other Indians from four to seven leagues outside the city—for that is the populated area, but not in all directions—are Otomíes, who speak the second principal language of the country. There is only one district, or parish, of Pinomes.[4]

4. On the *Pinomes,* see Sahagún (vol. III, p. 133). "These *yopimes* and *tlapanecas* . . . . speak a language different from the Mexican, and are properly called *tenime, pinome, chinquime,* and *chonchonti* . . . . all of these in general are called *tenime,* which means "barbarous people;" they are very crude and unskilled; they were worse than the *Otomis* and lived in poor, sterile land or in rough, mountainous country; but they know the precious stones and their virtues." (See also Orozco y Berra, *Geografía de las lenguas y carta etnográfica de Mexico.* Mexico, 1864; and Bancroft, *The Native Races,* San Francisco, 1882.)

CHAPTER XVII

Of how and by whom the city of Los Angeles[1] was founded; and of its characteristics.

THE city of Los Angeles, which is in New Spain in the province of Tlaxcallan, was built by the decision and at the command of the president and judges of the royal audiencia which sits here, the president being the bishop Don Sebastian Ramírez de Fuenleal, and the judges, the licentiates Juan de Salmerón, Alonso Maldonado, Ceinos, and Quiroga. The town was built at the instance of the Friars Minor, who begged these gentlemen to build a Spanish town to be settled by people who, instead of all waiting to have Indians assigned to them, would devote themselves to tilling the fields and cultivating the land in the Spanish way, for the soil was very good and suitable for cultivation. They argued that thus towns would begin to grow up in which many of the Christians who were now wandering about idle would collect, and that the Indians also would follow the example and learn to till and cultivate the soil in the Spanish manner; and that if the Spaniards had fields and work to do, they would lose the wish and longing that they felt to return to their country and would grow to love the land where they had estates and business. They claimed, moreover, that if this beginning were made, many other good results would come with it.

They worked and struggled so hard that at last the construction of the city was begun in the year 1530 on the octave of Easter, April 16,[2] the day of Saint Toribio, Bishop of Astorga, who built the church of San Salvador in Oviedo in which he put many relics that he himself had brought from Jerusalem. On that day those who were to be the new inhabitants came, and by command of the royal audiencia there were assembled on that day many Indians from the neighboring provinces and towns, all of whom came willingly to help the Christians. It was a sight well worth seeing, for the Indians from one town would come all together along the road, their people laden with the necessary materials for making their straw huts. From Tlaxcallan came some seven or eight thousand Indians, and nearly as many from Huexotzinco, Calpa, Tepeyacac, and Chollollan.

1. Puebla de los Angeles, now known as Puebla.
2. See Introduction, p. 6.

They brought some stakes and fastenings and ropes and a quantity of straw for houses—there is a forest not far away for cutting wood—and came in with their banners, singing and playing upon bells and drums, and others with groups of boy dancers and with many dances. That very day, after Mass[3]—the first Mass that was said there—the plan of the town was made and laid out by a stonecutter. Then without much delay the Indians cleared the ground and, to start with, forty lots were surveyed and assigned to forty settlers. As I was present, I say that in my opinion the original settlers of the city were not more than forty in number.

Then on that day the Indians began to build houses for all the settlers to whom lots had been assigned, and they worked so fast that they finished them that same week; and they were not such poor houses that they did not have plenty of rooms. This was at the beginning of the rainy season; that year the rains were heavy and as the ground in the town was not yet settled or tramped down and the proper drainage ditches had not been made the water flowed into all the houses so that there were many who laughed at the site and the town, which is built on a dry, sandy soil under which, at a depth of about nine inches, there is heavy clay and then limestone. Now, since they have made ditches along the streets to drain off the water, it runs off so well that even after heavy downpours and torrents of water, it all drains away and in two hours the whole city is as clean as Genoa. Later the city fell into such disfavor that it was nearly abandoned,[4] but now it has recovered itself and is, after Mexico, the best city in all New Spain, and His Majesty, having been informed of its character, has given it royal privileges.

The situation of the city is good, and the district the best in all New Spain. To the north, five leagues away, is the city of Tlaxcallan; to the west is Huexotzinco, also five leagues distant; five leagues to the east is Tepeyacac; to the south in the warm country lie Itzocan and Cuauhquechollan, seven leagues away; two leagues away are Chalollan and Totomiahuacán, and Calpa is five leagues. All of these are big towns. The harbor of Vera Cruz is forty leagues to the east, and it is twenty leagues to Mexico. The road from the harbor to Mexico passes through the city, and when the mule trains go with their loads to Mexico, as they pass

3. This Mass was said by Fray Toribio himself, and in his presence they did the surveying and distributing of building sites. See Torquemada, vol. I, p. 313.

4. Unfavorable reports on Puebla de los Angeles reached Spain, and in March, 1534, an official inquiry was made into the matter. See *Col. Doc. Inéd.*, vol. XVI, pp. 556 ff.

through here the people of this city provide themselves and buy what they need at a better price than the people of Mexico. When the mule trains are on their way back they take on loads of flour, salt pork, and biscuit for the provisioning of the ships, for which reasons it is hoped that the city will grow and improve.

This city has one of the best mountains of any city in the world, for it begins at a distance of one league from the town and extends in places for five or six leagues, covered with great forests of pines and live oaks. In one place, at a distance of three leagues, this mountain joins the range of Saint Bartholomew, which belongs to Tlaxcallan. All these mountains have good pasturage; in this country, although the soil of the pine forests may be sandy, it is always covered with very good grass, which, so far as one knows, is not true anywhere else in all of Europe. Besides this mountain, the city has many other fields and pastures to which the citizens bring great numbers of sheep and cattle. There is an abundance of water, both rivers and springs. Near the houses runs a brook in which already three dams have been built, each for two millstones; they carry running water which serves the whole city. Half a league away flows a big river which is always crossed by bridges. This river is formed of two branches; one comes from Tlaxcallan, and the other flows down from the mountains of Huexotzinco. I shall omit mention of other springs and brooks in the territory of this city, in order to tell of many springs which are close to or almost inside of the city itself. These springs are of two kinds. The ones nearest to the houses are of a somewhat heavy and brackish water, and for this reason they are not so much esteemed as those on the other side of the brook where the mills are and where the monastery of Saint Francis now stands. These are excellent springs of a very light and healthful water. There are eight or nine of them, some two or three fathoms deep. One rises at the door of the monastery of Saint Francis. The whole city drinks from these springs because the water is so good and so light. The reason why the water that rises near the city is bad is that it runs through veins of salt rock; all the other waters flow through veins and beds of very fine rock excellent for cut stone, as I shall now tell.

This city has very rich stone pits or quarries, and so near that at a distance of less than a crossbow shot one can get out all the stone one wants, both for cutting and for making lime. Being soft, it is so easy to break that, though most of the people take it out with crowbars and stone hammers, the poor quarry it with wooden levers and break up all that they need by pounding one stone with another. These deposits of stone are knee deep or half a man's height below the surface of the ground and the stone is soft because it is underground; when it is brought out into the sun and air it hardens and gets very strong. In places some of this stone is above ground, and it is so hard that people have no use for it because it is so hard to break, and what is underground, even if it be of the same piece of rock, is as soft as I have said.

This stone that the Spaniards quarry is very good for building walls, for they can cut it any size they wish and it is rather thin and broad to bind the structure and full of holes to take the mortar. As this country is dry and hot the stone and mortar set and become very hard. One can quarry more of this stone in a year than one could quarry in Spain in five years. The small stones and all the refuse from the cut stone are kept to make lime, which is very good; they make a great deal of it, for they have the kilns right near where they quarry the stone and the woods are near by and there is plenty of water. Even more noteworthy is the fact that this city has a quarry of white stone which has a very good grain, and the farther down they cut—to once and a half or twice a man's height—the better it is. Of this stone they make pillars and doorways and window frames, all very good and very handsome. This quarry is on the other side of the brook, on a hill about one crossbow shot from the monastery of Saint Francis and two bow shots from the city. In the same hill there is a vein of harder stone from which the Indians make stones to grind their *centli,* or maize. I believe that one could also make good millstones out of it.

Since I wrote this there has been discovered a vein of red stone, very handsome and with a very pretty grain. It is one league from the city. They also get, near the city, very good millstones. There are four mill dams, each for two stones. There is in this city very good earth for making adobes, brick and tile, although they have made very little tile because all the houses that they build are made with flat roofs. There is very good earth for making mud walls and fences. There have not been many allotments of Indians to the inhabitants in this city, but because of the very favorable conditions, there have already been assigned over two hundred large, fine building lots, and many houses have already been built and long, straight streets lined with very handsome facades. There are natural resources and land for making a very good and large city, and, to judge by its character, its trade and its commerce, I believe that before long it will be populous and highly esteemed.

Chapter XVIII

Of the difference between the frosts in this land and in Spain, and of the fertility of a valley called the Valle de Dios; of the mulberry trees and the silk that is grown there, and of other notable things.

The winter in this New Spain and the frosts and cold weather neither last as long nor are they as severe as in Spain; on the contrary, the climate is so temperate that it is no great hardship to go without one's cape in winter, nor to wear it in summer. But because the frosts are unseasonable and come at the wrong time, some plants and vegetables brought from Castile get frosted; such, for instance, as the orchard trees, grapevines, fig trees, pomegranates, melons, cucumbers, eggplant, etc. This is not because of excessive cold or frost, since these are not very severe, but because they come at the wrong time. About Christmas or Epiphany there come ten or twelve days as warm as summer, and as the soil is very fertile, the trees, even though they have not been dormant long and have shed their leaves only a short while before, put out new leaves; and as two or three days of frost follow—though not very heavy—it carries off all the leaves that have come out, because the trees are still tender.

Because of the goodness and fertility of the soil it happens that in many years the trees bud and bear leaves two or three times before the month of April, and get frosted each time. Those who do not know this and understand it are astonished that in Castile, where the frosts are so severe, the plants should not freeze as they do in this country. (What I am saying here is not beside the point, which is to tell stories of this land and describe its characteristics, nor am I straying from my purpose of praising and exalting the land and territory of this city of Los Angeles.) Therefore I say that in this New Spain any town, in order to be perfect, must have some warm land for its vineyards and orchards and fields, as does this one of which we are speaking.

Four leagues from this city lies an open plain called the Val de Cristo, where the citizens have their fields, orchards, and vineyards, with many trees of many kinds of fruit (especially pomegranates) which do extremely well. In their fields they harvest much wheat during the greater part of the year, whereas in the cold part of the country it ripens only once a year, as it does in Spain. In this place that I am speaking of, however, as it is warm country and the frost does not hurt the grain and as the valley has a great deal of running water, they sow and reap whenever they will; it often happens that one wheat field has just been planted, another is sprouting, another is in the blade, another in the ear, and another ready to harvest. What most enriches these fields is the mulberry trees that they have planted and are planting daily, for the conditions are very favorable for raising silk.

The plain known as the Val de Cristo, in which this valley lies, is so good that in all New Spain there is no better; people who are skilled in this and know how to recognize soils say that it is better than the plain of Granada in Spain, or than that of Orihuela. Therefore it would be well to give some brief account of a thing as good as this plain.

The Spaniards call this plain the Valley of Atlixco,[1] but among the Indians it has many names, for it is a very big piece of land. Atlixco, in their language, means a source, or spring, of water. This place, Atlixco, is really two leagues above the Spaniards' land, the Val de Cristo, and there rises in it a very big and beautiful spring, flowing so freely that it very shortly forms a great river that waters a large part of this plain, which is very broad and long and of very fertile soil. It has also other rivers and many springs and brooks. Near this big spring is a town which has the same name as the spring, that is, Atlixco. Others call this plain Cuauhquechollan la Vieja, because in truth the people of Cuauhquechollan planted it and lived in it at first. This is the place that is now called Acapetlahuacan, which—for those who do not know the name—is where the Indians hold their market, or tianquizco. This is the best part of all the plain. When the people of Cuauhquechollan had somewhat multiplied here, about the year 140,[2] they grew proud and decided to make war on the people of Calpa, which is four leagues

1. From this point on, it is often impossible to tell whether, when he says "this valley," Motolinía is referring to the Val de Cristo, or to the larger valley of Atlixco. Also, he seems to use the words valley (valle) and plain (vega) interchangeably.

2. The numeral is obviously incorrect, but there are apparently no data on which to base any valid correction. See Ramírez, *Historia de los Indios,* vol. 1, pp. 237 ff.

up at the foot of the volcano,[3] and taking them by surprise they killed many of them. Those who were left retreated to Huexotzinco and made an alliance and confederation with the people of that town. Together they attacked the men of Acapetlahuacan, killed many more, and drove them out of the place that they had taken. Those who were left retreated two or three leagues down the big river to the place that is now called Coatepec.[4]

Some years later, the people of Cuauhquechollan, or Acapetlahuacan, repenting of what they had done and realizing the superiority of the place they had left over the place that they then held and recognizing that they had been to blame in the past, assembled and with many gifts, begged the people of Huexotzinco and Calpa to forgive them and let them settle again in the land that they had left. This was granted because they were all related and descended from one line. Back in their original location, they rebuilt their houses and lived for several years in peace and quiet, until, having forgotten what happened to their fathers, they returned to their previous folly and again made war on the people of Calpa. The latter, seeing the wickedness of their neighbors, once more joined the men of Huexotzinco against them, and, killing many, they compelled them to flee and leave the land that they had given them, and drove them out to where they are now; and there the vanquished built Cuauhquechollan. And because these were the first settlers in this plain they called it Cuauhquechollan la Vieja. After the second battle the people of Huexotzinco and of Calpa divided the best part of the plain between them and have been in possession of it ever since. The Spaniards call this Tochimilco—I mean the whole of that province whose principal town is called Acapetlayocan. This is the oldest thing in this valley. It lies seven leagues from the city of Los Angeles, between Cuauhquechollan and Calpa; it has very good soil and is inhabited by many people.

Not to mention the crops that the Indians harvest in this plain—and they are many and very profitable, such as fruit and maize, which is harvested twice during the year—there are also beans, red pepper, garlic, and cotton. In this valley they plant many mulberry trees; just

3. Popocatepetl.

4. Torquemada (vol. I, p. 317) gives Ocopetayoca as the name of the town. Motolinía's Acapatlayocan seems to be merely a variant spelling of Acapetlahuacan (See above, bk. III, ch. XVIII).

now they are planting a piece of land for the king with one hundred and ten thousand mulberry trees, of which more than half have already been transplanted; they grow so fast that in one year here they grow bigger than they do in five years in Spain. In the city of Los Angeles some Spanish citizens have five or six thousand feet of mulberry groves, wherefore such quantities of silk will be produced here that it will be one of the rich things in the world and this will come to be the center of the silk industry;[5] for there are many plantations of mulberries, and with what is planted and raised in many other parts of New Spain, within a few years more silk will be raised in this country than in all Christendom.

The silkworm is so hardy here that it is not killed by being neglected, nor by being left for two or three days without food, nor does the heaviest thunder in the world—which is the thing that does them the most damage—do them any injury as it does in other places where, if it thunders while the worm is spinning, it dies and is left hanging from its thread. In this land, before silkworm seed was brought from Spain, I saw native silkworms and their cocoons, but they were small and grew wild in the trees without anyone's paying any attention to them, because their special character and virtue were not known among the Indians. The most remarkable thing about silk in this country is that there will be two crops in a year, for in this present year of 1540 I have seen worms of the second hatching, which by the first of June were fairly well grown and had already moulted two or three times. The reason why there can be two crops is that the mulberry trees begin to leaf out from the first of February and continue to grow and have tender leaves until August. Thus when they have harvested the first crop they hatch a new lot and have plenty of favorable time for it to mature, for as the rains begin here in April, the trees are putting out fresh leaves much longer than in Europe or in Africa.

This valley produces melons, cucumbers, and all the vegetables that grow in a cool country; it has no other characteristic of a hot climate

5. See above Introductory Letter, p. 30 and p. 220. Motolinía's hopes for the future of the silk industry in Mexico were not realized. Torquemada (vol. I, p. 319) states that in his time silk is no longer raised and even the mulberry trees have disappeared. "I do not know certainly," he says, "what the end of the business was, or what was the reason of its being given up." Humboldt (vol. II, p. 454) gives two reasons: 1, the policy of the Council of the Indies, which was always hostile to the development of Mexican industries, and 2, the increase of the China trade. Since 1900 sericulture has begun again in Mexico, so perhaps Motolinía's prophecy may be realized, some four hundred years after it was made! See Borah, *Silk Raising in Colonial Mexico*.

except that there is no damage from frost. In other respects the country is very temperate, especially in the part where the Spaniards have established themselves, so that the mornings are as cool as they are in the city of Mexico. Moreover this valley has a characteristic that many people have spoken of, which is that every day at noon there comes a wave of cool air which the Spaniards who live here call "embate de mar." This breeze is so soft and pleasant that it brings great relief to all. Finally, one may say of this valley that when they called it the Val de Cristo they gave it the name that suited it, because of its great fertility, productiveness, and the salubrity and mildness of its climate.

In the old days before the Spaniards came a very great part of this valley was uncultivated because the big towns throughout the area were constantly engaged in waging war against each other and using these fields as their battleground. It was the general practice in all the towns and provinces to leave, at the extreme boundary of each, a large barren stretch, cleared but uncultivated, for their wars. If by chance they did occasionally plant this land, which happened very rarely, those who planted it never enjoyed the fruits, because their enemies would lay it waste. Now the land is all being occupied by the Spaniards with their flocks and by the natives with farms, and the boundaries are being remarked. Some of these which are not clear are being decided by lawsuits, which means that many lawsuits are always going on among the Indians because the boundaries are confused.

Returning then to my intention and purpose, I say that on the river bank near the houses and the city[6] there are good gardens containing both vegetables and fruit trees; fruit with seeds such as pears, apples, and quinces, and fruit with stones such as *duraznos,*[7] peaches, and plums. These are not touched by the frost, and it seems to me that the land that Isaac planted in Palestine, from which it says in Genesis[8] that he harvested a hundredfold, must have been like this; for I remember that when the Franciscan monastery of Los Angeles was built, a citizen had planted wheat on the piece of land designated for the building, and it was good, and when he was asked how much he had sowed and how much he had harvested, he said that he had sowed a bushel[9] and harvested a hundred.

6. Puebla de los Angeles.
7. A kind of clingstone peach.
8. Genesis 26.12.
9. Spanish: fanega.

This was not because it was the first year that the land had been planted, for before the city was built they used to sow the bank of that stream for the Spaniard who had the town of Chołollan under his authority, and for more than fifteen[10] years now it had been planted every year. It is the custom here in New Spain for fields to be planted every year, and they produce very well without being fertilized.

In another part of New Spain I have been assured that from one bushel of Castilian wheat they harvested over one hundred and fifty bushels. It is true that this seed that produces so much is planted by hand, like corn; they prepare the soil in ridges, and with the hand they scratch a hole and put in two or three grains, and repeat this at intervals of a span, and later there comes up a compact tuft of stalks and heads. Corn has been planted within the territory of this city which has produced three hundred bushels for one. Now there are so many cattle that it brings almost nothing everywhere. They till the soil with yokes of oxen in the Spanish fashion. They also use carts as in Spain; there are many good ones in this city. It is a sight to see those that come in laden every day, some with wheat, others with corn, others with firewood for the lime kilns, others with beams and various kinds of wood. Those that come from the harbor bring merchandise and on the return trip carry supplies and provisions for the ships.

The chief thing in the city in which it surpasses older towns is the principal church. It is certainly very imposing and is stronger and larger than all the others that have so far been built in all New Spain. It has three aisles; and the pillars are of a very fine black stone with a good grain; there are three doors with their portals, very well carved and very elaborate. The bishop has his seat here with his dignitaries: canons, priests, prebendaries, and everything that is proper for divine worship; though they took possession first in Tlaxcallan, His Majesty has now commanded that the cathedral church should be here, and as such it is the seat of the ministers. This city also has two monasteries: one of Saint Francis and one of Saint Dominic. A very good almshouse is also being built. There are excellent houses, good-looking outside and with good rooms. The city is populated by honorable and virtuous people, who give great assistance to the newcomers from Castile; for as soon as the latter

10. Torquemada (vol. I, p. 315), in reporting this anecdote as told by Motolinía in his *Memoriales*, says: "and it was not the first year, but the fifth that it had been sowed." Motolinía's "fifteen years" is obviously an error.

land—which is during the months from May to September—many of them fall ill and some die. It is the occupation of many of the citizens of this city to give these newcomers gifts and attention and charity.

This city could easily be walled and made the biggest stronghold in New Spain; and a very good fortress could be built in it, although for the present the church is sufficient—so strong is it. If this were done—and it can be done at little cost and in a short time—the Spaniards of New Spain would sleep in safety, freed from the terrors and alarms that they have now suffered so repeatedly. It would also give great security to all New Spain, for the strength of the Spaniards lies in their horses and in a good terrain, both of which this city has: the horses are raised in the valley and plain of which I spoke, and the good terrain is the site on which the city is built. Also it is in such a district and so central that it could be mistress and subjugate all parts of the country, for it is only five days' journey to the harbor, and half of the citizens are sufficient to guard the city, leaving the rest to go about and make expeditions in all directions in time of need.

Until New Spain has one stronghold that will inspire some fear, the land cannot be considered very safe, because of the great multitude of the natives, for it is known that for every Spaniard there are fifteen thousand and more Indians. Since this city has so many great advantages and good qualities, and since, in spite of having had considerable opposition at the time of its founding and unfavorable treatment since then, it has risen and become so much esteemed that it is almost the rival of the city of Mexico, it would be only just that His Majesty, the Emperor and King, Don Carlos, its lord, and monarch of the world, should favor it and look upon it only as it deserves, without the addition of any false claims. If this were done, we can say of it that it would be a complete and perfect city, the joy and defense of all the land. It is very healthy because the water is very good and the climate very temperate. It has very fine and charming pleasure grounds, much game and beautiful views, for on one side it has the mountains of Huexotzinco—one of which is the volcano and the other the snow-capped mountain—and on the other side, not far away, the mountain of Tlaxcallan, and others round about. In other directions it has open, level fields. In short it lacks nothing, in situation, in views, and in all that goes to make a perfect city.

CHAPTER XIX

Of the tree or thistle called maguey and the many things that are made from it, both food and drink and clothing and footgear; and of its properties.

METL is a tree or thistle that, in the language of the Islands, is called maguey,[1] from which they get so many things that it is like what they say they make from iron. It is true that the first time I saw it, without knowing any of its properties, I said: "This thistle has great virtue." It is a tree or thistle like the aloe, but very much bigger. Its green branches, or leaves, are about a yard and a half in length and fit over each other like tiles, thick in the middle and growing thinner at the edges. The leaf is fleshy and must be nearly a span in thickness; it forms a sort of channel and tapers so much that the point is like a thorn or an awl. Each maguey has thirty or forty of these leaves, more or less, according to its size, for in some parts of the country they grow better and larger than in others. After the metl, or maguey, is full sized and its stock is well grown, they cut out its heart, and five or six of the pointed, tender leaves.

The stock that the plant forms above ground and on which the leaves grow must be about as large as a good-sized water jug. They keep hollowing out this stock to make a cavity as big as a good pot. It takes them about two months, more or less, according to the size of the maguey, to make the cavity and exhaust the plant entirely. Every day during that time they take out of the hollow a liquid which oozes out and is collected. This liquid, as soon as it is drawn, is like honeywater; when cooked and boiled over the fire, it becomes a clear, sweetish wine which the Spaniards drink, and they say that it is very good and very nutritious and healthful. When it is fermented in a jar, as one ferments wine, with the addition of some roots which the Indians call *ocpatli,* meaning an agent which produces fermentation in wine, it becomes so strong that it intoxicates violently those who drink it in any quantity. This wine the Indians used in their heathen days to produce a violent intoxication and make themselves more cruel and beastly. It has a very bad odor, and the breath of those who drink much of it smells still worse. In truth, when drunk temperately it is healthful and very potent.

1. The agave americana.

All medicines that are to be given to the sick are mixed in this wine. They put it into the cup or goblet and then pour on it the medicine that they are using for the treatment and cure of the patient.

From this same liquid they make good syrup and honey, though the honey has not as good a flavor as that made by bees, but they say that for use in cooking it is better, and is very healthful. They also make small cakes of sugar from this maguey juice, but it is not so white nor so sweet as ours. Good vinegar, too, is made from this liquid; some have better luck with it, or know better how to make it than others. From the leaves they get thread for sewing, and they make cord and ropes, cables and girths, and headstalls, and everything else that one makes of hemp. This plant, also, provides them with clothing and footwear; for the footgear of the Indians is very like that worn by the Apostles, being really sandals. They make *alpargatas*[2] like those of Andalusia, and also blankets and capes, all from the metl, or maguey.

The spines at the tips of the leaves serve as awls, because they are sharp and very strong—so strong that they are sometimes used as nails, for they will penetrate a wall or a beam reasonably well, although their real use is to serve as tacks, when cut short. In anything in which the nail has to be clinched they are no good, because they break at once. The Indians also know how to treat the leaves so that they can get a small thorn with its fibre attached, which serves as needle and thread.

The leaves themselves are also used for many things. They cut them—for they are very long—and on one piece the Indian women place the corn that they grind, for as they grind it with water and the corn itself has to be well moistened, it needs something clean to fall on. After they have made the corn into dough they put it on another piece of maguey leaf. These pieces of maguey leaves are much used by the craftsmen, called *amantecatl,*[3] who work in gold and feathers. On these leaves they make a paper of cotton mixed with paste, as thin as a very thin veil, and on the paper—on top of the maguey leaf—they work all their designs. It is one of the principal things that they use in their craft. Painters and other craftsmen make excellent use of these leaves. Even those who build houses use a piece of one of these leaves for carrying the mortar. They are also very good for drain tiles.

If they do not cut the metl, or maguey, to make wine, but let it

2. Rope-soled canvas sandals.
3. See above, bk. I, ch. XII, and note 9.

shoot up—as in fact many do—it sends up a bud as thick as a man's leg and grows from twelve to eighteen feet tall. When it has flowered and seeded it dries up. Where there is a shortage of wood this flower stalk is used for house building, for one can get good laths out of it and the leaves of the green plant serve as tiles. When it has sent up its stalk the whole plant dries up—even the root—and it does the same when they have taken the wine out of it.

The dry leaves they use for burning, and in most places this is the poor man's firewood. It makes a very good fire and the ashes are very good for making lye.

A leaf thrown on the coals is good for a cut or a fresh wound, and it is good to extract the juice while it is hot.

For snakebite they take the very small magueys, only about nine inches high, whose root is white and tender. They extract the juice, mix it with the juice of the kind of wormwood that grows in this land, and bathe the wound. It heals at once. This I have seen tried; it is a real medicine. This is true, you understand, when the bite is fresh.

There is another variety of these thistles, or trees, of much the same kind except that the color is somewhat more whitish—though the difference is so small that few notice it—and the leaves are a little thinner. This variety gives a better quality of the wine that I said some Spaniards drink; and I myself have drunk it. The vinegar from this kind is also better. This kind they cook in the earth, the leaves and the heart separately, and it then comes out tasting as good as preserved citron that is not very well prepared or not thoroughly done. The cooked leaves are so full of fibres that one cannot swallow them; one can only chew them and suck the juice, which is sweet. But if the heart is cooked by a good cook, it makes such good slices that many Spaniards like it as much as good preserved citron. More important is the fact that all the country, except the hot zone, is full of these metls. The temperate zone has more of the last-mentioned kind. These were the Indians' vineyards, and so they now have all the boundary lines and hedges planted with them.

They make a very good paper from the metl, or maguey. The sheet is twice the size of ours; a great deal of it is made in Tlaxcallan and circulates through a large part of New Spain. Paper is also made from other trees that grow in the hot zone, and they used to use great quantities of it. This tree and the paper made from it are called *amatl,* and from this name they call letters and books and paper all *amate*—although there is a special name for book.

In this metl, or maguey, down toward the root there is found a kind of whitish worm, as thick as a bustard's quill and half as long as your finger, which is very good to eat roasted, with salt. I have often eaten them on fast days when there was no fish. With the wine from this metl they make very good poultices for horses;[4] it is stronger and hotter and more suitable for this purpose than the wine that the Spaniards make from grapes. In the leaves of this maguey, travellers find water, for as the plant has many leaves and each one, as I have said, is about four and a half feet long, some of them hold the water when it rains. Travellers knowing this by experience go and seek it and it is often a great relief to them.

Chapter XX

Of how the idols were abolished, the festivals that the Indians used to hold, and the vanity and labor expended by the Spaniards in seeking for idols.

This chapter—which is the last—should be put in the second part of this book, where this subject is treated.

The festivals that the Indians used to hold, as I have told in the first part of this work,[1] with their appropriate ceremonies and pomp, all ceased from the time that the Spaniards began to make war on them. The Indians were so occupied with their tribulations that they remembered neither their gods nor even themselves, because they had so many troubles that in the attempt to remedy them they ceased to attend to the principal matter (*i. e.,* religion).

In each town they had an idol or demon whom they considered and called their principal patron; this one they honored and adorned with many jewels and robes, and offered it everything good that they could get, each town according to its size, the capitals of provinces

4. Spanish: *cernadas*. *Cernada* is the ash left from making lye. Mixed with wine, it is used as a poultice for animals that have caught cold.

1. See above, bk. I, chs. VI-XI, incl.

making the largest offerings. These principal idols that I speak of, the Indians concealed in the most secret place they could as soon as the great city of Mexico was taken by the Spaniards with all its jewels and riches. A great part of the gold that was with the idols and in the temples they gave in tribute to the Spaniards under whose authority they were placed. They could do no less, for at the beginning the tributes were so excessive that not all that the Indians could find or scratch together, nor what the lords and principal men had, would suffice. Under iniquitous compulsion they also gave up the gold that they had in the temples of the demons; when even this was exhausted they paid a tribute of slaves, and often, not having any slaves, they gave free men as slaves in order to meet their obligations.

These principal idols, with the insignia and ornaments or garments of the demons, the Indians hid, some underground, others in caves and others in the woods. Later, when the Indians were becoming converted and being baptized, they dug up many of them and used to bring them to the churchyards to burn them publicly. Others rotted underground, because after the Indians received the Faith they were ashamed to bring out the idols they had hidden and preferred to let them rot and not have anyone know that they had hidden them. When they were questioned about the principal idols and their dress, they would dig one up, all rotten—of which I am a good witness, for I saw it happen many times. The excuse that they gave was good, for they said: "When we buried it we did not know God, and we thought that the Spaniards would soon return to their own land; when we came to know God, we let it rot because we were afraid and ashamed to dig it up." In other towns these principal idols were in the possession of the lords or of the chief ministers of the demons, and they kept them so secret that scarcely anyone knew about them except the two or three persons who kept them; and of these they brought a very great number to the monasteries to be burned.

In many other remote towns, far away from Mexico, when the friars went there preaching, they would tell them in their sermons and before they baptized the Indians that the first thing they must do was to bring all their idols and all the emblems of the devil, so that they might be destroyed. In this way the Indians also brought a great quantity of idols to be burned publicly in many places. Wherever the teaching and the word of God has reached, nothing has remained in the way of idols, so far as we know, or nothing of any importance, for if a hundred years from now they were to dig in the courtyards of the temples of the ancient idols, they would always find idols, because the Indians made so many of them. For it would happen that when a child was born they would make an idol, and a year later, another bigger one, and on the fourth year they would make another, and as the child grew they would keep on making idols; and of these the foundations and the walls are full and there are many of them in the courtyards.

In the years '39 and '40 some Spaniards—some of them with authority and some of them without it—to show that they were zealous in the Faith, and thinking that they were doing something worthwhile, began to stir things up and disinter the dead and put pressure upon the Indians to make them give up their idols. In some places this reached such a point that the Indians would go and get the idols that were underground, rotted and forgotten, and some Indians were so tormented that as a matter of actual fact they made new idols and gave them to the Spaniards so that the latter would cease to persecute them.

Mingled with the righteous zeal that they displayed in hunting for idols there was no small amount of covetousness: the reason was that the Spaniards would say that in such a town or in such a parish there were idols of gold and of chalchihuitl, which is a stone of great value, and they would imagine that there were gold idols that would weigh a quintal or ten or fifteen arrobas.[2] As a matter of fact they came too late, for all the gold and precious stones were spent, and put safely away, and in possession of the Spaniards who first had the Indians and towns in their power. They also expected to find idols of stone that would be worth a whole city, and certainly, although I have seen many idols that were adored and highly valued among the Indians and much reverenced as important deities, some of them made of chalchihuitl, the one that seemed to me worth the most would not, I believe, bring ten gold pesos in Spain. And for this they upset and stirred up and scandalized the towns with their really indiscreet zeal; for even if there is some idol in some town, it is either rotten, or so forgotten, or kept so secret that in a town of ten thousand souls not five people know about it. These Indians consider them only for what they actually are, that is to say, pieces of wood or stone. Those who go about creating a scandal among

2. The *arroba* is one-fourth of a *quintal,* or 25 lbs.

the Indians, who are minding their own business, are like Laban who went out to meet Jacob to search his pack and upset his house looking for his idols;[3] for I have had plenty of experience of what I say here, and I see their mistaken ideas and the ways they have of disturbing and injuring these poor Indians who have forgotten their idols as completely as if a hundred years had passed.

3. Genesis 31, 31-35.

BIBLIOGRAPHY OF WORKS CITED

Bandelier, Adolph F. A. "On the Art of War and Mode of Warfare of the Ancient Mexicans." Peabody Museum of American Archaeology and Ethnology, Harvard University. *Tenth Annual Report.* Cambridge, 1877.

———. "On the Distribution and Tenure of Lands . . . among the Ancient Mexicans." *Idem, Eleventh Annual Report.* Cambridge, 1878.

———. "On the Social Organization and Mode of Government of the Ancient Mexicans." *Idem, Twelfth Annual Report.* Cambridge, 1879.

Bandelier, Fanny. *The Journey of Alvar Nuñez Cabeza de Vaca and His Companions from Florida to the Pacific, 1528-1536.* New York, 1905.

Borah, Woodrow. *Silk Raising in Colonial Mexico.* Berkeley, 1943.

Cabeza de Vaca, Alvar Nuñez. *Naufragios de . . . y Relación de la Jornada que hizo a la Florida con el Adelantado Pánfilo de Narváez.* In Biblioteca de Autores Españoles, *Historiadores Primitivos de Indias.* Madrid, 1877.

Casa, Fr. Bartolomé de las. *Apologética Historia Sumaria.* In Nueva Biblioteca de Autores Españoles, *Historiadores de Indias.* Por M. Serrano y Sanz. Madrid, 1909.

Castañeda de Nájera, Pedro de. *Relación de la Jornada de Cíbola.* Several translations—Winship, 1896; Hammond and Rey, 1940.

Cervantes de Salazar, Francisco. *Crónica de Nueva España.* Ed. by Francisco del Paso y Troncoso, *Papeles de Nueva España.* Madrid, 1914-1936. 3 vols.

Colección de Documentos Inéditos Relativos al Descubrimiento, Conquista y Organización de las Antiguas Posesiones Españoles de América y Oceanía. Madrid, 1864-1884. 42 vols.

Coronado, Francisco Vásquez de. *Carta al Emperador,* Tiguex, October 20, 1541. Usually included with the other Coronado expedition documents.

Cortés, Fernando. *Sumario de la residencia tomada a . . .* (1529) Mexico, 1852-53.

Díaz del Castillo, Bernal. *Historia Verdadera de la Conquista de la Nueva España.* Madrid, 1928. 2 vols.

Fernández de Oviedo y Valdés, Gonzalo. *Sumario de la Natural Historia de las Indias.* In Biblioteca de Autores Españoles, *Historiadores Primitivos de Indias.* Madrid, 1877.

Frazer, J. G. *The Golden Bough.* 3rd ed. London, 1912.

García Icazbalceta, Joaquín. *Don Fray Juan de Zumárraga . . . con un Apéndice de Documentos Inéditos ó Raros.* Mexico, 1881.

———. *Colección de Documentos para la Historia de México.* Mexico, 1858. 2 vols. Volume 1 contains Motolinía's *Historia.*

———. *Nueva Colección de Documentos para la Historia de México.* Mexico, 1886-1892, 5 vols.

Gómara, Francisco López de. *Conquista de México. Segunda parte de la Crónica General de las Indias.* In Biblioteca de Autores Españoles, *Historiadores Primitivos de Indias.* Madrid, 1877.

Hammond, George P., and Rey, Agapito. *Narratives of the Coronado Expedition, 1540-42.* Albuquerque, 1940.

Herrera, Antonio de. *Historia General de los Hechos de los Castellanos en las Islas i Tierra Firme del Mar Océano.* Madrid, 1730.

Hodge, Frederick W. "The Six Cities of Cíbola, 1581-1680." In *New Mexico Historical Review,* vol. 1, pp. 478-488.

Humboldt, Alexander von. *Essai Politique sur le Royaume de la Nouvelle-Espagne.* Paris, 1811. 5 vols.

Joyce, Thomas A. *Mexican Archaeology.* London, 1920.

Las Casas, *see* Casas.

Lizana, Bernardo de. *Historia de Yucatán* (1633). Mexico, 1893.

Martínez, Henrico, *Reportorio de los Tiempos y Historia Natural desta Nueva España.* Mexico, 1606.

Mendieta, Fr. Gerónimo de. *Historia Eclesiástica Indiana.* Mexico, 1870.

Molina, Alonso de. *Vocabulario en Lengua Mexicana y Castellana.* Mexico, 1571.

Morley, Sylvanus G. *The Ancient Maya.* Stanford University, 1946.

———. *An Introduction to the Study of the Maya Hieroglyphs.* Bureau of American Ethnology, *Bulletin 57.* Washington, 1915.

Motolinía, Fr. Toribio de. *Historia de los Indios de la Nueva España.* In García Icazbalceta, *Col. de Docs., op. cit.* Another edition by Daniel Sánchez García, Barcelona, 1914.

———. *Memoriales de . . .* Published by Luis García Pimentel in *Documentos Históricos de Méjico,* Vol. 1, Mexico, 1903.

Oviedo y Valdés, Gonzalo Fernández de. *See* Fernández de Oviedo.

Ramírez, José Fernando. *Noticias de la Vida y Escritos de Fray Toribio de Benavente, ó Motolinía.* In *Colección de Documentos para la Historia de México.* Publicada por Joaquín García Icazbalceta. Mexico, 1858-1866. 2 vols.

———. Editor. *Historia de los Indios de Nueva España,* by Fray Toribio Motolinía. In *ibid.*

Rebolledo, Fray Luis de. *Chrónica General de Nuestro Seráfico Padre Sant*

Rey, Agapito. *See* Hammond and Rey.

Francisco y su Apostólico orden. Seville, 1598.

Sahagún, Fray Bernardino de. *Historia General de las Cosas de Nueva España.* Mexico, 1938. 5 vols.

Sánchez García, Fray Daniel. "Bío-Bibliografía de Fr. Toribio de Benavente ó Motolinía." In his edition of *Historia de los Indios de la Nueva España.* Barcelona, 1914.

Ternaux-Compans, Henri. *Voyages, Relations et Mémoires Originaux pour Servir à l'histoire de la Découverte de l'Amérique.* Paris, 1837-1841. 20 vols.

Torquemada, Fray Juan de. *Monarchía Indiana.* Madrid, 1723. 3 vols.

Vázquez, Fray Francisco. *Crónica de la Provincia del Santísimo Nombre de Jesús de Guatemala.* 2nd edition. Notes and index by Fray Lázaro Lamadrid. Guatemala, 1937-1944. 4 vols.

Vetancurt, Fray Agustín de. *Teatro Mexicano.* Mexico, 1870-1871. 4 vols.

Index